# Praise for *Essentia[l]*
# *Interaction De[sign]*

"In *Essential Mobile Interaction Design,* Banga and Weinhold do a great jo[b o]
it takes to make a good-looking and easy-to-use app. The accessible language and visual
examples of quality work combine to make this book a great resource for those looking to get
into app design, or to take their craft to the next level."

**—Jon Becker**
  boom. reactive.

"*Essential Mobile Interaction Design* is not merely a book full of pictures and design concepts or
one of straight technical drivel. Instead, it is a guidebook for creating human-based interfaces
that feature simplicity, functionality, and value. Whether you have questions about how mobile
design is different from traditional desktop design, how to work with a developer, or even
what tools to use for the creation process, *Essential Mobile Interaction Design* demonstrates the
answer for that."

**—Phil Dutson**
  Lead UX and Mobile Developer, ICON Health & Fitness

"Filled with nuggets of useful information, this book is a solid resource for the many aspects
of designing a mobile app. I've found many recommendations in this book that we can use in
our apps."

**—Lucius Kwok**
  CEO, Felt Tip, Inc.

"A well-rounded, easy-to-read book that provides a good grounding in mobile design and how
to keep all those small details in mind so that your apps will really shine."

**—Dave Verwer**
  Shiny Development and iOS Dev Weekly

# Essential Mobile Interaction Design

# Essential Mobile Interaction Design

## Perfecting Interface Design in Mobile Apps

Cameron Banga

Josh Weinhold

**♦♦Addison-Wesley**

Upper Saddle River, NJ • Boston • Indianapolis • San Francisco
New York • Toronto • Montreal • London • Munich • Paris • Madrid
Capetown • Sydney • Tokyo • Singapore • Mexico City

For information about buying this title in bulk quantities, or for special sales opportunities (which may include electronic versions; custom cover designs; and content particular to your business, training goals, marketing focus, or branding interests), please contact our corporate sales department at corpsales@pearsoned.com or (800) 382-3419.

For government sales inquiries, please contact governmentsales@pearsoned.com.

For questions about sales outside the U.S., please contact international@pearsoned.com.

Visit us on the Web: informit.com/aw

*Cataloging-in-Publication Data is on file with the Library of Congress*

ISBN-13: 978-0-321-96157-0
ISBN-10: 0-321-96157-9
Text printed in the United States on recycled paper at RR Donnelley in Crawfordsville, Indiana.
First printing, March 2014

**Editor-in-Chief**
Mark L. Taub

**Executive Editor**
Laura Lewin

**Development Editor**
Michael Thurston

**Managing Editor**
John Fuller

**Project Editor**
Elizabeth Ryan

**Packager**
Anna Popick

**Copy Editor**
Melinda Rankin

**Indexer**
Jack Lewis

**Proofreader**
Anna Popick

**Technical Reviewers**
Jonathon Becker
Victor Lara
Francisco Velazquez

**Editorial Assistant**
Olivia Basegio

**Cover Designer**
Chuti Prasertsith

**Compositor**
Shepherd, Inc.

*I dedicate this book to Gavin. Although we've only just met, I couldn't be more excited to be your uncle. Hopefully, you'll be interested in interface design one day so that you can read through this and remind me how silly and archaic our phones and computers once were.*
*—Cameron*

*I dedicate this book to Mallory. Thank you for always encouraging me to take on new challenges and pushing me to always aim higher.*
*—Josh*

# Contents

# PREFACE

This text offers an introduction to and general overview of interaction design for all mobile computing platforms, with a particular emphasis on Google's Android and Apple's iOS platforms.

Mobile apps should feel natural and intuitive. Users should quickly and easily understand them. This means that effective interaction and interface design is crucial to the success of any mobile app. Few mobile app developers (or even designers), however, have had adequate training in these areas.

Touchscreen-focused, mass-market mobile applications are a type of technology that's only been possible to create since 2008, and the industry has seen monumental shifts and growth in the six years between the introduction of the "app economy" and the publication of this work.

This book aims to help put you in a place to succeed as a designer in today's app market by teaching proven principles and techniques that you can use in your next app, no matter what mobile platform, targeted device, form factor, or user base you're targeting.

In short, the tutorial style used here aims to help you master the mindset, processes, and vocabulary of mobile interaction design so that you can start making better choices right away. This book guides you through the entire process of app design, demystifying many of the tasks and issues that arise during the many stages of developing, releasing, and improving a mobile app.

Cameron Banga has been working in mobile application development since 2009, and in the nearly five years since releasing his first app he's contributed as a designer or as an adviser to more than 100 applications for iPhone, iPad, Android, and OS X. In that time, he's seen firsthand the growth and change experienced in the mobile industry and has worked to meet client and customer expectations throughout the many evolutions of mobile platforms.

This book aims to serve as a central resource for programmers or designers looking to best determine how to establish themselves in today's modern mobile landscape by offering advice formulated and acquired through Cameron's experiences over the past several years as a pioneer of the mobile app economy.

Topics chosen for this book were selected carefully by Cameron with advice from and in coordination with several successful and award-winning industry colleagues. The goal of each chapter was to focus on a particular strong primary skill required of any successful designer, breaking that skill down into a few key components that any novice could focus on and, with some strong advice and clear guidance, work to master quickly.

No programming knowledge and only basic design knowledge is required to understand this book, as it's been carefully crafted to be universally readable and helpful. In situations in which it does dive into extremely specific terminology or a topic for which prior information would be required, breakout boxes offer context and suggestions as to where the reader can look for further information that's beyond the scope of this book.

Only basic design tools were used to create the example work included in this book, and the software or hardware that was used is detailed where relevant. Much of this book focuses on general theories and somewhat universal design practices that can be slightly modified and fine-tuned to the reader's specific circumstances. Additional resources that are required or may be helpful have been posted online at http://cameronbanga.com/EMIDbook.

We hope you enjoy this book and that it helps you make progress toward your goal of becoming an outstanding mobile app designer. If you would like to share your thoughts or if you have a question, feel free to contact the authors at book@cameronbanga.com.

# ACKNOWLEDGMENTS

This book would not exist without the dedicated work of Laura Lewin (our gracious and ever-helpful executive editor) and Olivia Basegio (our wonderful editorial assistant, always willing to lend a hand and keep us on track). We'd like to give a huge thank you to the entire Addison-Wesley editorial team, especially Michael Thurston and Melinda Rankin.

Special thanks go out as well to our technical reviewers: Jonathon Becker, Victor Lara, and Francisco Velazquez. The book is significantly better due to their recommendations, nitpicking, and fact-checking.

## Cameron

I am extremely thankful for all of the people who worked with me and tolerated me throughout the lengthy process of book development, particularly my mother, father, brother, and sister-in-law. I can't explain the gratitude I have for my family and their ability to put up with the absences, stress, and limited schedule that comes with writing a book. Thanks to the entire 9magnets team: Dillon Carter, Nathan Feldsien, Michael Phelps, and Francisco Velazquez; they were amazing coworkers and even better friends throughout the entire process. I would also like to give special thanks to all the amazing people that I've had the pleasure to meet in the independent app development community that serve as my biggest source of inspiration every day. Cabel Sasser, I hope that this makes you proud.

## Josh

I am incredibly grateful for the patience and understanding of my wife, Mallory, who was amazingly focused on planning our wedding while I was off working on this book. I'm also thankful for my parents, who never stopped encouraging me to work hard and see what followed, and for the grandparents, aunts, and uncles who feigned amazement at the not-so-creative writing of my childhood. I'm also indebted to the many teachers and editors over the years who offered invaluable lessons and priceless opportunities, especially Jeff Burton, Greg Halling, Linda Jegerlehner, Marshall King, Pat Milhizer, Paul Oren, Mark Schwehn, and Susan Swift.

# ABOUT THE AUTHORS

**Cameron Banga** is the lead designer at a company he cofounded, 9magnets, LLC. He has worked on more than 100 mobile apps for clients ranging from professional sports teams, to educators, to large corporations. His first application, Battery Go!, quickly became an iPhone best-seller, and his apps have been recommended by the *New York Times*, *Fox Business News*, *Macworld*, *PC Magazine*, and many other media outlets. Cameron holds a B.A. in economics from Valparaiso University.

When not writing, Cameron is an avid photographer, novice runner, and coffee connoisseur in training. Cameron can be most easily reached via Twitter, at @CameronBanga.

**Josh Weinhold** is the assistant editor of the *Chicago Daily Law Bulletin* newspaper and *Chicago Lawyer* magazine. He spent five years as a political reporter and has written hundreds of news articles and feature stories published in the *Daily Law Bulletin*, the *Elkhart Truth*, the *Dubuque Telegraph Herald,* and on msnbc.com. He shared a National Press Club Online Journalism Award with other members of an msnbc.com and *Elkhart Truth* reporting team, and won The Chicago Bar Association's Herman Kogan Award for legal beat reporting.

He spends his free time slowly working through the long list of movies and TV shows he's been dying to see and fanatically following many real-life and fantasy sports teams.

# CHAPTER 1

# A LOOK AT MOBILE AND ITS MAIN PLAYERS

Apple may have popularized the use of smartphones and tablets, but a number of other companies followed its path and moved quickly to get in on this latest digital revolution. Now the marketplace is filled with hardware manufacturers and platforms. In this chapter, you'll find an overview of introductory topics that will be crucial to understand as you begin designing for iPhone, Android, and other mobile platforms.

You'll also find a brief history of mobile app design and information about how this industry grew. As a designer, you'll need to understand the past in order to successfully design for the future.

# The Field of Interface Design

There once was a very dark time in the world of mobile computing: a time when we navigated phones using small arrow keys or a rough scroll ball, a time when a calculator and an alarm clock were considered advanced features on a device that primarily made calls and sent text messages, a time when the most advanced game a phone could run involved a rectangular "snake" chasing after pixelized "fruit."

But in the late 2000s, a combination of two companies, touch-screen technology, and one ad campaign changed all of that.

Just a few years after Apple touted in print and television advertising that "there's an app for that," asserting that there was a way to accomplish anything you wanted to on the iPhone, it seems that there has become an application for any task our hearts desire to perform. Yet, there can't be an app for everything already; otherwise, you wouldn't be looking to jump into the world of mobile development.

Today, smartphones function as portable computers that respond to our every touch and that come equipped with a digital marketplace flush with programs for every imaginable purpose. In just a few short years, the world of mobile computing has gotten noticeably brighter.

Now there are a host of companies competing for consumers' mobile device dollars and even more companies competing for consumers' mobile application dollars. If you're reading this book, you're most likely a developer, designer, or project manager working in mobile, and you're looking to gain a better understanding of interface and interaction design on a mobile phone.

Over the course of this book, we hope to be able to lend a hand by explaining many of the most difficult problems that pop up in mobile interaction design. We'll offer in-depth analysis of the differences between mobile and traditional computing, the tools needed to optimize design, how to develop a visually attractive design, the best methods of gaining feedback, and much more.

If you're not a programmer or technically minded, fear not; this book is intended for everyone. The topics discussed—including theoretically optimal interaction design and operating-system-agnostic interface implementations—should be helpful regardless of the platform you're using.

This book may be most helpful for people who have some experience with general software design, perhaps on the Web or traditional desktop computers, and are now looking to learn how they can best apply their skills to mobile devices. If you've never worked in software before, though, don't fret; everything in this book is served up for easy digestion. Likewise, if you're a grizzled mobile veteran there are also a ton of tips and tricks you should find handy.

As with many technical volumes, this content is not necessarily designed to be consumed in a linear fashion. If only one or two chapters seem most applicable to your next app development project, feel free to skip ahead and take in the relevant pieces as you see fit.

Let's get started. You'll be jumping into the fine details of mobile interaction design soon enough, but first you need a short history lesson in mobile computing to lay the groundwork for the world you'll soon be exploring.

# The Dawn of the App

With the sudden explosion of the affordable smartphone market came the rapid ubiquity of apps: smaller, more focused, and often inexpensive programs that add value to the most advanced piece of technology individuals have ever owned.

What makes up these apps? Naturally, they have an underlying logic and are comprised of code, art, and images; but what actually *makes up* one?

Apps aren't a new thing or a recent advance in computing. An app—short for application—is just a piece of computer software designed to help a user solve a problem. Compiled from lines of code into a binary code (see Figure 1.1), typically written inside of an integrated development environment (IDE) such as Xcode or Eclipse, an app is seen as the most practical way for users to manipulate their computers or mobile phones into helping with an everyday task.

Today, you'll find apps most commonly on mobile phones, but they've existed on computers for decades. Generations of word processors, spreadsheet programs, first-person shooter games, and photo-editing platforms all qualify as "apps"; such apps just had to be installed via a floppy disk or CD-ROM. The abbreviated, seemingly new term grew popular in 2008 because of Apple's well-known "There's an app for that" marketing campaign and the launch of the App Store.

```objc
17    - (void)viewDidLoad {
18        [super viewDidLoad];
19
20        //[self setupRightNavigationButtons];
21        self.view.backgroundColor = [UIColor clearColor];
22        self.view.opaque = NO;
23
24        myWebView = [[UIWebView alloc] initWithFrame:self.view.bounds];
25
26
27        activityIndicator = [[UIActivityIndicatorView alloc]initWithActivityIndicatorStyle:UIActivityIndicatorViewStyleGray]
          ;
28
29
30
31    #if __IPHONE_OS_VERSION_MIN_REQUIRED >= 40000
32
33        myWebView.backgroundColor = [UIColor whiteColor];
34    #else
35        myWebView.backgroundColor = [UIColor blackColor];
36    #endif
37
38
39        myWebView.scalesPageToFit = YES;
40        //myWebView.autoresizingMask = (UIViewAutoresizingFlexibleWidth | UIViewAutoresizingFlexibleHeight);
41        myWebView.delegate = self;
42        myWebView.multipleTouchEnabled = YES;
43        myWebView.opaque = NO;
44
```

**Figure 1.1** Each pixel you design on screen will be manipulated by source code files, usually written in an IDE such as Xcode or Eclipse.

Most smartphones that came before the iPhone or Android phones shipped to consumers with a miniscule number of applications installed, typically curated by the hardware manufacturer or phone carrier. Because there wasn't much choice, these applications often had a high cost and limited feature set. There was no reasonable market for such apps because most developers were unable to get their software on the platform and carriers had little incentive to create apps that truly met consumer needs.

That environment changed radically, however, with both the advent of the touchscreen phone and access to a consumer-facing app store. Full-glass touchscreen phones, like the iPhone shown in Figure 1.2, were revolutionary in many respects. Gone were the days of phone interfaces limited by a number keypad or an extremely small keyboard that was difficult to type on. The glass screen became a blank canvas on which anything could be created, and it allowed developers to work with a fluid interface capable of handling nearly any type of application.

Although the technology within a phone gave developers unprecedented design power, an app store gave them unprecedented direct access to consumers. Almost instantly, developers with basic programming knowledge and a computer capable of compiling code could get their products in front of millions of consumers eager to see what this new, futuristic device could do.

**Figure 1.2**  The iPhone 5 is a great example of a modern-day smartphone with a large screen used to create a dynamic and fluid interface.

# Defining an App in Today's Context

In the practical sense, apps have been around almost as long as computers, but does the traditional definition remain the same as the modern one? When consumers ask you if you can make an app that fits their needs, exactly what are they asking for?

Today, an app is typically defined as a fully contained software application designed to run natively on a mobile phone, tablet, or even a traditional computer. Apps usually are downloaded from a store created and curated by the platform owner, such as Apple, Google, Microsoft, or BlackBerry. Often, an app is either inexpensive or free and serves a small, single purpose. Modern operating systems are now built around making it easy for the user to get in and out of apps, typically with some sort of basic launcher platform such as iOS's Springboard, shown in Figure 1.3.

From a technical standpoint, apps are typically compiled using code native to the platform, such as Objective-C or Java, and an IDE in coordination with software development kits (often

**Figure 1.3**  iOS's launcher, called Springboard, is a standard mobile application launcher; rounded rectangle icons depict each application.

referred to as SDKs) provided by the operating system creator. Application languages and pro-gramming, however, are topics outside the scope of this book.

Technically, HTML-based Web applications could also be considered mobile apps; they'll be discussed a bit throughout this book, but as a general rule of thumb, when apps are discussed the conversation involves writing in the native language of the platform rather than writing an app designed for one-size-fits-all access across a menagerie of devices.

Although it is possible to build a program with Web technologies such as HTML or JavaScript, most users don't think of those as "apps" unless they're downloaded from a traditional mobile store. Mostly this matters from a delivery standpoint, which we'll discuss later in this chapter.

There are many reasons a programming development team might want to build an app natively instead of on the Internet with Web technologies. First and foremost, the application will be reminiscent of the device's native language architecture and is thus likely to be much more responsive than applications written in Web languages such as HTML and JavaScript. Although there are some exceptions to the rule—some great applications have been cre-ated using such technologies—in general it is much easier for a developer to make a smooth, responsive, animated application when using a native language.

Another benefit of working in the native language of the system you're programming for is that you'll likely have much shorter communication with the hardware features of the device. If you're looking to integrate features into an app—to take advantage of the device's GPS, gyro-scope, accelerometer, camera, microphone, or other advanced hardware—you're probably best off building a native app using the platform's SDK.

## tip

Current mobile operating systems, such as Android and iOS, provide easy access to advanced hardware features such as GPS or gyroscopes by using a simple API. Take advantage of these features to provide exceptional interactions in your application.

As mentioned earlier, the interaction design techniques discussed in this book are designed to be platform agnostic and should be applicable whether you're working on iOS, Android, BlackBerry, or the Web. If you haven't done much mobile development, it's probably a bit difficult to understand the technical differences between a native iPhone or Android app and a mobile Web app, and that's no problem.

If you're reading this book, you may be a programmer fluent in a language such as Java or Objective-C; if so your platform decision has already been made, and now you want your interface to function a little bit better. Or you may be a designer or project manager who hasn't worked frequently on a mobile platform, and so your target platform has likely been picked already by your programmer or technical team. As we mentioned earlier, we won't dive too far into the technical aspects of each platform, but we will discuss important design constraints or limitations for each major platform.

## Build It and They Will Come

Ironically, the biggest players in this mobile revolution may not have even foreseen the potential of apps when they first announced their platforms. When launching the iPhone, Apple initially indicated there was no need for a marketplace for native software on the iPhone. Google likewise did not make a software store available for its Android mobile operating system at first launch.

It wasn't until 2008 that the typically unflappable Apple changed that plan. With the release of the iPhone App Store in July of that year, developers were finally given the opportunity to build native software for the platform. Google followed suit with the release of the Google Play Store (originally called the Android Market) just three months later (see Figure 1.4).

Apple's App Store and the Google Play Store were the first mobile app markets that prompted any significant customer response or gained traction with mainstream users. Today, however,

**Figure 1.4**   Consumers go to digital marketplaces such as Android's Google Play Store to find and download applications.

there are a variety of app stores available for nearly every mobile platform; popular ones include the Amazon App Store, BlackBerry World, the Windows Store, the Nokia Symbian Store, and Samsung Apps. Every major platform will be discussed throughout this book, but the premise remains the same for each; app stores are a place that users go to quickly download new software for their phones or tablets.

When Apple says "there's an app for that" now, it isn't kidding—and the same holds true for its competitors. The number of programs available on their stores continues to grow. To date, Apple has more than 900,000 apps in its store. Android has around 700,000. The Windows Store, though still young, claims to have 100,000 applications.

The astronomical growth of these mobile applications has greatly outpaced what any observer might have expected for such a marketplace. In a relatively short amount of time, applications for phones and tablets have redefined how we view computing. In the past, applications were viewed as larger, fully functioning operations: Web browsers, mail clients, and word processors that could be used for a multitude of tasks during an average computing day. Now applications are being built to target smaller, more specialized tasks.

On an iPhone or an Android phone today, for example, it's not uncommon to have three applications that handle e-mail, as they all serve different purposes for sorting through a user's daily messages. It's also not uncommon to have a handful of Web browsers—perhaps one for syncing bookmarks and another for sharing links socially. Additionally, many Web companies or services such as Facebook or Twitter now have their own applications; in the past, a user would simply open a Web browser to access such services.

Apps are easy to build. They're easy to get. And they're easy to use, thanks in large part to native application frameworks with features such as pinch-to-zoom, maps integration, and calendar support. All told, that makes apps the optimal experience on mobile devices.

# What Is a Mobile Device?

Apps and the smartphones that use them have been mentioned frequently already, but what truly defines a "mobile" device? One attribute commonly used to categorize nearly all mobile devices is the operating system that they're running. Most mobile devices today are based on what tech companies such as Apple and Google call a "post-PC" operating system: something that functions differently from the point-and-click only, window-based interfaces of desktops and laptops. (The term "post-PC" still doesn't have a technical definition, though. It's essentially a buzzword coined by Apple at the release of the iPad.)

A collection of mainstream operating systems now in the market meets this post-PC qualification: iOS, Android, Blackberry OS, and Windows 8. In this book, we'll be strictly discussing interaction design related to such operating systems.

These mobile operating systems are everywhere, so much so that it's difficult to get away from them. Phones, tablets, and even many laptops are now considered mobile devices running post-PC operating systems. Analysts estimate that in the beginning of 2014, mobile phones overtook personal computers as the type of device most commonly used for Web access. It's also estimated that two billion smartphone units have been sold worldwide, with iPhone and Android dominating almost 70 percent of the market.

So many devices in consumers' hands also means that there's a large quantity of potential users willing to pay to download apps. Apple alone has more than 575 million accounts registered with credit cards on the App Store, and the revenue generated by their app purchases, a few dollars at a time, really adds up. By summer 2013, app developers had already made more than $10 billion in revenue from sales inside Apple's App Store.

Smartphones aren't only making an impact in the United States, as areas including China, India, and many parts of Europe have been quick to adapt to these devices. In many countries with developing economics, potential users frequently pass over personal computers and instead choose a more affordable, versatile technology: mobile phones.

> ## note
> Mobile platforms today make it very easy to localize applications for numerous world languages. With a small amount of work, applications can become more desirable to people in different countries around the globe.

# A Portable, Pocket Computer

Although mobile devices today are largely defined as phones and tablets, their origins can be traced back to more humble, single-function products. MP3 players, including the original iPod and the Microsoft Zune, are often cited as the first mobile devices that mainstream users embraced in great numbers.

In fact, mobile computing devices themselves have been around since the early to mid 1990s. But the technology really hit its stride in the early to mid 2000s as cell phones became more accessible, lightweight, smaller, faster, and cheaper. Multipurpose devices such as the iPod or Zune made it easy for users to carry entire music collections, games, texts, and contact information in their pockets. Over time, these devices converged with cell phones to form an all-in-one device that was friendlier to users' pockets and wallets.

Smartphones, then, aren't exactly recent technology; they've been around for more than a decade. Running apps on these devices isn't really a new idea either, as phones have long had programs designed specifically for them. So what exactly led to the rapid rise of smartphones and the dramatic evolution in technology usage over the past few years?

This change was driven primarily by a refined definition of what it means to own a smartphone. Prior to the iPhone and Android phones, smartphone technology was seen as something best used for calls, text messages, and e-mail. The new wave of smartphones was revolutionary, because it took a device nearly as powerful as a home computer and shrunk it down to a size that could fit in a pocket or a purse. For the first time, a phone was effectively capable of browsing the Web or running programs on par with the type computers had featured for decades.

With the creation of mobile app stores, it also became simple for nearly anyone to create software for these devices. To spawn a mobile application in the past, a developer would be forced to go through restrictive mobile carriers or hardware manufacturers—a difficult task for even seasoned software veterans. Only a few privileged developers then were able to make programs and sell them to consumers worldwide; now it only takes a few months, a computer, and a connection to the Internet for any of the tens of thousands of developers to release their creations to users worldwide. This new "app economy" is a flat playing field in which anyone can make an impact with little experience or few resources.

The combination of extremely capable smartphones, an abundance of great mobile software, and previously unimaginable Internet speeds from mobile carriers created a perfect storm for the industry in 2008 and 2009; as a result, a modern economy now exists in which smartphone adoption rates are approaching 80 percent in major markets such as the United States, Canada, Japan, England, and France.

## Tablets, Too

Since 2010, the world of mobile computing has grown to include tablets, especially with the proliferation and success of Android and iOS operating systems. Devices such as the iPad and Google's Nexus 7 are now seeing even faster adoption rates than smartphones ever did.

Tablets aren't a new, unprecedented computing experience either. Microsoft was an early proponent of tablets that featured a pen stylus and touch interface, but the company marketed them with little to no success throughout the 1990s and early 2000s. Over the past 20 to 30 years, tablets have been seen as the computing device of the future, making frequent appearances in science fiction movies and TV shows, and for good reason; a carryable computer that can be written on or interacted with by touch just seems to make sense.

> **tip**
> Currently, all major tablet operating systems are essentially siblings of and based off of systems that were also successful and popular on phones. Don't try to pick up

both Apple and Android tablets when first learning about design in an attempt to diversify your knowledge of mobile interaction types. Instead, focus on one mobile operating system and become an expert at its phone and tablet interface designs.

Most early tablet devices failed or were targeted for extremely niche markets, but they finally found success in 2010 when Apple released the iPad (although even that device was met initially with a mixed response).

In the years since its release, the iPad has been nothing short of a dramatic, industry-disrupting device. It has seen incredibly strong growth and adoption rates: even better than those of the iPhone, considered one of the most profitable products ever.

With the success of the iPad, competitors have followed suit. Google has now moved its Android operating system to the tablet format, allowing apps to take advantage of the larger-screen devices. Google now partners directly with hardware manufacturers such as Asus to create its own hardware as well, and their Nexus 7 is viewed as the most successful Android tablet to hit the market. Due to the operating system's open-source nature, a variety of hardware manufacturers have built unbelievable tablets with a multitude of screen sizes to choose from—ranging from 7 to 13 inches—on hundreds of devices released worldwide.

Microsoft also jumped into the tablet market with its own touch-centric tablet. The Surface, released in 2012, is a popular piece of hardware that integrates closely with the company's Touch and Type Covers. Users can quickly attach or detach the tablet's keyboard, which makes typing in apps such as Microsoft Word or Excel simple and easy. The Surface has developed a dedicated user base, but it still has room for improvement. It hasn't picked up a large market share, although many designers and programmers are keeping an eye on this device as one that could have future potential.

## Other Devices That Are Part of the Revolution

So far, this discussion has focused only on smartphones and tablets, all of which have touch-screens, but mobile devices don't necessarily need to have a panel that responds to swipes and pinches from fingers. Hardware that uses more conventional navigation tools has had some success as well.

Microsoft's Surface, for example, includes a touchscreen but also comes with a keyboard and a standard laptop trackpad that allows users to operate the device as both a tablet and a traditional laptop. And in 2013, BlackBerry released its BlackBerry 10 operating system which, although capable of supporting touch interfaces, also supports the classic QWERTY keyboard devices that were once the dominant smartphone feature (see Figure 1.5).

**Figure 1.5** Although many current device interfaces are touch-screen only, some still come with physical keyboards.

# The Industry's Key Players

Now that you have a background in apps, mobile devices, and the operating systems involved, it's time to dive further into the key players in the industry. Mobile's growth has been characterized by big, bold moves by the companies detailed ahead, and some historical context can be helpful in understanding what drives the systems that you're creating software for. From Apple's revitalization to Microsoft's reimagining of Windows, the critical events explained here present some perspective on what's led to today's current mobile app landscape.

## Apple

The foundation for the emergence of so-called post-PC operating systems was laid by Apple with the release of the original iPod in 2001. At the time, most didn't see the device as a revolutionary mobile computing platform, but the iPod was one of the first devices that truly allowed the average person to simultaneously carry their music, videos, podcasts, contacts, and calendar: essentially, their entire digital personas. Apple hit a gold mine when it discovered that people wanted the capability and functionality of a computer in a smaller, pocket-sized device.

At Apple, the impending mobile revolution was being designed and refined over a period of several years. Steve Jobs, designer Jony Ive, engineer Scott Forstall, and other Apple executives led a secret project to merge Apple's expertise in desktop computing with its new hit mobile music and video player.

It wasn't until 2007, though, that Apple was finally able to crack the code and deliver a miniature computer. The device was so incredible at the time that many critics and competitors didn't believe that the product shown off during the initial press conference was even real. Many thought that Apple was using gimmicks or tricks to make the device as fast, smooth, and responsive as it appeared in initial video previews. At the time, storing all that media on one device with a remarkably long battery life was seen as something just shy of magic.

The release of the iPhone sparked the mobile-computing revolution. For many, it was as simple and fun, if not more so, to use than a laptop or desktop computer for browsing the Web, watching videos, reading PDFs, or playing games.

Not only did the iPhone change the way users saw computers (to the point of ignoring them altogether), it also significantly advanced touch computing. Although touchscreen computers had been available for many years, the technology never saw mainstream adoption, primarily due to inaccurate screens hindered by poor build quality. But after the iPhone, other vendors took notice; operating systems such as Android, BlackBerry, Windows, and the now-defunct WebOS integrated first-class touchscreen functionality.

Apple followed up the iPhone in 2010 with its iPad, which pushed growth in a market that had never seen widespread commercial success. As noted, the iPad has experienced phenomenal growth, and tablet computers are poised to soon eclipse the yearly sales, market share, and Web-browsing rates of desktop computers and traditional operating systems.

## Google and Android

Android has been a breath of fresh air for mainstream open-source computing since Google announced it in 2007. Early versions of Android were defined and led by operating system cofounder Andy Rubin and were mostly inspired by his work at his previous company, Danger.

Android was designed from the ground up to be an open-source system run by the Linux kernel, which would power the smartphones. The original Android operating system was focused on bringing a truly great e-mail and messaging function to mobile phones that traditionally had very limited capability for such features. Although originally created by a small startup team led by Rubin, Android was acquired by Google and rolled into what would be the foundation for the Web giant's now strong mobile strategy.

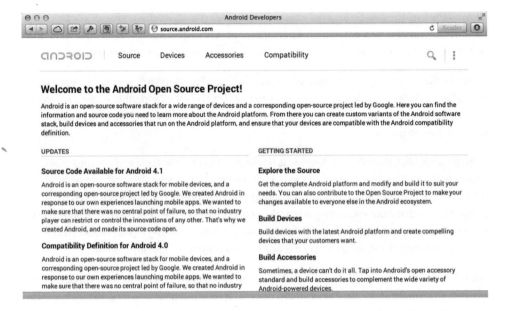

**Figure 1.6**    Because Android is open source, you can visit Google's resource Web site to download the entire operating system source code.

Because Android is open source and available to any manufacturer that's able to compile the source code and willing to work within the platform's license agreement, it's now available on more than 4,000 distinct hardware devices worldwide (see Figure 1.6). A new iPhone only hits the market once a year, but Android device makers can literally release dozens of new implementations with a variety of different specifications every month.

These contrasting strategies lead to many of the differences in operating systems that will be discussed throughout this book. Although the specifications of iOS devices are strictly dictated by Apple, Android devices can be found with nearly any screen size, processor, RAM, and hardware configuration imaginable.

Consumers love this functionality, as they can buy a device to match any need they might have, but it makes interfaces a bit tougher to build. Yet, the success of Android and the large market size it has built means that there are millions upon millions of customers waiting to use applications.

## The Other Players

Aside from Apple and Google, there are a few other players of note. Although you may never design anything for these platforms, it's important to know what they mean for the mobile industry.

## BlackBerry

The first major competitor is BlackBerry, a company credited with being the driving force behind the original smartphone craze. Before Apple took over with the iPhone in 2007, Black-Berry stood alone atop the mobile summit, primarily due to demand from the business world. Once renowned for phones with full QWERTY keyboards, BlackBerry had significant difficulty adapting once touchscreens emerged and became popular. The BlackBerry 10 operating system is the company's latest offering in the mobile space. This new design focuses on dynamic interactive messaging, making it easy for users to quickly move back and forth between e-mail, text messages, social networks, and more.

The most difficult hurdle for BlackBerry to overcome has been a lack of applications. Because its post-PC operating system didn't arrive on the scene until January 2013, most developers had already established themselves on either Android or iOS. Although the interface is clean and intuitive—and available with both touchscreen and physical keyboard options—BlackBerry 10 has seen relatively slow market growth to date.

## Microsoft

Another strong mobile competitor has been Microsoft and its Windows 8 and Windows Phone 8 platforms. A rash departure from its typical style, Microsoft overhauled a long-standing operating system strategy, converging mobile and traditional desktop computing into a single platform that uses the same interface styles and design language. This vast change was somewhat uncharacteristic for the computer behemoth out of Redmond, Washington. For nearly two decades, Windows was renowned for its consistency. Today, Windows phones, tablets, and desktops feature a new flat design, which Microsoft previously labeled "Metro" but is now calling the Microsoft design language. This new format is characterized by bold colors, large text, and square, sharp-edged buttons. The initial version of Windows 8 received some criticism because it did away almost entirely with its famous "Start" menu and desktop format. In later updates, Microsoft backtracked on its uncompromising devotion to its new idea because some long-term users had found the new interface hard to work with.

To date, Windows 8 has faced relatively mixed reviews as well as mixed success in the market. The new Windows desktops and tablets were greeted with adoption rates similar to those of their predecessors, but Windows Phone has had a difficult time gaining wider public adoption. For application developers, it would be advantageous for Windows to see greater worldwide popularity because the unified design structure and language among platforms makes app creation easier; however, customers just aren't jumping on the bandwagon.

### tip

If you're struggling to decide which platform you should target with your first mobile project, try either your favorite platform or the platform that you currently use on your phone every day. If you can't think of a type of project you want to work on, build something that solves a personal need or something you would use every day. Designing a project for yourself will help provide extra motivation when picking up and learning a development platform.

## Mobile Web Sites

Finally, don't forget about mobile Web sites. As discussed earlier, they don't offer the same experience as native apps, but they've still had success and are turned to frequently by users. A variety of new operating system choices that focus on using the mobile Web as the primary application-delivery framework have surfaced recently. Popular Linux distributors such as Ubuntu are proposing a completely open-source take on mobile software and operating systems. Browser stalwart Mozilla is also promising to take Firefox and use it as the foundation for a mobile platform.

Later, we'll take a look at the variety of benefits and potential pitfalls that the mobile Web faces regarding interaction design. The goal of working with HTML, CSS, JavaScript, and other Web technologies is quite simple: Developers should be able to write once, and designers should be able to design once, creating a Web application that runs on any hardware and any operating system. In theory, that sounds amazing, but in practice it hasn't worked out so well. Browsers simply aren't completely consistent between operating systems or rendering engines. Although much work has been done to help mobile Web sites work well in any browser, these applications take a lot of tinkering and fine-tuning in order to function properly. Most of the best mobile applications currently being built use native frameworks such as Objective-C or Java. Although Web apps do look promising, it appears that they're still a few years away from offering the same responsive, animated interactions that users demand from their mobile phones.

This is changing rapidly—even daily—and there could be a time in the near future in which mobile Web sites overtake native applications as the platform Web developers and designers target first. It's best to remain open-minded and consider developing a mobile Web application whenever it can provide the same experience as a mobile app. This results in a product that allows you to have an audience much larger than any single mobile platform's customer base while also helping to keep a development team small and design resources focused.

# Distinctions between Platforms

As a designer, you often won't play a major role in choosing the platform you'll be working with. Typically, engineering resources on a project dictate the direction in which you head. Because this book will focus on interface design, we won't dive too far into which programming languages are the most efficient or simplest to learn, but you should be cognizant of the technical hurdles surrounding a project.

Designers typically see themselves as artists, thus becoming too focused on the creative project and not enough on the technical cogs that spin in the background. This is one of the biggest mistakes designers make, especially early in their careers. Mobile interface design is much more than pretty pictures and perfect typography.

The essence of mobile interaction design is defined by the way an application feels in your hands, the way it responds when you are most dependent upon the information contained within it.

Users expect an application to feel alive on the phone. They expect consistency, reliability, and sophistication. They don't just expect these traits inside your app; they also demand them from how your application functions within the entire ecosystem of their chosen operating system. Therefore, it's important to understand the technical choice you're making with a platform so that you can design to the delight of your user base.

If you target Apple's iOS operating system, it's likely that you're building an application rich in animation with an aesthetic much like that of a piece of fine woodwork. The best applications in Apple's ecosystem feel handcrafted, like something passed down from generation to generation. It's this "Garden of Eden" feel that draws users to the Apple infrastructure.

If you're targeting Apple's platform, your primary goal should be to focus, focus, and focus some more on your interface. To Apple users, details matter, so be sure that you take seemingly insignificant font-size decisions or color choices into consideration.

Google, meanwhile, has long lived by the mantra of "open and free." Android is an open-source operating system, and the majority of applications available for the platform are either free or open source as well. This strategy has been effective as Android has built a reputation of being a perfect haven for individuals who want to tinker around or start their own hobby project. As such, applications on this platform are notorious for being quick to market and a little rough around the edges. This can be an advantage for good designers, though, because it can make it much easier to stand out from the rest of the often ragged crowd.

The reluctance of Android users to pay for apps can cause some issues with monetization strategies, however. Because most applications for Android are free, it's very common to see advertising contained within the application itself. Banner ads, splash screens, or entirely branded applications have become a very real by-product of the mobile app world, and as a designer you will have to live with that reality.

Currently, there's a lot of potential for Android tablet applications. Although Android phone apps are more than plentiful, there are actually very few tablet applications, especially compared to the iPad market. Android provides many tools to help scale applications from small screens to large screens, and with a bit of extra work you can create an outstanding tablet experience, which is rare for Android users.

In the post-PC market, Microsoft has entrenched itself as the leading platform for enterprise deployments. For users who must have their long-standing powerhouse applications, such as Word, Excel, or PowerPoint, Microsoft has emphasized that they are the only significant player around.

Microsoft also offers a unique opportunity for designers as it now uses the same operating system on desktop computers and tablets. Although Apple has OS X on its desktops and Google pushes the Chrome operating system for traditional computers, Microsoft has championed the "no compromises" system in which users conceivably can have their cake and eat it too.

This cross-platform strategy leads to some interesting design decisions, many of which are in direct contradiction to established interface-design principles such as Fitts's Law (discussed in the following Note). It's still too early to decide how this strategy will play out, but Apple and Google seem somewhat open to copying this idea. In OS X Lion and Mountain Lion, Apple brought many of its successful iOS features to the desktop, and Google recently began working to unify the design language between Android and Chrome.

## note

Fitts's Law is a common model for user-interface design and a common principle that designers work with when building software for desktop applications.

The idea is fairly long and complex, but it can be most simply stated like this: Because your computer mouse stops moving either vertically or horizontally once you hit the top or bottom of a computer screen, buttons or interface objects placed on the edges of the screen essentially have infinite width or height. Look at your computer and you'll see this with menus or important navigation buttons appearing near the corners of the screen.

This principle doesn't apply to mobile devices for which fingers are used to manipulate objects, as your finger doesn't need to scroll from one target point to another; you just pick it up and move it where it needs to go.

We could write an entire volume discussing which operating system is best suited for your software, but this small overview is enough background for now on which design elements make each platform unique. Throughout this book, we'll continue to discuss the unique design factors of each operating system, so by the time we're done you'll feel at home as a designer regardless of the platform you're tackling.

IN-DEPTH

What's the best way to get familiar with the interface design of a new operating system? Study the prepackaged applications of an operating system, programs that companies like Microsoft, Apple, or Google ship to users. These are constructed by the same people who created the design language and human-interface guidelines for the platform; thus they're prime examples of what the developer sees as model software for the platform.

- Examine them carefully until you understand why each and every decision was made regarding the user interface.

- Look at the human-interface guidelines for the system. These documents go deep into the design decisions of the system and are like the designer's bible for building a platform.

- Spend a few hours using the built-in applications; set up the native mail app to check e-mail and look at forecasts on the weather app. Soon, you'll be able to understand why the interface works the way it does.

Interface design isn't just about making something look pretty; it's about building a functional piece of software that serves its purpose intently and efficiently. Prebuilt apps are often prime examples of projects with those goals in mind.

# Conclusion

When kicking off a first or second mobile design project, it may be a bit confusing to determine an initial direction. Between various operating system providers, device sizes, and target audiences, there's a lot that can make it difficult to get comfortable and to feel like you're in control of the design.

But by sitting back, relaxing, and tackling these problems one at a time, it will be easy to focus your work and begin building an interface with exceptional interaction design. First, decide whether to use iOS, Android, or another operating system; then choose whether to work for a phone or tablet; then prepare to begin your project.

Interaction design, and design in general, is about making choices. A target operating system and device type are just two choices in the long process of building a product. As you continue to explore the mobile design process, you'll learn how to focus choices into small and simple decisions. Before long, you'll be isolating problems and making informed decisions like an expert mobile designer.

# CHAPTER 2

# DESIGN FOR HUMANS, BY HUMANS

Now that the history lesson is complete, it's time to dive headfirst into the pool of mobile interaction design. Over the coming chapters, we'll cover the various interaction foundations that we should master and the potential roadblocks that stand in the way of building mobile interfaces. The first step of that quest involves determining what exactly mobile interaction design is. Next, it's critical to learn how to avoid the first big mental pitfall that traps many designers working on interfaces: learning that they are designing for humans—impressionable, sometimes confused, unforgiving humans.

# What Is Interaction Design?

Mobile interaction design can be a somewhat confusing term—and one relatively advanced for those just beginning careers in interface design. Often used interchangeably, interaction design and interface design are completely different concepts, and it's important not to mistake one for the other. In fact, the two ideas can appear to be so similar that a casual reading of this text could make it seem as if we are confusing the two as well. They have separate definitions, however, and although they do work together to achieve the same goal, they are actually quite different.

Interface design involves the technical pieces and intricate design language created and mandated by a platform developer for use in a specific operating system. On a popular mobile system such as Android, this includes standards such as using Roboto as a system font or applying the Holo Light or Dark visual theme styles that specify suggested color, font size, line height, or other properties of phone interfaces. Apple has its own carefully defined set of interface design standards, as pictured in Figure 2.1.

**Figure 2.1**   In iOS 7, the use of attributes such as Helvetica Neue-Light as a system font or white as a font color are examples of interface design elements.

Interface design revolves around a standard look for specific elements—for example, the way an icon appears or the type of text used in error messages—throughout an interface. Modern operating systems typically have long human interface guidelines documents that detail how to establish the correct look and feel for each and every visual asset in an application. As an interface designer, it's your responsibility to understand these documents and to be capable of building an interface that meets their requirements.

Interaction design, meanwhile, is a more abstract term. If interface design is like chemistry class, then interaction design is a philosophy seminar. Interaction design has much more to do with the design concepts and interface tools used to present information to a user.

With interaction design, you're going for something much more powerful than slick fonts or an appealing logo; you're looking to understand and influence users' behaviors once they load an application. Though you will use interface tools such as buttons, switches, typography, lighting, audio sound effects, icons, or color to help do this, interaction design is also more focused on the user's reaction or on habits that develop in response to each of these elements. Your goal is to learn how the average user will respond to your interface—ultimately, you hope, in a predictable manner—and then refine and evolve the interface so the user experiences exactly what you intend.

> ## warning
>
> **NO PERFECT USERS**   Unfortunately, when building the interactions contained in an app there is no exact "ideal user" you can target everything toward. In economics, problems that need solving reference "homo economicus": a hypothetical person who makes rational and well-thought-out economic decisions. For mobile designers, though, that person doesn't exist.

Interaction design is a fluid, ever-evolving field. Although interface design changes are somewhat like the world of fashion, dominated by color schemes, background types, and gestures that go in and out of style, interaction design remains a slower-moving industry, one primarily driven by the way users interact with the human-interface tools the operating system offers to applications.

Interaction design, for example, changes when tools like the mouse and keyboard change. Major advancements in interaction design occur when users flock to new technology such as mobile phones, forcing designers to learn how to adapt and build software that takes advantage of features like the pinch-to-zoom and swipe-to-unlock gestures, similar to the examples in Figure 2.2.

**Figure 2.2**    On the same iOS 7 lock screen, the use of a slide-from-left-to-right gesture to unlock the device or a tap-and-drag-up gesture from the camera icon are examples of interaction design.

The field will also continue to evolve in the future. Who knows what will drive the devices and interfaces of the coming years? In just the past few years, major advancements have been made through new technologies such as the Siri voice-command personal assistant and the Google Glass visual platform. If the advanced worlds imagined by science fiction writers continue to manifest in our realm, perhaps previously unthinkable elements such as brainwave control or holographic interfaces could play a role in the interface design of the future.

**tip**

Interaction design isn't strictly limited to mobile applications; everything we use involves interaction design. Practice your design critical-thinking skills by finding ways to improve the interaction design in common, everyday items. How would you improve the design of your car, refrigerator, or vacuum cleaner? Look for the beauty and simplicity in items that function well (or the clutter and difficulty posed by poor interaction design), then use these as inspiration to help improve your apps.

# Goals When Designing an Interface

Now that you know what you're trying to achieve with interaction design—efficient and easy-to-use interfaces—what should your goals be when you embark on this journey? Is an ideal interface one that's simple or full of features? Should you try your best to blend in with every other application and operating system, or should you try to be unique?

Building a product involves making lots of decisions, so your primary goal as an interaction designer is to be in a position to best understand what the right choice is. The end goal is always to create the "ultimate" interface. Unfortunately, that notion is subjective, and in reality it will never happen. Yet, it doesn't hurt to try.

## tip

In a perfect world, you'd be able to design for "homo interacticus": a hypothetical person who makes rational, well-thought-out decisions when they interact with a mobile app. But because he or she doesn't exist, it's often helpful when designing to refer back to the applications built by the platform creator (Mail or Safari on iOS and Gmail or Chrome on Android) to see examples of near-perfect applications.

Because you can't build an ultimate interface, your goal should be to refine your interface as you learn about your customer base and work to retain users and increase their opinion of your application (something measured quantitatively in app stores through ratings and reviews). If you take a systematic approach, you can hopefully solve the seemingly unsolvable equation that reveals which parts of an application increase or decrease user satisfaction.

## Designing for Humans

It sounds silly, yet it's so simple. You're designing applications to be used by humans; if not them, who else would use your work? Grasping that concept, however, is the most difficult obstacle designers face when attempting to build the perfect app interface.

When you design computer software, you're making it for users quite similar to yourself—and ideally your software will scratch the itch of some problem they're trying to solve. But although it's important to remember that they are like you, also keep in mind that they aren't *entirely* like you. When using interface pieces to plan out an interaction design, you must be careful that the design doesn't make sense only inside your own head.

Although that might seem simplistic, redundant, and perhaps even patronizing, it's still the most important primary lesson of designing user interfaces. The vast majority of users, although human, aren't interface designers and may not even be extremely tech-savvy. By reading this book, you are acknowledging that you know more about computer interfaces and interaction design than 99 percent of your potential user base. Users are normal people that come in all different shapes and sizes. They may speak different languages, be older or younger, be better or worse readers, know more or less about computers, and even have various disabilities (such as color blindness) that hinder their ability to use your application. Your users will be simultaneously a lot and hardly anything like you.

Comprehending that you are building for all types of people quickly reveals how difficult interaction design can be. For many, it's this diversity and challenge that makes the job of an interface designer exciting. Understanding your audience helps you see software problems differently and in a way that will help you create an effective design.

As you'll learn through experience, humans are by no means the perfect users. Interface designs need to be forgiving, preventing the user from messing everything up in an instant. Designing for humans is in stark contrast to designing for computers, which automatically run all programming instructions defined in the code. In the apps developed for mobile platforms, human users often won't listen to what they're told even when you think you've laid out everything in a clear and deliberate way. Meeting that challenge is both the most rewarding and the most frustrating aspect of building an interface and interaction design for humans.

So what's the best design for human users? It's one built with forgiveness in mind. Ideally, strive to create something that gives the user a sense of freedom and the ability to explore without fear or apprehension. The biggest way to comfort users through interaction design is to guard against data loss, clearly explain the results of major actions, and allow users to start over when they feel they've made a mistake. When building apps, you want to create experiences that give the user a sense of security to explore your work.

Apple's App Store (see Figure 2.3) is a great example of a design built toward encouraging user exploration while also confirming content. To pay for an app, a user must tap on an app's price, tap a subsequent "buy" button, and then finally enter a password before a purchase is confirmed. This gives users the comfort of browsing without fear of making a mistake and accidentally purchasing something.

That threat of losing massive amounts of important information was one of the biggest dangers of early computing. If the user didn't know how to properly manage applications, it was quite

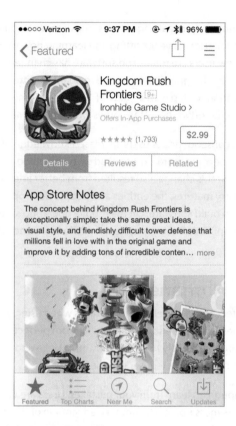

**Figure 2.3** Apple's App Store for iPhone makes prices clear, and purchases require specific confirmation actions from the user.

easy to delete important work documents, treasured family photos, or entire folders of important system information.

In post-PC operating systems, however, there's been a reimagining of how documents are handled, and it's a shining example of great interaction design. Developers working in iOS, for example, don't get full access to the photos a user takes with the iPhone camera. Instead, the applications seeking to alter or enhance photos—by cropping, removing red-eye, or adding a filter—must first create a duplicate of the original photo.

This is a drastic change from the era of traditional computing, in which applications had direct access to original files and any changes made could potentially overwrite or damage precious user photos. Knowing this—and knowing that it made users fearful of working with photos— Apple retooled the way files lived in an operating system, and with this change they paved the way for the significant growth of applications that allow users to get creative with their photographs.

Designing for humans brings other challenges too; some of them are fun, like working around the impatience and aversion users have for sitting and learning how to use an app via a tutorial or help menu. The way new users are trained on software has changed significantly in recent years, something interaction designers have needed to adapt to. Fifteen years ago, it was not uncommon for an application to ship with a guide of 100 pages or more, but today modern software—especially mobile software—often comes with no help manual.

That evolution is a direct consequence of users' increased knowledge of and familiarity with computers: as individuals become more experienced with technology, there is less need for generalized instruction. But this change also resulted from better interaction design. As the computer software industry matures, the entities and people developing applications increase their knowledge of how to build software. On the mobile operating systems of today, navigation menus have been simplified, making a more straightforward and clear process for users to work through.

## Designed by Humans

Though users are imperfect and will likely make mistakes when using your applications, it's important to note that designers are also human and far from perfect. In building interaction design for any application, you're likely to make many mistakes—and any design is capable of being improved in order to offer a better user experience.

There are many ways, though, to learn from your mistakes. Users are very good at pointing out spots where designers mess up, so why not take advantage of that fact? Let users get their hands on your application, test it out, and offer feedback. Be sure to listen to their comments and criticisms, as taking in negative feedback and growing from it is among the most difficult things a person has to adapt to when making work public. It's just like waiting for a grade on a test in high school; you inherently don't want to see or hear what you're doing wrong. As a result, it takes an intentional effort on your part to open up an interface design for comment from the general public and then use that feedback to improve your work.

> tip
>
> Design is not a profession for the shy. In order to be a great designer, you'll have to show off your work frequently and deal with constant criticism about your products. Be warned: Once work has gone public, everyone (and we mean *everyone*) will have an opinion on your work.

That doesn't mean you have to unveil your in-development app to the entire world right away, though. There are many design-focused communities on the Internet that can get your work in front of experienced eyeballs for input on how to improve it. Dribbble and Forrst are communities geared toward designers who want to improve their craft. In these networks, users are encouraged to post their upcoming work on a public forum so that others can comment and suggest improvements. Consider joining one of these sites to gain constructive and well-intended criticism on designs for upcoming projects.

Likewise, it's often valuable to build a small pool of trusted friends and colleagues who are willing to review your work and offer thoughts on what you're doing correctly and what needs improvement. Most successful software development teams implement formal processes such as peer design reviews or code reviews to help make sure their work is being checked internally for improvement.

When working by yourself or on a small team in which you are the only designer, however, it can be difficult to find close friends who are talented and knowledgeable enough to provide this type of insight into your project. If you find yourself in this situation, tech conferences are a great place to meet like-minded individuals who you can build friendships with based on a shared passion for mobile application development. Because you're building digital software, it's easy to instantly share Photoshop designs, wireframe workflows, or early software beta builds with anyone around the globe. Plan to attend a few conferences and make a concerted effort to meet other designers and software developers while you're there.

Finally, there's often nothing more helpful than a beta-testing group that allows you to experiment with interaction design types and play with test builds of upcoming applications. When finding users to test prerelease software, it's important to select a diverse group of potential users. Look for friends and family who are known for vocally sharing their opinions, and be willing to listen when they offer their thoughts. It can often be a valuable experience to sit next to them and watch as they use your software for the first time. While observing, you can see what parts of the design they had problems with and where it could be clarified, simplified, or better explained.

## tip

When choosing one of your first beta groups, try to recruit a group about two or three times larger than you imagine is necessary. Unfortunately, people get busy or will offer less feedback than you desire, so grow your group in order to get adequate amounts of feedback.

By realizing that you, like your users, are also imperfect, you can give yourself a stronger chance of success with software designs. The importance of listening to users with an open mind can't be overstated. Sure, they probably don't know as much about user interface or interaction design as you do. They won't understand whether the technique used in an application is thought out well or applies the proper implementation suggested by the operating system provider. The same users don't know all the work that goes into making a Hollywood blockbuster or the construction of a pro sports team's roster—but that doesn't mean their criticism isn't spot-on sometimes. These people are your users—potential customers—and as the saying goes, the customer is always right.

# Where to Begin

Now that you've admitted that you're a self-doubting designer permanently cursed to a lifetime of consistent pixel-by-pixel second-guessing, it's a good time to start thinking about how to launch an app project. To begin, it's important to know how software and interfaces work together to build a complete product. This leads to a new spin on an age-old question: Which came first, the software or the interface?

## note

The neck-bearded and nerdy amongst us may snidely comment here that the answer is obvious: Software came before interfaces, you might say, with the introduction of punch-card computers or even text terminals. But remember, text is an interface too. As long as a user is interacting with data or a computer, an interface of some sort is required.

There's a distinct difference between software and interfaces, and it's even possible for a single piece of software to have several different interfaces. Consider the Windows 8 operating system shown in Figure 2.4. When running an application on a traditional desktop computer with a keyboard and mouse, users have a distinctly different interaction experience than they do when using a finger as a pointing device on a Windows tablet that runs the same software on the same operating system. Regardless of the hardware, users want the same experience with the different interface mechanisms.

Your software should be fine-tuned so that regardless of interface, operating system, or device size the experience is unique and effective. It's your job as the interaction designer to thoroughly understand the difference between software and interface. In essence, the user is paying for you to make the tough design decisions for them, relying on your skill and expertise to provide an experience that is both delightful and intuitive. But because the user's experience with software is so dependent upon the interface and because an outstanding interface requires responsive and well-programmed software, it can often be difficult to tell the difference between interface and software. Let's take a minute to examine how these two important aspects of software design intertwine when building a product.

Advancements in interface design will sometimes allow for novel software ideas and concepts. In other situations, changes in software will create new interface opportunities. Processing power advances in the original computer terminal, for example, paved the way for the use of

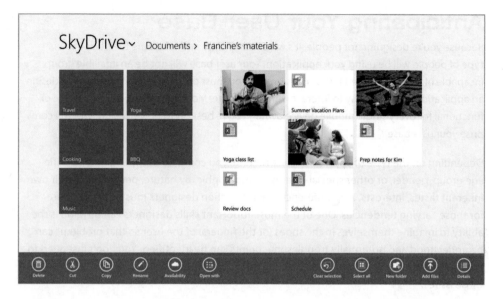

**Figure 2.4**  File management and cloud storage app SkyDrive effectively utilizes the advantages of Windows 8's user-interface changes. It features large touch targets for tapping with a finger while also providing function buttons toward the bottom of the screen for optimal accessibility with a mouse.

computers as word processors. In the early age of computers, it was clear they would at some point replace typewriters and pen and paper as the most common writing tools; it just took time for software to get there and be capable of handling such an interface.

Inversely, the advent of a new interface—the accurate touch screen on the first iPhone—allowed for novel software opportunities thanks to new powers such as pinching two fingers together to make photographs larger or smaller on the screen. Today, nearly every photo application on every mobile platform with a touch screen allows the user to swipe or pinch in order to see new photos or zoom in to tiny details. This hardware change fostered a type of software design that quickly became intuitive.

Computer interfaces, be they hardware or software, work hand in hand with applications. With new methods constantly being invented, it's our job as interaction designers to keep up with trends in the industry. The best way to do this is to follow the announcements and major unveilings made by key players in the mobile industry. Large hardware producers such as Samsung, Apple, and Microsoft frequently have conferences and press announcements at which they roll out new hardware designs. Operating systems likewise are often updated on a yearly or even more frequent basis, and the providers of software development kits typically keep developer portals up to date with information on system roadmaps and software changes. Be sure to frequently check these portals; information in the mobile software world usually has a short shelf life before it's cleared away for newer technology.

# Anticipating Your User Base

Because you're designing for people, it's wise to step back and take time to anticipate what type of people will be using your application. Your user base will not be an infallible group incapable of being confused by your designs, so you must prepare for that and work to design an application that is as easy to interact with as possible. Most apps won't be marketable or functional for every single mobile device owner; you're best off to first envision who will comprise your user base.

Depending on the type of app you're constructing, you could be designing for a specific age group, gender, or other special-interest demographic. By nature, people have their own inherent tastes, interests, and preferences, so interaction designers must build software for those varying tendencies. One of the most important skills designers can develop is the ability to imagine themselves in the shoes (or the fingers) of the user so that problems can be understood and potentially troublesome points can be identified. You don't just need to know where they're having problems, though; you need to understand why they're having those issues.

Many designers are apprehensive about the idea of catering their work to people of different tastes or abilities; after all, it's easiest to build what you know. But by not panicking over the notion of constructing software for different types of people and embracing this reality of design, you'll have a leg up on competing applications and open up the possibility of wider success.

There's an urban legend frequently passed around Silicon Valley that Facebook's logo is blue because its founder, Mark Zuckerberg, suffers from red/green color blindness and thus has the easiest time seeing things that are blue. As a result, it was a supposedly natural choice for him to pick that color as the primary design accent for his Web interface and branding.

This story is an effective parable that should guide your work as a designer. You'll be building tools for people who have disabilities or who experience computer software differently than you do. One of the biggest mistakes you can make as a designer is to lose sight of the fact that your users are a very diverse group.

There are many ways to help your apps cater to segments of the population with capabilities that differ from your own. There are a number of tools available, such as xScope by Iconfactory, that help designers get a better understanding of how applications look to people with various forms of color blindness. Likewise, Apple has built a variety of accessibility tools into iOS. AssistiveTouch, for example, is a feature that allows various iPhone gestures to be performed with a single hand, helping those users who may have disabilities that make using two hands to operate a device difficult or impossible.

> **tip**
>
> When building applications, enable operating system features such as text-to-voice, color blindness controls, and enhanced zoom modes to see how your on-screen interactions work with these features. It would be a disservice to users with disabilities if you didn't test an app to make sure it's usable by as many people as possible.

Instead of ignoring this reality and allowing the iPhone to be unusable for people with disabilities, Apple has built a special tool developers can take advantage of to provide an accessible application for all. Not to be outdone, Google is well known for its industry-leading voice search function, which allows users who find typing difficult to browse the Web as easily as any other mobile device owners. Google has also built other powerful accessibility options into Android, such as text scaling for users who have trouble reading standard font sizes.

Certainly not every app developed can have such focused or advanced design considerations, but these do serve as strong examples of the way the titans of the industry have rethought the traditionally single-faced form of interaction design applications, making them work better for a number of users who otherwise would have been left out in the cold. When designing interactions on screen, it's important to be creative and imaginative in order to push the envelope of efficiency and create groundbreaking mobile interfaces.

So what's the best way to formally undertake the process of planning for your user base? Many designers practice a concept called preparing personas. Personas are hypothetical people who might download your app; for practice, try to role-play as those personas in an attempt to understand the problems your application is trying to solve for them, how they'll use the application, and what their impression of your interface and interaction designs might be.

Designers for the popular image-centric social-networking site Pinterest, for example, might create personas—a bride-to-be, a person looking to redecorate their home, or someone looking for a new wardrobe—to put themselves in the mindset of people who would check out their photo-sharing service. Each type of user will have very different needs and desires for their application, and all need to be considered when making design choices. Similarly, a personal-health application might try to envision what avid runners would do when using their software, or an educational app developer might consider how kindergartners would respond and react to their reading-instruction tool.

Through an app such as MindNode for Mac (see Figure 2.5), you can quickly create simple personas that can be shared among your design team and project stakeholders, allowing you to better analyze and critique potential app interfaces for a specific type of user.

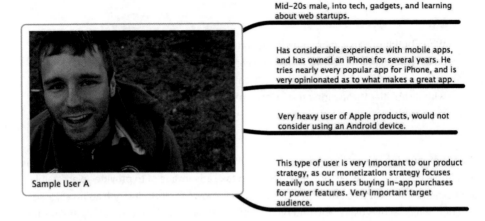

Mid-20s male, into tech, gadgets, and learning about web startups.

Has considerable experience with mobile apps, and has owned an iPhone for several years. He tries nearly every popular app for iPhone, and is very opinionated as to what makes a great app.

Very heavy user of Apple products, would not consider using an Android device.

This type of user is very important to our product strategy, as our monetization strategy focuses heavily on such users buying in-app purchases for power features. Very important target audience.

Sample User A

**Figure 2.5**   With MindNode, you can draw up hypothetical personas to help you envision how potential users will react to your interfaces.

Another solid strategy for learning more about potential users is to peruse the field for existing applications that aim to solve similar problems or that have similar user bases to the app you plan to build. The success of the app store model means there are now hundreds of thousands of applications to compete against in the marketplace, but that also means there are hundreds of thousands of apps to use as inspiration. Don't hesitate to look at other successful applications, especially the top downloads on the platform you're designing on, for quality examples of design, implementation of special features, and use of interface components. Mobile app stores have now enjoyed five years of success and growth, so learn from the wealth of experience gained by designers and developers. Most stores police their top-download lists, so the apps you find at the top of the charts will almost always be admirable pieces of quality development work.

Finally, a lot can be learned by directly discussing application ideas with potential users. Beta testing was mentioned earlier, but that effort can often come too far into the development process to make a drastic overhaul of major ideas or interaction design. Beta testing is a great way to figure out small quirks or bugs that need to be fixed before shipping the app to the marketplace, although there's usually not enough time remaining to fix issues deeply rooted in the interaction design.

Instead of waiting until then to identify major issues, it's useful to reach out to anonymous potential users before typing the first line of code or opening the first Photoshop file. Although it sounds simple, many designers advocate hitting up a local coffee shop with sketches or early interaction wireframes in order to pick the brains of random possible customers. Grab a sampling of various ages and genders, offer to buy them a cup of coffee, and use them as a focus group to gather reactions to and feedback on your early ideas. Often, those few dollars will go a long way toward figuring out whether you're on the right or wrong path to developing a successful mobile app.

# Mobile's Role in User Workflow

Because your audience is composed of humans, you need to recognize not only their faults but also the great things about them: namely, the fact that they have very busy lives. Many users are likely to be juggling hectic jobs, a busy social schedule, sometimes a full family, and perhaps a hobby or two. No matter how helpful an app may be or how much time you guarantee to save the user with it, it will still be a struggle to convince your intended audience that an application can provide value to them.

Because most applications cost very little (if anything at all), there's not much incentive for the user to sink time into learning a program's interface or features; they didn't pay much for it, so they don't lose much if it just sits on their device's metaphorical bookshelf collecting dust. Most people are unable to find the time to review the user manual for their new $30,000 car or $2,000 television, much less a $1 app buried amongst the dozens of others on their phone. That places just a little bit of pressure on designers to make sure software is simple, intuitive, and easy to learn, doesn't it?

With this understandable impatience in mind, it can't be stressed strongly enough that applications should have simple, easy-to-understand interfaces and user interactions that are readily apparent and require little thought. If the user is unable to pick up an application and figure it out quickly, he's likely to leave it and never open it again. With so many apps fighting for users' attention, the opportunity cost is simply too low for them to spend more than a few minutes attempting to understand how a program works.

Some startling math helps put this point in perspective. If an iPhone user wanted to test out every application in the App Store for just one minute, it would take nearly two years— without sleep—to finish that quest. With this incredible amount of software available, does anyone have an incentive to pick up an application and continue using it if it can't be easily understood?

When developing an interface and interaction design on a mobile phone, it's also important to keep in mind that mobile computing is still in its infancy and ultimately serves as a companion to the functions offered by traditional computers. Many designers often forget that their phone applications are in fact properly named "mobile" apps; they're used on the go, with only a few glances given to them at a time. It's important to remember that these applications are not running on powerful computers with large displays. At least for the time being, it will be difficult to replace traditional workstation applications such as word processors, advanced photo editors, or other programs that require significant typing and a steady hand with a mouse. But mobile phones do handle portable, simple software extremely well.

> ### note
>
> Remember that users might be using not a single traditional computer but a variety of traditional computers. Work desktops, home laptops, Windows PCs, and Macintosh and Linux machines could all be things your users encounter on a daily basis. Try to imagine any potential use case that a potential user could fit into.

Finally, it's also crucial to be cognizant of the types of situations users will be in when accessing your work. Laptops, obviously, are not very convenient for use at the grocery store, on a subway, or at a youth soccer game. Yet, thanks to smartphones it's now possible for anyone to send

**Figure 2.6**   iBiker by ITMP Technology, Inc. features large text and a simple interface, making the app useful for runners or bikers looking to access it while exercising. (Courtesy of ITMP Technology, Inc.)

e-mails or check Twitter while in those locations. Thus, it's imperative that you not only consider the interaction methods you use in applications, but also the situations a user will be in when attempting those interactions.

Suppose you're building an app for avid cyclists to use to track workouts, one like iBiker (see Figure 2.6). It's very likely they will access this program while riding their bicycles. As a result, it would be a terrible idea to pick small typography or pile a host of buttons on the most prominent interfaces. As a designer, you must anticipate where your application will be called upon if you want to provide the best experience. Mobile apps will often complement traditional computing experiences, not replace them.

### IN-DEPTH

Looking for an application that was built to meet the needs of as wide a range of users as possible? Browse different mainstream social-network applications such as Facebook, Twitter, or Foursquare.

Applications like these have enjoyed worldwide success and are now used by people of all languages, ages, and genders and in dozens of countries around the globe. There is not a single demographic that isn't found in these applications' user bases. With this in mind, their designers had to build extraordinarily wide-reaching applications.

Take some time to browse these applications and think deeply about why their designers made the decisions they did. How would you design an app if you knew it had to be viewable in nearly every language spoken on the planet? Which gestures and interaction types would you integrate if you knew your application would be used by both the most novice and most advanced users on a platform?

These applications may not be perfect in every way, but their designers have inevitably tackled a plethora of questions related to the broad scope of their user base. They are great case studies of design that show how to walk the fine line of creating something that works for everyone.

## Conclusion

If your applications are going to find success in the marketplace, it's your job as a designer to remember that you're building for people like you. No matter how brilliant a concept is or how sensible you are with interface principles, an app won't go far if the user doesn't find it engaging, coherent, and easy to use. This can be anticipated and accounted for by reaching out for input both before you start work and during the development process.

Although you might want to design an application with every feature imaginable, the most successful apps on any mobile platform often do only one thing extremely well. As long as you know what you're trying to provide a user with, you can strip away the unnecessary fluff or problem points; as a result, it's much more likely that the app will climb the popularity charts.

# CHAPTER 3

# DYNAMIC DIFFERENCES IN MOBILE DESIGN

Clearly, no two mobile computing devices are created alike. With a variety of operating systems, platforms, and screen sizes, there's a lot to keep in mind when attempting to cater an application to a certain piece of technology.

It's time to start tying interaction and human-interface design together as you begin breaking down how to design for specific form factors and for the ways people use software on their devices.

# Understanding the Role of Mobile

As advanced as mobile devices and software have become, they still play a complementary role to traditional computing. Applications often tie into more traditional digital setups, be they word processors, spreadsheet managers, slideshow presentations, PDF readers, e-mail clients, or anything else used to perform work or personal functions. When not uploading photos from a hike, watching a movie, or playing a game on a mobile phone or tablet, some other form of hardware or software—most likely the kind that predates smartphones—is being used.

But as smartphones and tablets increase in power and potential, users are using these devices for an increasing number of tasks, and this growth has led to a remarkable point in computer history. PC sales consistently climbed for years, but numbers are now beginning to drop, while tablet sales are rising exponentially. The trend reported by various hardware manufacturers is largely the same; PC demand is way down and mobile demand is way up.

The drop in demand for PCs may also, ironically, be due to improvements in the quality of desktops and laptops. Processing power, hard drive space, and other features that previously advanced radically on an annual basis throughout the 1990s and 2000s no longer change so quickly. Owners now get more bang for their buck because computers live significantly longer and don't seem outdated shortly after leaving the store shelf.

Some manufacturers, it appears, saw this problem coming. If their products became so reliable and so advanced that purchases were necessary only once every decade, their bottom line would gradually become frighteningly small.

Enter the tablet. When Apple announced the iPad in January 2010, Steve Jobs tried hard to make the case for the need for his new electronic product. Everyone he knew owned a laptop and smartphone, the Apple executive said, and the iPad would fit somewhere in between those two devices. Jobs believed there was a place for a device bigger than a phone but not as hefty as a laptop.

Over time, though, tablets may end up playing an even bigger role in users' daily lives than even Jobs expected. As the large yet holdable devices begin to permeate the marketplace, fewer people see the need for a traditional computer and instead opt to use only mobile platforms.

Just six months after he defended his product's very existence, Jobs sat on stage at the All Things Digital conference and made a now famous statement: Traditional computers are like trucks and iPads are like cars. In the early days of transportation, he pointed out, many people drove trucks merely because there was no other type of vehicle available. But as people and products evolved, the car became the preferred method of transportation and dominated the world's roads.

Jobs saw tablet computing as a digital interaction method primed to become the sedan of the information superhighway. Tablets, he contended, could emerge as the computing device for the common person.

As the battle for users' dollars and attention plays out between desktops, laptops, tablets, and phones in the coming years, the market will remain volatile and cluttered, while the industry will be full of opinions on what should drive computing forward. Perhaps in the end mobile will continue to outpace other computers and push laptops to the brink of extinction, or maybe the two will serve unique purposes and play separate roles in the daily lives of the public.

Today, though, there's a wealth of services that help developers build software that can be made available to users of all types of devices. Cloud database and file-hosting services such as Parse, Apple's iCloud, Google Cloud Messaging, or Microsoft's Windows Azure have made it incredibly easy to build complex and feature-rich software that shares data across many platforms. This gives development teams the ability to target all users on native platforms as long as they optimize for device characteristics and interaction methods.

> **note**
>
> Where technology is today, it's much easier to provide a responsive experience and optimal interaction using native code and frameworks. As your development team advances, you'll probably be targeting software toward multiple platforms. This is where software such as iCloud or Azure comes into the picture, because simple cross-platform compatibility and easy data accessibility is very much an important aspect of successful modern interaction design.

Mobile and its influence on the way people use digital systems is still in its infancy. As interaction designers, it's essential to understand our users and the way they work with devices but also to know the history of the technology they're using. It's all part of the effort to comprehend how current products solve user problems and meet user needs: valuable information we can use when developing products that define how we solve similar problems in the future.

# Mobile-Only Interactions

By now, you know that interaction design is the process by which software is iterated and fine-tuned into a form that delivers the best possible experience for the user. As an interface or interaction designer, it's your job to sit down and strip away all unnecessary details and excess in your software so that you can minimize its complexity for potential customers.

Although interaction design often relates to software interfaces, hardware plays a major role in that concept as well. Let's take a look at user-interaction methods and potentially problematic situations that only arise when working with smartphones and tablets.

# Interactions Only Possible with a Smartphone

In the early days of advanced mobile phones, processing power was the most significant limiting factor in interaction design. It was also the reason phones had been seen as second-class computing citizens; the devices just didn't boast the juice that desktops and laptops have long had, and as a result performance suffered. Early smartphones often stuttered and were generally unresponsive.

> ### tip
>
> While working on interface design, it's important to remember that responsiveness is a subjective term and can change greatly when moving across devices and operating systems. It's important to use a variety of devices on a platform in order to gain a better idea of relative performance context.
>
> When using an iPhone or Samsung Galaxy device that's a year or two old, it will likely feel slow and sluggish, but remember that these devices once provided the most responsive experiences for their respective platforms, and current devices that feel fast will one day be very slow.

Only with the launch of the iPhone did on-the-go devices finally start to enter the conversation as having major multiuse potential. This new class of device didn't bring an exponential jump in processing power, though, as its major advancement was the result of a remarkable decision by Apple's design team. They chose to key in on the interface's responsiveness to touch. Many competitors had focused on giving phones desktop-style functionality, but Apple focused on interactivity and simplicity.

The design goals were simple in concept. When pinched, photos should resize dynamically without delay or slowdown; Web pages should scroll immediately when flicked up or down; dragging an icon around on screen should be fluid and should feel as if the pixels below are magnetized to our fingertips.

Creating these interactions is easier said than done when working with limited phone processors and RAM. Mobile operating systems today still work within these constraints, although hardware improvements have increased significantly with dual- or quad-core processors, and cloud-hosting solutions make limited storage space less of an issue.

Any remaining lack of power is made up for by the dramatic difference in hardware functionality and capabilities that smartphones now provide over their predecessors. For example, pinpointing the precise location of a laptop wasn't an essential function 10 years ago, but now that feature is essential to many smartphone apps thanks to GPS receivers and cell-tower triangulation. Location identification has significantly enhanced mobile interaction design and has been a major force of smartphone growth. With a device that can quickly locate exactly where a user is, there's no longer a need to spend time entering a ZIP code or address when attempting to find show times at nearby movie theaters or when determining where the best Chinese food restaurant is in a 10-block radius.

Taking advantage of previously unimaginable smartphone features like GPS helps teach a critical early lesson of mobile interaction design: You should always minimize the amount of user effort required to interface with your service. Thankfully, many new mobile tools and hardware features are there to help us accomplish this goal.

You can use a phone's gyroscope to determine the device's orientation, customize a profile using photos taken with the phone's camera, or create augmented reality applications using a device's magnetic compass. The features you're able to take advantage of continue to develop, evidenced by new technologies such as near-field communication or infrared sensors, and will only continue to grow more impressive in the future.

When designing an app, it's important to ensure these functions take advantage of smartphones' inherent mobility. When working on a platform, it's useful to think of the features and functions at hand as if you're playing a sport; laying out an interaction plan for an app is like working out a team's lineup and game strategy. If you want to be the best manager you can be, you need to fully understand the way the wind is blowing on any given day, and play to your personal design strengths, all while de-emphasizing the design weaknesses for your team.

A great example of this is the Hourly News application produced by Urban Apps, shown in Figure 3.1. Its exceptional interaction design capitalizes on the various hardware and software advantages offered by a mobile phone.

The app is fairly simple; its sole function is to allow a user to listen to hourly news updates from notable news, sports, and finance media outlets. The app's designers, though, assumed it would most frequently be used when a person is in motion: driving a car, walking, or riding public transportation. Therefore, when the app is opened the first newscast is started automatically, with no interaction with the interface required. The gorgeous main interface contains only a single, primary interface button. Very large and in the center of the screen, the button's only function is to pause or play the audio. The feed can be skipped through or moved backwards with an on-screen swipe gesture. A cell phone connection or Wi-Fi network is needed in order for recent news updates to be downloaded at the application's launch.

By understanding how a user would interact with the app and integrating common hardware capabilities, a simple and wonderful app was created that offers a prime example of software that would not be possible on any device other than a smartphone.

**Figure 3.1**   If mobile interaction design was a sport, Hourly News would be on a long winning streak with its exceptional design focused on optimizing utility for mobile use. (Courtesy of Urban Apps, LLC.)

## Interactions Only Possible with a Tablet

Smartphones don't have a monopoly on unique mobile experiences, though. Tablets also boast a host of interactions that are unique to their platform—though they do share many of the advantages that smartphones feature, because the two devices share a common ancestry.

Tablets are much smaller and lighter than laptops and also contain advanced microphones, cameras, location-tracking chips, gyroscopes, and other features that typically do not ship with traditional computers.

Much like when building a phone app, key features should be taken advantage of when constructing tablet software, but it's important to recognize that not all of these advantages are guaranteed. The iPad, for example, comes in two models: one with cellular connectivity and one without. Similarly, the first-generation Nexus 7 has no rear-facing camera, and the Microsoft Surface has no cellular connectivity option.

The features that are available on a device vary greatly by manufacturer and platform, so it's important to identify the necessity of each and every function in an app and how it will operate if certain hardware qualities are not available on a device.

> ### note
>
> How do you determine the hardware features that will be available for the platform you're targeting? It's a constant question for designers and developers. It can vary heavily by platform, but most operating system providers offer some sort of official page, usually on their primary developer portal, that offers some type of running statistics of or insight into devices prevalent in the market.
>
> Bloggers and developers with an interest in a platform often publish data and attempt to identify the prevalence of features on a certain device or operating system in order to know what's most common. If data is unavailable from the platform provider, these posts can be useful, but the limited number of sources they draw from means that they shouldn't be considered authoritative on the subject.

This influences interaction design, as an app needs to offer a uniform experience regardless of device capability. For example, designers need to ensure software doesn't crash if a device isn't constantly connected to the Internet, because some devices come with Wi-Fi only or with cellular data options. If you're integrating photos into your app, it should be designed so that a user can pull an image from the local photo library if a camera is unavailable to take a picture to fill that space.

It's these subtle, sometimes overlooked device differences and hardware issues that often lead to terrible experiences for users. Interaction design is not only about producing great experiences for users in the most ideal situations, it's also about guaranteeing they don't have an atrocious time attempting to navigate an app because their device doesn't contain a hardware feature a designer erroneously assumed would be there.

The tablet's biggest advantage is simply that it brings the world of touch screens and dynamically interfaced applications to a device that is sized for reading, writing, and interacting with data. Once a designer first begins designing an app for a tablet, he or she is often struck by how similar it is to creating a poster, book cover, or other graphic for a paper product. For users too, this is the device's most exciting feature; it's the size of a book, yet eliminates the need to keep track of hundreds of pages of paper. In many respects, tablets are better than books because they allow for an interactive experience that a bound collection of dead-tree fragments simply doesn't provide.

For these reasons, Fortune 500 companies have been big early adopters of tablets despite historically being some of the slowest movers when it comes to information technology.

"Enterprise customers," as they're known, are notorious among software developers and contractors for needing to use an operating system or software package for long beyond its anticipated lifespan simply because the existing product is too familiar and upgrading requires too much time or money. Because this group of purchasers—people and companies who normally would be averse to adopting a technology early—has embraced tablets so readily, there's a large potential market for products that replicate traditional work or productivity tasks that require traditional filing systems or high performance in situations in which traditional computers may be impractical.

Tablets also have great potential as individualized entertainment devices, and that market should not be ignored either. Phone devices are often too small to make watching videos or playing games enjoyable for long periods of time, but tablets are the perfect devices for users who want to sit back and be entertained in a location other than the living room. By optimizing the interaction experience and focusing on content and clarity, many apps in recent years have offered immersive experiences akin to ones featured in movie theaters and on modern-day video game consoles.

# Interactions That Aren't Possible on Mobile

So far, this chapter has done nothing but sing the praises of next-generation mobile devices and the new types of app experiences they offer. However, there are several potential interaction designs and features that are impossible or extremely difficult to achieve on a phone or tablet.

Returning quickly to the "interaction design is a sport" analogy, the following experiences and interaction methods would be a team's worst players. Ideally, these individuals would sit on the bench and stay far away from the field of the interaction plan for our app.

## Keyboards and Data Entry

Applications that require extensive text entry or typing are standout examples of mobile-problematic experiences. It's hard to recreate the ease and familiarity of the full QWERTY keyboard on a glass surface. Many have tried custom keyboard configurations, but text entry is still a key feature for which mobile devices trail traditional computers.

There are ways to get around this deficiency, including the Bluetooth support that allows external wireless keyboards to connect to tablets or phones, but this remains more of an obstacle than a solution as users must constantly remember to grab an extra device in order gain full functionality.

Third-party hardware manufacturers, and even Microsoft with its Surface tablet, have launched efforts to create covers that also function as QWERTY keyboards, but these attempts often involve shape, size, or other format compromises that still make them less useful than traditional typing setups.

When creating an application of any kind, be aware of this data-entry difficulty as the interaction design is developed. Many programs make inputting numbers and letters too difficult, and as a result users shy away from using those apps. A little bit of work focused on making text entry more efficient can go a long way in interaction design.

Most operating systems, for example, provide multiple keyboard types that can be chosen in the programming stage. iOS and Android both have several layouts to pick from—including one optimized with buttons for entering common Web URL endings such as .com and .edu and another designed for typing text paragraphs efficiently. When laying out the various points for data entry in an application, take time to learn all the native interface components that are available, including the different switches and button styles. The designers who created these components spent significant time deciding what the easiest ways to manage entry on the platform would be. They've probably thought about a lot of the issues you haven't and definitely considered the issues you already have. Go for the simple answer: If a component looks well suited for the type of data entry your app requires, don't second-guess that hunch.

## Click, Tap, Point

A discussion of interaction types would not be complete without mentioning pointer devices—the tool used to click, tap, or manipulate content on screen. For mobile computers, this means fingers; for traditional computers, it's the mouse.

The most important difference between the two involves the interaction radius the user has to engage with content. When moving a mouse, the user directly interacts with a small number of pixels at a time, usually only a handful. But when tapping with the finger, the user comes into contact with a much larger radius—sometimes as many as 40 or 50 pixels. Human fingers clearly aren't as precise as mouse-pointer icons. Thus users have a much harder time making small, precise inputs on a screen, which is why larger buttons and icons are often seen on mobile devices.

User pointing devices won't be the only variable designers need to consider; user dexterity is never the same either. When working with a mouse, users don't directly interact with content; instead, they move a device sitting on a table that then interacts with content. The software that operates computer mice can be adjusted for a variety of speed settings, giving the user flexibility in determining how his ability will affect the computing experience. A finger, though, comes with no such options menu, and some users may find it difficult to accomplish advanced gestures that come naturally to others.

## Expandability

Mobile phones and tablets come with their own limitations as well. Namely, they lack the expandability and added-feature compatibility that traditional computers have offered for years. It's tough, for example, to find a mainstream smartphone with USB ports, HDMI inputs, or connections to output to multiple monitors or hard drives. In some ways, this makes your job easier, as designers can focus on a single user experience and not worry about outlying features that are not commonly used. But like many tradeoffs in the mobile realm, this is a double-edged sword; many enthusiastic potential customers gain satisfaction from features or capabilities that are difficult or nearly impossible to implement on modern mobile devices—leaving potential profit on the table as a result.

# Universal Appeal

So far, this discussion has focused on the difference between phones and tablets, but designers will often have to tackle a situation in which they need to create an application that works well on both, or they'll need to build a program that can function easily across a variety of operating systems. So what essential design and interaction practices are important to know while attempting to put together a one-size-fits-many app?

## Interaction Experiences for Phones and Tablets

When discussing the design of an app that will work on both phones and tablets, let's first assume that it will be built for the same operating system platform. If you start out designing an app for iPhone, it's most likely you'll be adapting it for iPad next; an Android phone app will convert most easily to an Android tablet. Although it's possible, albeit unlikely, that an iPhone app you design will be quickly ported over to an Android tablet or vice versa, we'll save discussion of techniques for creating multiplatform apps for the next section.

When creating an app for both phones and tablets, the primary goal should be to scale interaction types for the two devices from the very beginning of the project. If an app targeted for both small- and large-form devices appears anywhere on a potential project roadmap, it's highly recommended that you consider how your design will work on various screen sizes before moving too far along in the creation process.

For inspiration, look to how leading Web sites have developed in recent years—especially the way they've implemented responsive Web design techniques. While mobile app designers have enjoyed the luxury of being able to target native interface elements or specify interaction types based on a device's screen size, Web designers have been working since the pre-iPhone era to provide identical content and functionality on screens both large and small as well as in situations in which connectivity is limited. Many of these Web sites may be less interactive than or have limited features compared to a mobile application, but they provide valuable insight into the way content can flow on a page and be rendered effectively for mobile.

Most responsive Web sites with multiple pages stacked in a hierarchical menu, for example, found that the way to function best depended on the platform used to access the page. On a mobile phone with a small screen, the menu remains hidden and requires interaction with buttons to bring the menu into focus. On a larger touchscreen device or a desktop browser, the entire menu stays visible and appears above or next to content.

Take a look at the Google.com homepage (Figure 3.2) as an example. When moving from the desktop site to the mobile version, the search window is scaled, different menus appear, search buttons are reconstructed, and the displayed interface is reduced. Google clearly knows how to slightly modify the browsing experience based on form factor, an essential principle of responsive Web design.

It's a simple design element, but a key one; like most good interaction decisions, it involves stripping away unnecessary clutter when on a small screen and emphasizing controls and enhanced navigation opportunities when on a large screen. Designing an app that can be scalable to screens of any size relies on a key concept: questioning whether every feature added during the development process simplifies or clarifies the interface. Designers can easily be trapped by the temptation to add features that seem to enhance functionality without realizing that such decisions come with consequences.

Far too often, designers work out a full interface concept complete with related interaction techniques for a mobile phone application before they begin to contemplate how it will look and feel on a larger tablet. Don't wait to consider concepts of scalability until after the design is complete or, even worse, the app design is being programmed. Once the design is pixel perfect

**Figure 3.2**  Google offers a scaling interface for users that looks great on both laptops and phones.

in Photoshop or lines of code have been written, it's essentially too late; changes are much more expensive and time-consuming when implemented in a near-final state than they are when the design is in the form of wireframes and pencil-and-paper sketches.

Take typography, for example. Text that may fit easily on a large iPad screen can frequently fit poorly or even be illegible when scaled down for an iPhone. Thus it's important to discuss things like menu copy and paragraph length with the rest of your application team to determine how the words will best flow on a variety of screen sizes.

Before kicking off the design process, it's also important to research how the platform you're targeting specifically handles the movement between large and small device styles when it comes to interaction design and program logic. Each platform deals with these issues differently, so it's best to keep up with the strategies recommended by the operating system's creator.

On iOS, for instance, designers and engineers typically work together to produce two separate XIBs (Xcode Interface Builder files) for any universal binary (an application that will run on both iPhone and iPad). This strategy allows for versatility when moving between screen sizes as well as the opportunity to easily pick different interaction types or gesture methods based on the screen size a user engages with.

The introductions of iOS 6 and 7, however, also brought Apple's announcement of a new method of managing mobile interfaces called auto-layout. This allows just one XIB to be created for use on a variety of screen sizes.

> ### note
>
> An Xcode Interface Builder file is a proprietary file type that can be used in the creation of iPhone and iPad application interfaces using an Xcode feature called Interface Builder. These files are extremely common, as they allow interfaces to be designed graphically while also allowing an easy tie-in to programmed code.

Currently, auto-layout is something still a bit complex and not fully embraced by designers as a way to easily move apps from iPhone to iPad. The most common implementation method is still to create separate XIBs for each screen size or to create interfaces completely in code. Yet, the new auto-layout process is growing in popularity, and Apple continues to make considerable advancements with the technology. It became much more useful with the introduction of the larger iPhone 5, because designers needed to implement interfaces that could adapt to both the new 4-inch diagonal screen size and the 3.5-inch version of older iPhone generations. As a result, it's not unforeseeable that at some point in the near future a single XIB could be used for both iPad and iPhone.

Android, meanwhile, is much better suited to adapt to multiple interface sizes. Because Android was a system built from the ground up to support various screen resolutions, the tools for creating Android apps have always focused on easily forming scalable interfaces. Today, most design work is aided by creating XML files that dictate how an interface should scale based on the size of the device's screen.

Currently, the Android system supports four screen sizes for phones and tablets: small, normal, large, and extra large. Devices are classified based on screen size and resolution, and Google dictates the acceptable ranges for each screen type. When working with Android, it's up to the designer to decide how the app should respond to each size.

The action bar, for example, is a common Android interface item that allows the user to access the app's main menu and switch between different application views or functions. The bar also often serves as a home for common interactions inside an app, such as searching or sharing content. Finally, the action bar often contains a title to indicate a user's current location inside the app.

An action bar may have multiple items, not all of which can fit on the screen at one time. While working with Android interface XML, a designer can specify which fragment functions are the most important and should appear on screen regardless of the device's size. Likewise, a designer can specify the font size based on a screen's specifications. With multiple screen sizes to target and the ability to modify based on screen density or resolution, Android designs can be tailored to work well with the wide range of tablets on the market.

On Android, the action bar anchored to the top of the view and right below the main navigation bar shows the variety of different fragments available to the user for displaying content. For the Google Play app shown in Figure 3.3, content such as different app categories and top lists are available for easy tapping.

Although scalable applications and shared code between phones and tablets are great, there's no shame in avoiding such strategies from time to time. If an application idea has too much potential but will fundamentally change with a move from phone to tablet, consider scrapping the design conversion completely and instead building separate applications for each screen size. There's no requirement to build the same interface for a phone and tablet, and there's no requirement to even build the same application for each form factor.

## note

"Form factor" is a smartphone or tablet's size, shape, aspect ratio, or other physical attributes that vary between devices even though the operating system may remain the same or be extremely similar. For example, two phones may both run

Android, but one may have a 3.5-inch screen and be very thin and another may have a 5-inch display and be very thick. These devices are both Android smartphones, but they have very different form factors, and as a result they can feel very different when used in practice.

In fact, for some apps it may make sense to focus on bringing the features and functionalities best suited for both devices to their respective screens. This creates two different design directions along with two different potential feature sets and the potential for even more work. But if your application does not seem well suited for small screens and large screens using the same feature set and design style, it might be best to make the extra effort and focus on creating exceptional applications for both devices.

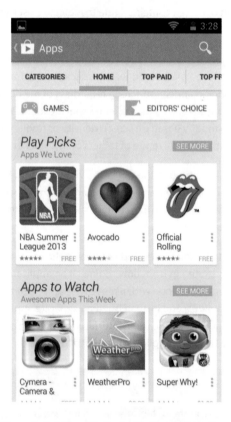

**Figure 3.3**   The Google Play app uses the standard action bar to help the user navigate.

# Interaction Experiences for Multiple Platforms

A more difficult task than designing an app for phones and tablets on the same operating system is designing one for multiple phones and tablets on different operating systems. When moving from Android to iPhone, it's as though a designer or programmer is crossing a border into a new country with a completely different language and culture. Making such a transition involves adapting to new programming conventions and growing accustomed to a new design style.

Far and away, the biggest mistake that can be made when planning such a project is forcing an initial design onto another platform. If an app has been detailed and customized for iOS, don't try replicating it attribute for attribute on Android or BlackBerry 10.

Aside from games, most applications depend on the use of several native interface pieces and as a result don't work well when forced onto a foreign platform. Unfortunately for designers, there's no universal interaction implementation that translates an app to all operating systems, so porting an iPhone interface to Android is likely to make a program feel extremely out of place and unintuitive to a user. Most iOS applications, for example, rely on tabs to navigate the user between different views, but that interface style looks confusing and is unlikely to scale well on Android and its various device sizes.

Building an application for multiple operating systems is much like building one for multiple devices: You will benefit greatly if planning begins from the get-go. In many respects, that's a difficult task either because it's impossible to predict the future or because the project's budget doesn't allow for such forethought. But if designers are capable of beginning work for both platforms at the same time, it's ideal to start with interaction and interface wireframes for a general mobile application, ignoring any specific target platform. By building such a wireframe, a designer worries less about the specific interaction methods or interface pieces—such as a tab bar or navigation bar—and instead focuses on the source of the content inside the application, including tables, maps, videos, and how those elements connect coherently for the user.

Once an understanding is developed of the general path a user will take to move inside an app, a designer can begin to apply the specific interface pieces needed for the targeted operating system. This is the time to decide whether the tab bar will be used for an iOS app or the action bar will be featured in an Android app. It's also the time to implement Android's system-wide "Back" button to return through application hierarchy or to include iOS's "Back" button in the standard navigation controller.

At this stage, take a look at the app's content flow, and decide how interaction should be implemented in accordance with the established and defined conventions for each operating system platform. Although interface controls may have different styles or interaction gestures on each platform, the content will likely be similar between operating systems; the designer just needs to determine the most appropriate way to display the content on the target platforms.

> ## note
>
> Human-interface guidelines for the target platform should be the most important document a designer refers to when deciding the appropriate interaction methods for his work. These guidelines are typically found at the platform's online developer portal.
>
> Specific interface components and interaction methods will evolve over time. Just look at the changes between Apple's iOS 6 and iOS 7 for an example of how much can change in a year. It would be impossible and likely irresponsible to claim that a specific interface style or interaction gesture was appropriate in all mobile situations, as these conventions change drastically and extremely rapidly. As such, it's important to refer to a platform's design documentation and interface guidelines, as they will instruct you how to proceed in presenting content.

Once designers determine the pieces they will use to put the puzzle together, they can then go and tie the app together across platforms by using similar colors, backgrounds, and general art design. This allows the application to feel unique to the platform it calls home while still being part of a unified brand.

As new operating systems and platforms become available in the future, you'll most likely want to create something on one piece of technology that might not work on its ancestors. Avoid the inclination to mimic or port any new design features backward onto earlier technology; it won't go nearly as smoothly as you anticipate.

Remember Cover Flow? The OS X-introduced design style is still prominent in the Finder application (shown in Figure 3.4) used to navigate through files and folders on Apple computers. At the time of the original iPhone, it was a groundbreaking way to display album art, allowing listeners to swipe left and right to browse their digital music collections.

This method of displaying album covers proved so popular that many developers attempted to implement it on other operating systems and hardware that weren't up to the task of such a graphic-intensive visual design feature. As a result, the hardware couldn't keep up with the advanced swipes and scrolls necessary to display images or files that way and ended up stalling and stuttering.

Although the look proved great for selecting music albums, it wasn't a particularly useful way to navigate through other file types. Nevertheless, developers tried to catalog many other types

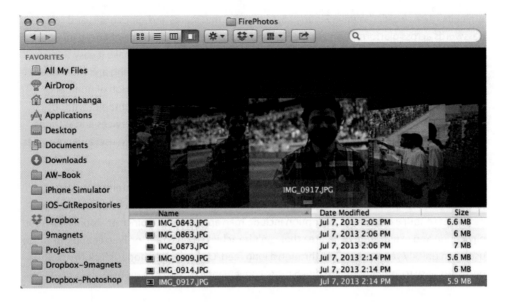

**Figure 3.4** Apple removed the Cover Flow technology from its mobile devices, but it still lives on desktops and laptops.

of data with scrolling images. This trend quickly became overused and misappropriated, and now it stands as an example of an interaction design convention that harmed applications and didn't help users. Apple removed Cover Flow from its applications, and it's now rare to see the concept in use in modern apps.

# Complementing Traditional Workflows

Because your mobile applications will often be used to complement traditional workflows, it's important to focus interaction design on aiding users with their traditional work. Much like you did when working on scaling an application from phone to tablet, you should consider ways in which your application could be improved through a design that focuses on working in collaboration with users as they move through their day.

A common way many applications do this is through the incorporation of sync services such as Azure, iCloud, or Dropbox. Unfortunately, it can sometimes be difficult to build a service that relies on users interacting with documents, because the mobile world has largely thrown file management by the wayside. Yet, despite the simplicity that the no-file system was designed to bring to users, an application can be significantly easier to interact with if a user can easily import and export documents between a phone, tablet, and desktop. By spending time allowing document interoperability, an application becomes much more usable.

AgileBits's 1Password, shown in Figure 3.5, is a service that stores and syncs notes and secure passwords across platforms and is a great example of an application with enhanced interaction aided by interoperability. 1Password uses a variety of methods that make it easy to share between devices. Because 1Password requires a gratuitous amount of typing and the management of usernames and passwords, which often require a heavy combination of numbers, different letter cases, and symbols, it is a hassle to manage it on a phone or tablet without the aid of a desktop computer. Through the inclusion of simple syncing services and settings, interaction design is greatly improved and the application becomes easy to use, as it now gives an alternative way to handle the difficult task of data management.

Another way to enhance a user's traditional work experience via mobile interaction is by providing an interface or capability that is difficult to perform with a traditional keyboard or mouse. Standout examples of this notion include map apps, in which pinch-to-zoom allows for navigation and exploration of an area that can't be achieved on paper, or Twitter apps, in which users can quickly yet precisely flip through a long feed. On a mobile phone, a flick-to-scroll gesture is easy to implement and much more convenient to use than a mouse.

**Figure 3.5**   Through syncing with Dropbox, 1Password users have access to their data on iPhone, iPad, Android, a desktop or laptop, and a plethora of other devices.

> ## tip
>
> Designers aren't limited only to touch gestures when attempting to improve an application's interaction experience. Actions such as a device shake or rotation can also be used to offer shortcuts or another way to solve an interface problem that is not easily fixed through touch.

Finally, another interaction type that benefits the user is one that expands or supplements a pre-existing Web or desktop application on mobile—especially one that is used most often or is most necessary when on the go. Consider software used to manage employee time cards. Most of the work within this system, of course, will be done by employees or managers on a desktop computer when logging vacation time or approving hours worked over a pay period. But occasionally a person may need to track time when on vacation or out on a sales call. In this case, a simple mobile application that allows access to only a single feature—say, time tracking—would add considerable value to the original desktop application.

> ## IN-DEPTH
>
> Somewhat ironically, it's often easiest to learn good design through the intentional exposure of incredibly flawed design. In experiencing the bad, you can better see the subtle nuances that make other projects good.
>
> There are some simple ways to experience mobile apps in an unflattering light. One way is to use an iPad to run an application that has only been built or optimized for iPhone or, likewise, find an Android application that has received no optimization for tablet-sized screens.
>
> After a few minutes of using these applications, the lack of focus and optimization for the large form factor should be more than apparent. Text will be poorly spaced, images may be stretched, and interaction methods may be out of place or feel inappropriate. Through using these application and understanding why they provide bad experiences, we can easily see why it is important to prepare and modify an application to feel at home on its target platform.

# Conclusion

Thanks to the commoditization of device components and desire for mobility, software that functions while remaining consistent between devices and form factors is no longer a luxury: It's now a reality of software development. If you design a successful app, it's extremely likely that you will be required to make that app available for a variety of platforms and devices.

Through a grasp of the techniques and concepts discussed in this chapter, designers should be prepared for the critical thinking that is required when porting an app to a tablet or across platforms.

So long as you keep focusing on the long-term strategy and break designs down to their most critical and basic components before building them up to a specific device size or operating system, it is more than possible to build a great multiplatform experience that provides consistent content and brand no matter where it's released.

# CHAPTER 4

# FIRST SKETCHES
# OF AN APP

You won't need a hammer or a screwdriver; maybe you'll need a tape measure—though preferably one in digital form on the top and side of your computer screen. Like any job, there's an established set of tools that most interaction and interface designers use to create their projects. Programs such as Photoshop, Balsamiq, xScope, and others are critical components of the interface-building process. In this chapter, you'll find a general strategic outlay for planning the design of a mobile application. Using the steps and techniques presented, you'll be prepared for the different phases a design evolves through during its infancy, before a programmer writes the first lines of code.

# What Tools Do You Need?

A mechanic is only as good as his or her tools, or so the saying goes. The ones that care about their work the most are the ones that most significantly invest in their tools. It's true for auto body shops, and it's true for design shops as well.

Before making a serious effort to create an app, designers need to make sure they have the best equipment available at all times. When starting out, this can be a bit difficult, as new computers and professional software are often quite expensive. To avoid wasting money on improper tools, it's important to get the best bang for your tech buck.

Many of the tools and tips recommended in this chapter developed from labors of love: fondness and expertise forged over a couple of years and a hundred apps worth of experience. But it's important to note that there are no one-size-fits-all solutions when it comes to choosing tools or selecting a process to draft a design. The following recommendations come from a process that has led to the creation of several successful apps, but if you come across a piece of software better suited to your task at hand don't be afraid of going your own route. Likewise, the tools available to designers grow and evolve at a lightning-quick pace, and new products are constantly hitting the market that make design faster, easier, and more efficient. It's always worth giving new products a try, as any learning curve involved may pay off significantly down the road.

The first tool needed in a designer's supply kit is one that's essential to everyone from elementary school students to rocket scientists: a quality notebook, journal, or word processor. Being a successful interaction designer requires taking notes consistently and excessively. Everything from trends in the industry seen in other apps to thoughts on personal work should be documented for future reference.

> ## note
>
> Remember that the tool suggestions in this chapter are just that: suggestions. If you currently have a workflow that functions better than what's recommended, feel free to diverge (or, even better, share your setup with other designers online). The goal is to do apps well, regardless of the tools and methods used.

Interaction design focuses on the constant development of a product in order to increase usability and value, so there's always room to improve a work. As is also true for painters and comedians, inspiration doesn't always strike at the most convenient moments. Some of a designer's best ideas will come when he or she isn't working; they'll arrive while walking down the street or in the middle of the night. Always having a notebook or phone-based word processor handy is a great way to quickly jot down thoughts as soon as genius strikes. Try Field

Notes by Draplin Design Company and Coudal Partners. These handy, portable notebooks come in a standard size that's roughly the same aspect ratio, width, and height as a smartphone screen and, likewise, work well to approximately portray a scaled-down tablet screen. They fit well in a pants pocket or purse, and they're great for scrawling out quick ideas or sketching out design prototypes.

When it comes to computer hardware for a designer's utility belt, it's tough to suggest anything other than an Apple laptop running OS X, preferably the most recent version available so there are no issues with compatibility for Apple's development applications. There's no denying that all iOS development and interface design implementation and most Android development takes place on computers running OS X. Access to Windows is required, however, for Windows phone app development, so designers planning on taking that route will need to keep that in mind.

If you don't plan on doing any coding at all and most of your work will be focused on creating visual designs, you could be perfectly fine with a Windows PC. Do consider using a machine, however, that will allow you to commit code for the projects you plan on contributing to, even if you don't see yourself as the programming type. It can be very valuable for designers to have access to source code for modifying art files or making basic code changes, typography selections, or color choices. If you plan on developing for iOS, it will be well worth your while to have an Apple laptop or desktop so that you won't be limited in case you want to tinker with code in the future.

The most frequently recommended computer for mobile design is Apple's MacBook Pro, ideally one with a Retina display. The benefits of the mobility a laptop provides far outweigh the added power provided by a desktop. Apple's most recent laptops with Retina display are great for designing work that looks fantastic on the high-resolution displays found in most phones and tablets. Designing on a low-density display can be difficult, because in some cases you may not be able to preview app designs from Photoshop or a similar program in full resolution. If cost is an issue, the MacBook Air is an excellent laptop, but steer clear of the 11-inch model; such a small screen size will make design work difficult.

If a stationary computer is preferable based on your personal needs, a designer can't go wrong with an iMac, either. These need to be capable of professional-level functionality, so it's best to purchase the most well-equipped computer you can afford. If you're low on budget, Apple's Mac mini is a more than capable machine for design and development. The biggest and best system isn't always essential; for most practical purposes, Apple's recently redesigned Mac Pro is probably overkill for the type of work you'll be doing.

### warning

**UPGRADES CAN BE DIFFICULT**   It's important to note that for many Apple computers, specifically the MacBook Air, MacBook Pro, and iMac, it can be difficult or impossible to upgrade RAM or hard drive storage space after purchase. Carefully consider your spec decisions before ordering a computer.

Preferences for design software can vary greatly based on personal taste, but there are a few essential tools to look for in any program. First and foremost, designers need some sort of wireframe or mockup function that can take interaction ideas and translate them into a visual element programmers can use to begin their work.

Balsamiq by Balsamiq Tools LLC (see Figure 4.1) is the multiplatform industry standard for quickly creating visual wireframes. The application is built specifically for digital design work and comes equipped with many templates and styles that cater to building Web sites and mobile software. Balsamiq balances speed and style and also quickly visualizes interaction thoughts into something others can see, understand, and offer feedback on.

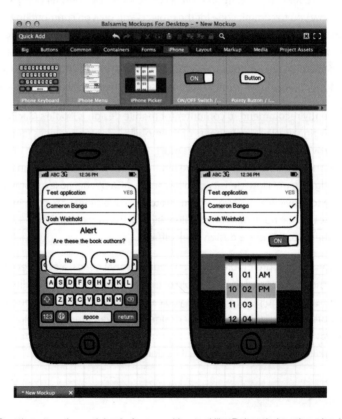

**Figure 4.1**   Creating attractive, quick wireframes with a tool like Balsamiq is rather simple, as designs take just minutes and can be extremely helpful in the visualization process.

Two other valuable sketching and early prototype applications of note are OmniGraffle by The OmniGroup and MindNode Pro by IdeasOnCanvas GmbH. OmniGraffle is a wireframing and digital prototype application in the same light as Balsamiq, but OmniGraffle focuses more heavily on creating work that looks close to reality. Such a feature offers output that's visually appealing for clients or stakeholders, but it does add time to the concept process. MindNode Pro, shown in Figure 4.2, is a mind-mapping application that's used for creating general text outlines. It's a fairly simple tool, but it allows a designer to take a simple idea, spread it out into actual words and thoughts, and then transform those thoughts into patterns that outline a more complete thought process.

MindNode Pro is a favorite tool of designers due to its ability to easily and quickly visualize ideas. It's also useful for a variety of non-app-related tasks. For one example, look no farther than this very page; MindNode Pro for iPad and OS X was used to visualize and outline each chapter of this book.

When it comes to rendering anything in pixels, meanwhile, Adobe's Photoshop is far and away the most popular choice for computer graphics creation and editing, and it's a piece of software that's used heavily in interaction and interface design. If it's something visual and not something done in code, odds are it'll need to be done in Photoshop. Adobe recently made a major model shift to its Creative Cloud platform, which is basically an all-you-can-eat buffet for their products. For a monthly fee ($50 currently), users have access to Adobe's entire Creative Suite. This is a great shift for designers who previously found the high cost of each Adobe program prohibitive, as they are no longer limited to one program but can instead now use other Adobe products when creating software, such as Illustrator for vector art creation or Audition for audio editing.

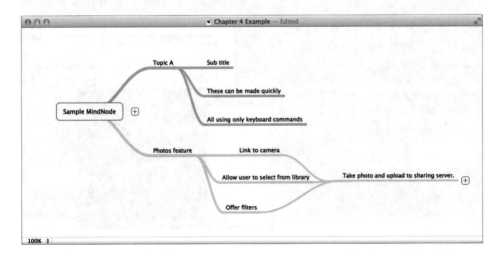

**Figure 4.2**   MindNode Pro offers a simple, clean interface for creating mind maps.

Still, there are other options available for small app-creation teams who find that monthly expense to be a creative barrier or for designers who simply want a product not offered by Adobe. Several strong—and extremely affordable—competitors have emerged recently, including Pixelmator by Pixelmator Team Ltd. and Sketch by Bohemian Coding. The downside of going with less popular products, though, is losing out on the wisdom of the crowds. Countless online tutorials, books, and instructional videos have been developed to walk users through basic and advanced Photoshop techniques, so individuals not experienced in visual design may have some trouble instantly mastering alternative programs.

Finally, a software gem that's absolutely imperative to have in a designer's tool kit is xScope by The Iconfactory. It's essentially the Swiss Army knife for interaction designers, offering a variety of magnification and pixel-measuring tools to use when analyzing an application on the iOS simulator or an Android virtual device. The tool is priceless because designers sweat to make sure every pixel is in exactly the right place while debugging and testing software.

It's somewhat difficult to describe what xScope does (or appreciate how well it does it) without using it. Essentially, the application makes it simple to measure a variety of important on-screen metrics when designing and developing apps. In Figure 4.3, you'll see an on-screen ruler and magnification loupe being used to inspect the visuals of a Web site.

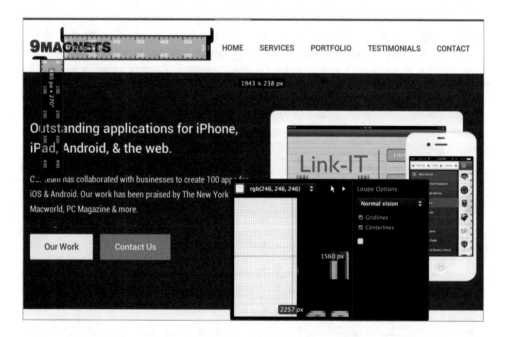

**Figure 4.3**   xScope helps designers measure a variety of on-screen metrics.

# Becoming a Designer

Once your design utility belt is firmly buckled and your tool kit fully equipped, it's time to determine how to actually tackle the job of becoming a designer. There's no certification exam to pass or credentials to acquire, but there are many classes to enroll in (for a fee) and even some universities offering to teach the trade of design; but are they worth your time and money?

If you're young and either in college or about to head off to it, by all means enter a program that's focused on design and product creation, even if it's not specifically geared toward the development of mobile apps. There's a great deal of benefit to be derived from going through a full college or trade-school program on how to become highly proficient in computer software creation.

But if your college years have passed you by or the cost or time required for a full course load is daunting, there's a nearly endless supply of free information available on the Internet that can help you become more adept at this craft.

Currently, most mobile app designers are either self-taught or have some background in computer engineering or another traditional visual design field. Eventually, though, the leaders of the industry five, ten, or twenty years from now will have gone through some post-high school program focused on software development.

Another way to hone your skills or grow your knowledge base is something often discussed by those looking to get into the world of app development: conferences. There's certainly no shortage of events, ranging anywhere from a day to a week in length, vying for developers' time and dollars. These sessions are often quite expensive, but they remain one of the only ways a programmer or designer can spend hours upon hours listening to or talking with titans of the industry.

Based on personal experience, conferences offer the opportunity to draw from a wealth of knowledge and enjoy a healthy dose of much-needed social interaction and networking. The face-to-face benefits of a conference cannot be understated, especially in the tech industry. Many mobile developers work alone at home or at small companies of two to three people and each one is perhaps the only person in town with such a hobby or profession. Thus, conferences offer a valuable opportunity to foster camaraderie between people with similar interests, providing both inspiration and motivation.

With many conferences making audio and video of lectures and roundtable discussions available via the Internet, though, any technical expertise gained by attending in person becomes less and less valuable. If you're paying your own way to an event, aim for the ones that are most affordable—something in line with what you'd spend on a short and cheap weekend getaway. Look at conferences as the entree of establishing friendships and interacting with individuals with shared passions that just happens to come with a side dish of learning. Don't break the bank on pricey conferences, and you won't be saddled with overeater's remorse the day after.

> tip
>
> For a good list of various conferences that anyone can attend regardless of their mobile platform of choice, check out http://lanyrd.com. The site is dedicated to helping connect users to different professional conferences.

## Planning for a Specific Platform

Once the basic wireframes of an application are drawn up, it's time to move on and begin preparing for the intricacies of a specific platform. Now, you should start thinking about how an application will look and feel on one specific mobile device or another.

First, it's essential to find the developer documentation for the appropriate platform. The human-interface guidelines will be the most important document for a designer, along with any other design-specific documentation available from the platform's developer center. For iOS or Android, Apple and Google frequently update documents on human interfaces much like they do for API and other technical processes. Major mobile platform developers also have other documents available detailing how to implement specific looks and feels for common interface features, and they often update these style bibles after a major operating system update. Even if you're comfortable with a platform's interface guidelines, it's always important to check back with the developer's recommendations to see if anything has changed. Human-interface guidelines are most definitely a living document, sometimes even more so than the platform programming guides themselves.

While reading over a platform's documentation, it's valuable to make sure that one or more test devices are available at a designer's disposal. Ideally, a minimum of one fairly new and up-to-date physical device should be handy, and some virtual devices should be installed and loaded. These can be things such as an iOS simulator that's prepackaged with Xcode, an emulated Android device from the Android SDK, or something similar that allows a designer to run test applications on a computer. These vary by platform, so visit the manufacturer's developer resources page to learn what options are available.

> **tip**
>
> A good rule of thumb is to always have three devices for testing: one device that's new and uses the most recent technology, one that's old and contains the least powerful technology that you plan to support, and one dedicated for use in offline or other edge-case scenarios.

Once you get your hands on a device, ensure that you're comfortable using it. One recommended strategy during app development is to carry the targeted device as your primary phone or tablet for at least a week. After using it for several consecutive days, you'll become familiar with its common interaction practices and begin to appreciate how users work with the device in professional and personal settings.

New designers often make the mistake of using only screenshots or the human-interface guidelines document to draft their interface work for a new platform. Interaction design, though, is less about the look of an application and more about the feel and flow of how an application works. It's impossible to accurately judge what feels natural on a platform based solely on screenshots, and the guidelines document is written using colloquial terms that only make sense after using a device for a couple of days.

In Apple's human interface guidelines for iPhone and iPad, for example, the author uses the following sentence: "And, although people might not be aware of human interface design principles such as direct manipulation or consistency, they can tell when apps follow them and when they don't." Users will know if an application feels out of place, and there's no way for a designer to know if he or she has implemented principles correctly unless the operating system has been used personally for day-to-day tasks.

Once a device is in your pocket or backpack and you've studied up on an interface's official documentation, take a look at some third-party development resources such as books or blog tutorials on the design for your target platform. Although the interface guidelines will be your rulebook going forward, and the device itself will help you experience how to use the platform, advice and instruction from leading developers is one of the best ways to learn about real-world user expectations. Follow some top developers and designers on Twitter or RSS feeds to get a constant flow of information on how platform design changes daily. The mobile development community is still a very tight-knit group, and many bloggers or book authors are approachable and more than willing to discuss your interaction plan online or over lunch at a conference, so don't hesitate to reach out and ask for help.

And again, don't underestimate the power of social interaction. Find local groups or meetups with like-minded mobile developers; most medium- to large-sized cities have clubs with monthly meetings to discuss trends and evolutions in the industry. Getting together to chat and interact is crucial for members of an industry known for having its fair share of people working alone at home. You're designing for some of the hottest platforms in the world, and people love offering up their opinions, so go out and be social.

# Starting with a Workflow

Now that you've got a device and have a plan of attack for learning about a specific platform and staying up to date on its news and trends, it's time to begin the real work: developing an application's interaction design. The best place to start is by composing a wireframe and building a general overview of the application's workflow.

If the world of interaction design is like a house, an application's workflow is the cement foundation, and the wireframe is the wood that supports the walls. It's not time yet to pick what type of doors to install or what color to paint the living room, but a number of important decisions are made at this early stage that will influence how an application works—decisions that will be very difficult to change once you progress further. It's crucial to make sure these choices are thought out well and thoroughly evaluated.

Begin this process by writing down or drawing a graph of a basic plan for what users will experience when first launching the application and then how they will move through it to accomplish a certain task. This initial phase of the workflow should be extremely abstract initially. The general purpose of this exercise is to understand the reasons why users will download this app, what their first impressions of it will be, and how information can be presented to them as quickly and efficiently as possible. You can conduct this process by using an application such as the previously mentioned MindNode Pro or you can simply use a large piece of paper with boxes, lines, and text that describes the setup and flow. You're essentially developing an advanced connect-the-dots process while also working to remove as many dots from the system as possible.

Figure 4.4 shows a relatively simple workflow design, starting with the user entering the application and ending with the user's purchase of a pair of jeans. The goal with the design is to minimize the steps needed to reach that end result and properly identify places in the interface at which a user might find interaction difficult. That helps a designer determine where to devote the most time during the development process. The key at this stage is simplicity, making rapid iteration easy as you see the need for changes while working on your ideas.

In this example, we realized it might be difficult to present a way for the user to quickly and easily pick out the exact size of jeans they want. We've got a couple of strategies in mind that might solve that problem, but we're not sure which one we like best yet, so we've jotted down a few notes to return to later.

Even at this early stage of working with a wireframe, it's not too soon to begin gauging user experience. One of the most common ways to evaluate an application is to calculate how many

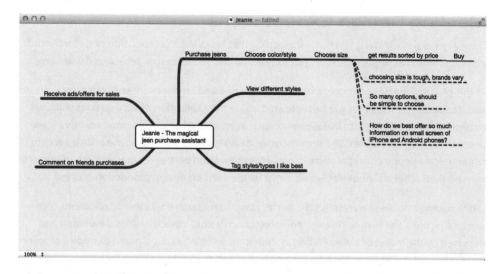

**Figure 4.4** MindNode Pro can be used to build a plan for a hypothetical application designed to help a user pick out a pair of jeans at a store.

taps the user must make or the number of page transitions required to go from launching an application to completing the desired task. As designers, we have two factors that are very much in our control: how easy it is for users to understand where to make input decisions on an interface and how many screen-to-screen transitions they must go through. Decisions made about those elements directly influence how much time a user spends moving through an application, and you're unlikely to find someone who enjoys an application that fruitlessly wastes his or her time. Respect the user, and always find the quickest way to get from Point A to Point B.

Ideally, designers should strive to strip away as much complexity and as many obstacles from an application as possible, removing until they can't remove anymore. Interaction design is all about creating an optimal experience for users, and for many reasons apps are optimal when they are the most simple. They're used on the go and on small screens, so complex experiences often do nothing but frustrate the average person. Designers should always be aware of those factors and aim to avoid complexities when designing a workflow.

> **tip**
>
> Another valuable metric—aside from measuring the number of taps or screens required to get to a solution—is measuring how much time it takes the user to complete tasks after entering the app. The faster the experience, the happier the user.

# Meeting Design Expectations

Once a general workflow is laid out—something that looks like a combination of general word associations and a connect-the-dots puzzle—it's time to move on to a generalized wireframe.

At this phase of the design process, it's time to imagine and render every single interface piece and interaction method that will be replicated inside the application. Now, decisions will have to be made about whether to use elements such as integrated voice commands or advanced uncommon system gestures. The documentation created here will also be the primary way to communicate design concepts and philosophies to involved parties—programmers, managers, marketers, or other stakeholders—that might be involved in the app production process.

While wading into these waters, it's the perfect time to research how other applications with similar functions and features implement interaction design, especially ones developed and designed by the maker of the operating system itself. Keeping in mind prime examples of software on a platform helps guide how your own application should look and feel. It also allows you to spot flaws or problem areas in competitor apps, presenting an opportunity for your app to offer something different that helps it stand out in the marketplace.

> ## tip
> Constantly peruse the "Top Apps" lists for all major platforms that you plan to support and take note of how they handle complex interaction challenges. Hundreds of new applications are released each day, and the best of the best often tackle difficult problems in unique ways.

Once you've gained a good understanding of the way other applications address the problems your app might face and you've analyzed the best work on the platform by the people who made it, you can begin crafting a voice for your application. Will it be one that truly fits in with the rest of the apps on a user's phone, or will it be something that boasts a truly unique design and aims to stand out from the crowd? There are positives and negatives to both approaches, and now is the time to thoughtfully consider where your application will fit. Because most operating systems have a rather coherent universal design philosophy, it's important to remain cognizant of what breaking from that pattern will mean. If a user is aware of that design outlook, they know it by name—or at least by sight—and expect applications to look a certain way. Offering something strikingly different can be eye-catching, but it can also sometimes be unsettling to a user.

An operating system design philosophy is a deep concept that permeates an entire platform. Just look at Apple's Aqua visual interface design in OS X, unveiled in January 2000 but still in use today. Aqua (shown in Figure 4.5) is easily recognizable in the standard OS X window, with polished metal chrome capping off the top edge of the view; bright, glass-styled red, yellow,

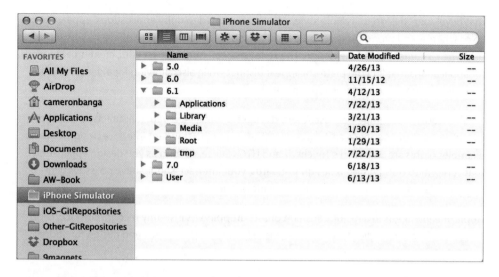

**Figure 4.5**  If you've worked with OS X before, you'll recognize Apple's Aqua visual interface design by its steel window appearance and blue tint.

and green buttons in the top-left corner; rounded rectangle buttons; and bright blue that highlights selected items.

Apple, though, sees Aqua as something much more than a basic visual look. To the company's designers, Aqua represents the foundation of the operating system's entire graphical user interface; it presents elements with a goal of "incorporating color, depth, translucence, and complex textures into a visually appealing interface," according to Apple's OS X Human Interface Guidelines.

Apple's plan was to use these principles in combination with an animation system that appeared to be as fluid as water itself to create designs that looked so great that (especially in the early versions, which far outpaced competitors at the time) you can understand what the writer is talking about and how that design principle set a standard for every single application on the operating system.

Clearly, Aqua is not just a visual style; it represents a design goal, one that Apple makes easy for developers to achieve in their own work. Aqua is also a great example of iterative design. The style was introduced nearly 15 years ago and has gotten better through 10 (and counting) major releases. The design language contained within it has evolved, but Aqua's core design philosophy remains unchanged.

As with Aqua, current mobile application platforms also have their own sets of design goals. It's extremely important for designers to understand the intentions and aims of these design goals and not just view them as a visual style to occasionally abide by. Currently, Google recommends that developers design to its Holo style, a system designed to unify applications' appearance, color scheme, and typography after a period in which Android software offered a very mixed bag when it came to interface design. The style has been hugely successful, creating a standard for applications that lets the platform appear distinct while also allowing for a design that is scalable and usable on multiple types of devices.

It's also worth noting that, because Android is open source, hardware manufacturers are free to customize the experience and make modifications to the standard interface design. Popular examples of this are Samsung's TouchWiz and HTC's Sense. As long as you design applications that conform to Google's Holo design standards, your interface should have no issues with being displayed on these manufacturer-specific designs.

Apple, meanwhile, is in a major transition phase, dropping its instantly recognizable iOS 6 look and feel in favor of a radically reimagined, visually simplified aesthetic and design functionality in iOS 7.

Well-designed interaction and interface designs often share an important trait: The designs are consistent across all applications on the operating system, and the user can easily predict how a common button, gesture, or interface structure will respond to interaction. There's much to be learned from using these operating systems repeatedly; you gain an understanding of the feel of the system, but you also develop a sense of what the creator's design expectation is. Through that, a designer can decide if it's wiser to stick to the platform norms or venture out onto a creative new path.

In most situations, especially for novice or inexperienced designers, it's best to stick to the platform's design conventions. As a result, you're less likely to make a serious design mistake or create an interaction design method that is confusing and discouraging to users. The interaction methods that are baked into an operating system are tried and true, tested with a multitude of usability drills and established as the common (and often best) practices on a system. By venturing out and attempting to create a new interface and interaction style, a designer risks stepping too far away from a user's comfort zone.

> ## tip
> New designers may see sticking to standard user-interface conventions as boring, opting instead to get wild and pursue their own creative ideas. But remember, the first goal of interaction design is to create something that works, not something that breaks the mold. Simple and boring trumps complex and confusing every time.

That's not to say there aren't wonderful examples of designers taking risks and reaping big rewards as a result. Look at Loren Brichter, a digital designer renowned for his creation of the pull-to-refresh interaction method, now common among thousands of apps on multiple platforms. Brichter took an action that was fairly common—scrolling up and down to view content—and used an "excessive pull" gesture at the top of a page to launch a screen-refresh function. The design is beautiful, immediately discoverable, easily comprehensible, and visually hypnotizing, and it in no way interferes with the rest of the application's interface.

Keep in mind, though, that Brichter was originally an Apple designer who worked on software for the first iPhone. When he created this new interface technique, he was already an accomplished expert in the field and understood the ramifications of what he was building. His story presents an important lesson on attempting to create new application interaction types: When choosing to throw caution to the wind and ignore pre-existing conventions, a designer had better know full well what he or she is doing.

## Wrapping Up Design Documentation

Once the relatively primitive sketch of an app's general look and feel is complete—and thought has been put into its interaction and usability—it's almost time to move to the next big phase of the process and begin turning your design ideas into pixels and programming code. Work in the wireframe and early design stages shouldn't be brushed aside, however, as it's important to create as detailed a preliminary document as possible. Often, a designer will be tempted to jump quickly to Photoshop files or other advanced design work, but devoting extra time to these early steps will pay off down the road. An extra hour or two spent creating documentation can save dozens of hours further along in the project.

Keep this key guideline in mind: If you can't describe an animation, gesture, or other piece of interaction implementation to a programmer or teammate in a simple sentence or two, it probably needs additional refinement or further thought. The documentation you create at this stage of development will be the foundation for everything else on the project, from programming, to art, to testing. Be as direct and explicit as possible when discussing and writing directions for implementation.

Software development can often be like the "telephone" game that kids play in which a phrase is whispered from one person, to another, to another. Usually, the sentence the last person in the chain says out loud is far different from the one the originator first uttered. In app development, the lead designer is much like the person at the start of that game. If the direction and plan isn't clear, concise, and simple, it's likely that the vision will get misinterpreted somewhere along the development chain, resulting in an application that's much different than the one the designer intended.

## Creating Pixel-Perfect Digital Mockups

After fully documenting the application in a wireframe or sketches, it's time to start creating art assets for the implementation of the software's design. Some designers may only be working on interaction design and concepts—such as interface feature implementation or gesture utilization—and as a result won't be implementing the actual visual design of the project. If that's the case for you, feel free to skip this section.

Creating art designs for a project is often one of the most difficult concepts to teach in any field of design, not just app development. Although interaction is very much an objective concept, and a platform's descriptive documentation clearly outlines when to use gestures, aesthetic design is much more subjective. Ahead are general tips and recommendations for creating app art, but for those looking to get additional help on aesthetic design, consider taking an art class or reviewing books on visual design principles.

Most of the example work described in this section is performed using Adobe's Photoshop, an industry-standard tool for anyone in the creative arts. The program allows designers to use a variety of visual tools such as brushes, shapes, and erasers to create nearly anything imaginable. Developing your own style and skills in Photoshop is something that takes time to master; the best artists in the industry often have a dozen or more years of experience and are still learning and growing.

If you're a new designer and uncomfortable with Photoshop, consider searching for tutorials online that best mimic the specific visual style you hope to achieve in your app and then use blog posts, podcasts, or videos to walk you through the steps needed to create this look. There are thousands upon thousands of Photoshop instruction sources online, and they can be an invaluable resource. Likewise, there are many books on Photoshop that can help you tap into the potential of every tool the program has to offer.

> ## note
> Photoshop talents and design skills require a lot of practice and plenty of trial and error to develop. Do you see an icon design or app style that you like? Practice by trying to recreate the look in Photoshop. Your first few attempts will be difficult, but with repetition you'll quickly learn how to create similar designs.

A great visual design is a very important component of interaction design; if a designer can't fully represent how to interact with an app via simple text, iconography, and interactive features users won't be able to understand the software, and in turn the app won't see much success.

Visual cues create a path for users, helping them find safe ground so they don't fall astray. That's a reason why it's often wise for a project's interaction designer to also be the visual designer, because a uniform thought process by a single individual helps maintain coherence between interaction intention and visual implementation. Imagine interaction design as the artistic idea, Photoshop or programmed code as the paintbrush, and the visualization of the app as the canvas. It's much easier to bring a work of art to life if only one person is in control of the paintbrush from start to finish.

The amount of art required for an app can fluctuate from project to project based on the technical requirements of the software, the desired visual aesthetics, and the platform, so there's no straight answer for how much art will be needed every time. A thorough discussion with the project's lead programmer is the best way to determine how to bring a wireframe to life with both art and code. Once again, this is where that extra time spent developing a detailed wireframe and application design document comes in handy; a programmer can review these and instruct the designer how they want the project's visual assets to be created.

On iOS and Android, most art will be produced in the PNG file format and will be imported and referred to in code to make the visuals appear on screen. It's best to create as little art as possible in Photoshop or another image-based program, instead implementing elements with code for native interface design pieces. Code is typically more nimble and able to be altered more easily while also being rendered on screen more quickly. Applications will thus be more responsive and require less work while also being less likely to break down when the operating system changes in the future. Each programmer has a different opinion, however, on what they prefer to do in code and what they want to do using other assets, and so constant communication with the app programmer is required.

# Reiterating Before It's Too Late

One of the primary goals of interaction design is to be constantly iterating on an implementation in an effort to improve upon the original work. Although you've already done this for a wireframe, you now have actual art assets in PNG or another format along with full Photoshop design files that will aid in a more complete analysis.

> ## note
> Remember, iterating on a design is the thoughtful and intentional process of taking original work, questioning decisions, and potentially revising and recreating parts of the project in an effort to improve its design.

Now is the perfect time to sit down and review your design work with every stakeholder in the project, from the client who's funding it to the programmer that's implementing the design. The following five questions are often simple and easy to answer when working only with concept art designs, but they'll grow more difficult and expensive to resolve once the application becomes actual lines of code, so it's best to address them now:

1.  **Does the app look like it will fit in with the platform?**

    It's a designer's prerogative whether he or she wants the work to blend in on the platform or not, so this question can often be answered either positively or negatively and still be OK, depending on the person's intentions. What's most important, though, is creating a coherent design that looks and acts like mobile software.

2.  **Will users be able to use the application with no guidance?**

    Long gone are the days in which each piece of software came with a hefty instruction manual. Mobile apps must be capable of remaining useful while standing alone, because the production team won't be there to guide the user along the way. This question can often be answered by showing the Photoshop work to another tech-minded person who can offer an outside perspective while also understanding what the designs in the program are intended to represent.

3.  **Can the programmer implement the design with art assets and design documentation only?**

    Most likely, a designer will be working hand-in-hand with the programmers on a project, who will hopefully be able to ask questions about why something was designed the way it was and how it should be implemented. This isn't always the case, though, and designers should be prepared for that possibility. Once design documentation is handed off to a manager or programmer, they should be able to deduce the designer's intentions and planned interaction design without being required to check in with concerns every five minutes. If a programmer can't create a design with only the documentation provided, more work is likely.

4.  **Will the design age gracefully?**

    Age can wear heavily on things, and mobile apps are no different. There's an adage frequently quoted when creating logos for corporations or businesses that says that the goal should be to design something that would have looked outstanding 100 years ago, would look outstanding today, and will look outstanding 100 years in the future. Strive for a general style and brand that will remain tasteful and visually appealing as an operating system or platform changes over time. This can vary in difficulty based on platform, but it's wise to avoid trendy "flavor-of-the-week" design practices that will fall out of fashion quickly. Instead opt for classic, traditional, platform-friendly looks.

5.  **Does the design meet future project goals?**

    A lot of new designers get tripped up in their development by creating a great first version of an app but failing to allow space for future feature improvements that will be necessary in subsequent releases. Designs shouldn't be handcuffed by hypothetical "maybes," but it is important to consider how an application's design might evolve after another six or twelve months of work. Take a journaling application, for example, in which a designer uses a swipe interaction to open various menus but fails to recognize that the app's 2.0 release will include a photo-adding function in which users will swipe to move through pictures. This will cause an interaction conflict, leading to a complete design overhaul a few months after launch, complete user confusion, a completely unreliable design, or some other terrible cocktail of those poor-design consequences.

> ### note
>
> Identify each stakeholder in a project long before work begins, especially if your project is for a client. Stakeholders will be managers, bosses, programmers, and anyone else who has a vested interest in a project. Moving too far along with the design before receiving stakeholder approval on a feature or style may result in work disapproval and unsatisfied clients.

As you get more and more involved with the world of software, you may run into an increasingly common programming approach called agile software design that runs in direct contradiction to the strategy just outlined. Agile software design involves design and programming team members working out basic features and plans to constantly add more to the product based on user response, testing, and developer experience. It's a great strategy, but only for those who are quite familiar with software development and are comfortable with how to handle a product constantly in motion. If you're new to design and programming, hesitate before adopting this strategy; you may be better off thoroughly thinking through a design prior to the start of programming.

# Preparing for the Next Stage

Although the app remains in its infancy at this phase of the development process, it's not too soon to take formal opinions of it from potential users or colleagues. As designers, it's often our job to dictate or direct the development path and make important decisions about the project, but we're by no means dictators. Don't let yourself be above healthy discussion or critiques of your work from *anybody*. Each and every voice that responds to your output can be valuable, so don't jump to dismiss the opinions of others who don't have design experience. Apps aren't just for the tech elite; everyone from mothers to bank tellers to baristas are potential users too. Inevitably, someone in such a position will point out a bad design idea.

Ultimately, if you can't defend your own design it's probably not that great of a design to begin with. Be willing to question and evaluate your own ideas with the goal of an improved user experience in mind. Developing apps is very much a team sport, and your work will inevitably grow with thoughtful critique and constant iteration.

IN-DEPTH

In order to build apps, you need apps. A few great software-development tools were briefly mentioned in this chapter, but here's a more detailed look at these favorites, along with a few additional gems that you might come to depend on. These pieces of OS X software will give you a leg up on the competition when designing your app.

- **Adobe Photoshop** is the gold standard by which all other design tools are judged. Originally released by Adobe in 1990, the software has been used for a variety of graphic design purposes and has permeated society to such a point that "to Photoshop" has become a household verb. Regardless of the platform you're designing for or the platform you're building with, Photoshop will be an indispensable tool.

- **Skitch** is a simple application currently owned and managed by Evernote that allows for simple text and graphical markup on screenshots captured by a computer. It's very quick to use; just take a screenshot and then mark up the image with arrows to point out errors, text to explain intention, or simple shapes to note where content should be. When building work in a preproduction emulator, Skitch is a useful tool for quickly noting where interface errors exist so that programmers can fix bugs and improve the app.

- **Balsamiq** is a multiplatform tool that allows for rapid creation of a basic software wireframe, which is used to show stakeholders and programmers how an interaction design works when programmed. Clear communication is a necessary skill for any interface designer, and Balsamiq is a great tool to graphically indicate design intentions to the people who will be coding your work.

- **xScope** is the Swiss Army knife of interaction design, with a variety of invaluable tools to help improve and iterate on an interface. The application includes various measurement utilities, color indicators, and magnification tools that allow a designer to zoom in and view tiny details easily. xScope—created by Iconfactory, a team known for building some of the most beautiful interfaces available on OS X and iOS—provides a great way to double-check that you've properly placed all of your interface pieces.

- **Pixelmator** is renowned as a worthy competitor to the almighty Photoshop. It's an extraordinary digital art enhancement tool currently available for much less than a single monthly subscription payment to Photoshop. If you're a novice designer looking to get your feet wet with as little cash overhead as possible, Pixelmator is your soulmate.

# Conclusion

A carpenter doesn't build a house the first time he or she picks up a hammer. A writer doesn't crank out a great novel the first time he or she sits down at the keyboard. Likewise, it takes time and development for designers to become comfortable with—much less master—using the tools of their trade. You've just begun to crack the surface of the work involved in creating an app by learning about the early steps of design. With a solid foundation laid, you can now begin building the framework of your original mobile creation.

# CHAPTER 5

# FINDING THE RIGHT DESIGN FLOW

Not all apps are created equal. Even if it accomplishes a desired task, how effectively an app does its job can vary greatly based on its type of application. As a result, it's critical for designers to understand the various categories of apps their work falls into. Although the number of applications for various platforms is almost beyond comprehension, most of them fit into one of several broad categories. In this chapter, you'll find examples of apps that fit into several simple and easily recognizable categories that will help you understand the work they're doing at a root level.

# The Big Three App Types

At their most basic foundational level, applications fall into three general types regardless of the platform they're on: native, Web, and hybrid. As long as the device on which the app runs has the capability to load software and access the Internet, it fits into one of these three designations. Although the differences between these types are subtle, it's important to recognize the distinctions and determine what type you're looking at when analyzing a piece of work. Identifying these three different categories can help you learn a lot about how an app works and make good assumptions about how its interface was set up.

## Native Apps

A native app is composed of pieces of software completely written in the native language of a platform. For iOS, the native language is Objective-C; for Android it's Java or C/C++. Native applications are written entirely to the specification of the platform owner by using the technologies and best practices prescribed by whoever has built the operating system.

If an app comes preinstalled on your phone or tablet, it's most likely native software. In Figure 5.1, you'll see a collection of 27 applications that come preinstalled with the

**Figure 5.1**   These are all native applications that come preinstalled on a first-generation Google Nexus 7.

first-generation Google Nexus 7. Created by Google, the native apps are built using the Android SDK.

Native applications will usually be the most powerful applications on any given system, because they have the ability to most easily tie in to the various advanced hardware functions (GPS, motion control, etc.) of a phone or tablet. Likewise, the platform providers will also produce diverse APIs that make it easy to integrate features such as maps, advanced-interface user interactions, easy file storage, and much more. Native applications will persist as the most dynamic and fluid applications on a device, providing superior hardware power thanks to their direct framework integration with the various device components. That allows for better integration of animations, advanced 3-D rendering, and anything else that may require high processing power.

Simple and responsive animations may be the most common interaction implementation that is well served by using a native app, as providing a quality experience often requires creating animations to instruct or delight a user.

## Web Apps

The complete antithesis of the native application, meanwhile, is one that actually offers the best explanation of what a native app really is. The native app's polar opposite is the Web application, something all smartphone users will inevitably come across. These are pieces of software that run completely inside of a Web browser. They feature interfaces built with HTML or CSS; are powered via one of a variety of popular Web programming languages, such as Ruby on Rails, JavaScript, PHP, or Python; and can typically be run on any phone, tablet, or computer with a standards-compliant, modern Web browser.

For a well-done example of a Web application, check out weather software Forecast.io (Figure 5.2) by The Dark Sky Company, LLC. It effectively uses Web resources to provide an exceptional user experience. The application is written with an HTML/CSS front-end interface, yet it provides rich graphics and animations that are on par with native experiences.

The ability to run on nearly any phone, tablet, or computer does also come with several big hurdles that must be overcome, however. First and foremost, designers won't have access to the native frameworks and interface-creation tools provided by Apple, Google, or another platform creator. Instead, designers must create their own user interface entirely from scratch.

For an experienced interface designer, this may not be that big of a challenge, but for a beginner this is often a substantial undertaking. Likewise, designers will be missing many animation tools, meaning that the application will not look as fluid or responsive as a native piece of software. Designers will have to pay careful attention to small details, as many of the pieces put into place automatically for a native app will not be available.

**Figure 5.2**   Forecast.io features a clean user interface that neatly presents weather data. (Courtesy of Adam Grossman.)

## Hybrid Apps

The hybrid app combines attributes of both native and Web apps. The ultimate goal of hybrid applications is to use some sort of redundant, common code that can be used across platforms while also tailoring required attributes to the native system.

Take an application designed, for example, to display topics hierarchically in a standard iOS or Android table while also relying on HTML-based text views when a user moves forward to view specific information in a topic area. This presents a designer with HTML formatting language that is capable of providing advanced text styling on multiple platforms using just one document but can still take advantage of the native device presentation offered by using tables.

The definition of a hybrid application can vary a bit depending on who you ask, but most describe it as an app in a situation similar to the one detailed previously or as an application whose primary logic and functionality is completely reliant on back-end server infrastructure code, with the native mobile system serving as little more than an interface shell to control and power the app. Hybrid applications usually have some benefits of native interfaces and advanced hardware capabilities. Full use of the app can be limited at times, though, when connectivity is poor due to the constant requirement that an Internet connection be available, because the code driving the application resides on a Web server. Hybrid applications are typically the middle of the road when it comes to responsiveness, often falling behind native applications but still performing better than Web apps.

For guidance on what a strong hybrid development toolkit looks like, research Appcelerator's Titanium SDK. Their kit allows developers to use a single JavaScript framework and a single code base in the creation of applications for iOS, Android, and Windows Phone.

# Common App Navigation Methods

Now that you know the difference between three major types of applications, how will each change the way you go about building ways for users to navigate through and interact with your programs? Each app type has its own set of common navigation-interaction methods that will change how you operate, depending upon the platform you're working on.

Before this breakdown, though, it's important to understand one simple-sounding, yet key, term: *view*. In apps, views are windows or screen areas that contain various interactive interface attributes. System views are components that were created by the operating system provider and that contain specific functionality through which the user can take an action. After that, the app presents more information in the same view or transfers the user to a different view.

Now, let's take a look at a variety of common interface components and view windows found on iOS and Android.

## Single View

Single-view applications are easily the simplest type of applications that you can build, containing merely a single page of information that can be interacted with on screen. What users see upon opening the application is all they get. Although remarkably basic, this type of app is still rather common; most calculators, built-in cameras, and utility apps use this form of simple interface, as shown in Figure 5.3.

Because of their relative simplicity, these apps often have significant similarities across platforms and software types. The most important attributes to target when building a single-view application are clarity and organization, because where each interface item is placed and how it responds is of the utmost importance.

Look at the Voice Memos application on the iPhone, for example, and how it emphasizes clarity in a single view. In the app, two different pseudo-views are available, and an animation slides

**Figure 5.3** Apple's Calculator is a solid single-view application; it focuses on one simple and specific task and achieves it in a polished, focused manner.

to place emphasis on either the audio-recording meter or a list of saved memos, depending on what action state the user is in. The user can either record more content or share existing recordings, and an elegant animation makes the change between those two states apparent and easily comprehensible. Although this is an app exclusive to the iPhone, a similar design would be easy to replicate on Android; likewise, its key features and style could be replicated in a Web app.

> **tip**
> Other single-view applications worth checking out include Reminders on iPhone and Google Earth and Google Now on Android.

# Stacked Navigation Bar

Stacked navigation views are popular on a variety of different mobile operating systems and are perhaps even the most common interactions interface a designer ever works with. On modern-day iOS, this interface is called the "Navigation Bar" and on Android it's typically referred to as the "Action Bar."

Regardless of platform, this interaction piece is often anchored to the top of the view and remains a constant figure spanning the width of the screen. This navigational tool is quite familiar to anyone who has ever used a mobile operating system; it presents several interaction pieces in the main part of the screen, and tapping one pushes forward to a new view. As it does so, a navigation stack anchored to the top of the screen animates to visually indicate to the user that a foreword movement has taken place. A back arrow appears at the top left of the navigation bar, as you can see in Figure 5.4, allowing the user to reverse to the previous view.

This is one of the most common interaction types seen in mobile today: It's used to navigate through e-mail, text messages, and many other applications. On Android, however, it's not

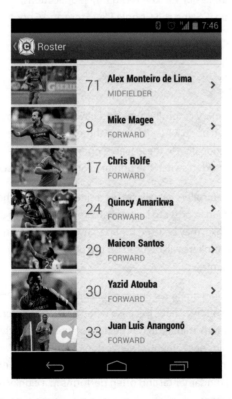

**Figure 5.4**  On both Android and iOS, a left-facing chevron is the most common way to indicate a "back" function. Here, it appears as the left-most item in the action bar.

always necessary or even especially common for the action bar to contain a back arrow icon after the user has advanced through multiple views. Instead, the hardware or software standard back button on the device is touched in order to return the user to the previous view.

Navigation stacks are frequently seen in native and hybrid applications, but they are more difficult to pull off in Web applications. Many Web apps take the standard navigation stack and anchor it to a static bar at the top of HTML Web pages. This is rather unadvisable yet fairly common. In Web applications, the preferred method is to use the standard Web browser navigation buttons so that the application can operate like any other Web experience. By attempting to recreate the standard navigation stack through art and a Web browser, designers are likely to create a messy situation that can be better handled using the more familiar browser controls.

> ## tip
> For other good examples of stacked navigation applications, take a look at Mail and Contacts on iOS and the Google Play Store and Google Play Music on Android.

# Tab Controller

The tab view is another primary controller type and navigation view found on a wide range of platforms. This style is called upon when there are three or four different views that will contain all of the application's functionality. In these views, opening one of the tabs or using a slight swipe from left or right is used to switch the primary content view on screen.

On iOS, segmented view controllers can also serve a similar function, though the segmented control is usually only applied in order to switch between two or three different types of views. The tab controller, meanwhile, may be used for up to five or six different views of content. Sometimes, navigation controllers will be used on top of tab controllers to provide multiple levels of hierarchy for content.

This control is most often seen on native and hybrid applications for iPhone and Android and is rarely used in Web applications. That's because when a tab or segmented control is used the expected behavior is a smooth animation for the data managed directly by the segmented control. Controls such as tabs or segmented views don't work well in Web applications because HTML Web pages are arranged in a linked, individual-page fashion. Dynamic content on one page is a bit less fluid and fundamental and often performs in a clunky manner, resulting in a below-optimal user experience.

**tip**

Want to see more examples of standout tab-view applications? Load Clock or Music on iOS and Clock on Android.

## Scroll Views

Scroll views have been an extremely popular element throughout the history of computing, and anyone who has grabbed a mouse or touched arrow keys on a keyboard over the past few decades is familiar with them. On mobile, though, this interaction method handles a bit differently. Scroll views are used for groups of photos, text, or any other information that surpasses the width and height of the device, as we can find in the iOS Weather app in Figure 5.5. In this

**Figure 5.5**   Scroll views don't need to only scroll vertically in a constant, fluid motion. The iOS Weather app scrolls horizontally on fixed-width intervals to show weather forecasts and information for different cities.

method, only a piece of the entire content is visible at a given time, and the user must flick right or left to view additional elements outside the current view.

Scroll views can be also be used in combination with the navigation bar, tab controller, or a variety of other interaction types and is common on both iPhone and Android. It is also used and is prevalent in native, hybrid, and Web applications.

> **tip**
>
> Great scroll-view applications you might want to take a look at include Weather and Calendar on iOS and Google Keep and Google Play Movies & TV on Android.

## Search-Driven Navigation

Another common navigation type—search-driven navigation—is an interaction method not often thought of as one that moves users between views. It's commonly used on both iPhone and Android, though, and can be implemented without taking up much space on screen because the search bar is usually fairly small. Incorporating search functions helps to navigate and drive a user through an application, as you can see in Figure 5.6 with Terminology by Agile Tortoise.

Designers can also use voice search in a way similar to how Apple has integrated Siri and Google has incorporated Google Now into their respective devices, or a designer can keep it simple and use a more standard, text-based search. Both Android and iOS offer simple interaction tools that help implement search-centric applications via text, although you may have to put in a bit more effort and integrate a third-party framework into an app binary in order to include voice search.

Search is an ideal tool to implement for navigation when an app contains a large amount of data a user may potentially have an interest in, especially if it's likely the user will have a solid idea of what data to seek out. How painful would it be to navigate through a music library full of thousands of songs on a mobile screen without a search function? Scrolling through a seemingly endless list just to find a single, three-minute tune would quickly become frustrating. By using a simple search function, though, the song can be found in seconds.

> **note**
>
> It's common to have two or more of these interaction and navigation types in any application. In the iOS music player alone, users come into contact with a tab controller, a scroll view, a navigation bar controller, and a search controller.

**Figure 5.6**  In the Terminology app, search helps a user locate one specific word and its definition in the midst of a database of thousands.

## Modal Controller

One of the more common control types—modal—is used so frequently that designers are likely to implement it without ever realizing it. Modal controls are used when an application forces the user to make one choice or interaction decision specifically before moving on to a further view or seeing more information. A modal setup can contain several specific views or multiple controls within it, but it's always seen as somewhat of an interjection into the typical application flow, helping to focus the user on the task at hand.

Implementing an e-mail sheet in an application is a nice example of effective modal control. If a user, say, taps an image that looks like an envelope, he or she could be presented with a system-standard view that allows for information from the app to be shared with another person. The experience, remember, is disruptive, but it focuses the user; the e-mail form sheet (a modal view) pops up on top of the app's standard content, forcing the user to send an e-mail or cancel out of the window.

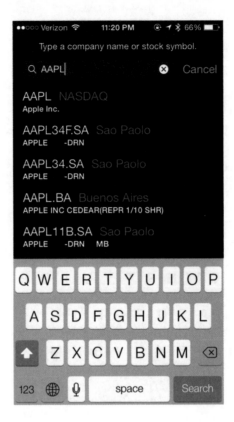

**Figure 5.7**    A modal-interface view forces the user to make a specific choice in order to proceed.

The method used to add a financial listing for iOS's Stocks app to track, as shown in Figure 5.7, is a modal view that requires the user to either enter a stock or cancel in order to proceed. The user has no other choices; hence, this view is modal.

## Gesture-Based Navigation

Another navigation interaction—one that's relatively new to the mobile landscape—is a pure, gesture-based navigation control. Gesture techniques such as two- or three-finger scrolls, pinches, and others are now often used to move the user through different parts of an application.

This application-flow model is not very common, but it's possible on both iOS and Android and on native and hybrid applications; however, a gesture-focused-navigation app would be very difficult to execute in a Web application. Trouble arises there due to the lack of the direct use of essential gesture-recognition frameworks that are built into mobile platforms such as Android and iOS. Instead, a Web browser controls most of our touch-based interaction, and browsers aren't programmed to recognize and take advantage of the advanced gestures required for these controls.

Clear for iPhone by Realmac Software is an app that uses this method notably well. This to-do list software functions entirely on gesture-based-interaction techniques and does not contain standard interface chrome buttons for creating new lists or tasks. Instead, a user simply pulls, pushes, and pinches to move through the app.

### tip

Don't confuse the term "interface chrome" with the Google Chrome browser. Interface chrome is somewhat common computer software design slang used to describe buttons of an interface.

The term's origin is disputable, though it seems to have been used as early as the mid-1980s and is included in Eric Raymond's *The New Hacker's Dictionary,* often considered to be one of the most definitive sources for programming slang and popular terminology.

Gesture-based application navigation structures are extremely advanced and require a significant amount of mobile interaction experience in order to implement correctly. It's best to reserve the strategies used inside apps like Clear for designers who grasp how gestures are typically used within mobile operating systems and who understand how to make these gestures obvious to users so that they can easily interact with the app.

# Picking an Interaction Type

How should a designer go about considering which interaction type is best suited to an upcoming app project? Ideally, by now you've read through the full set of human-interface guidelines for the platform you're targeting. Once you have a pretty solid grasp on the interaction methods and controls that are available to you, it's time to start constructing strategies.

When attempting to determine which control to use, it's often tough to predict which piece will be best for an app. It's wise to adopt a mentality of using the piece that will allow for the most unobtrusive interaction. Quite frequently, less is more, and an interface that allows content to be front and center to the user is best. Having users struggling to wade through an interface in order to find the content they want benefits no one.

In most situations, the standard navigation bar or action bar is a great tool to use, because it allows the user to be presented with considerable content in the view but also allows for jumping forward if there is a need to learn more about a specific topic. The primary content resides in a large view, and the navigation bar at the top of the screen is visually unobtrusive, sitting back and only animating into an obvious hierarchal structure when the user has the ability to move backwards. It's also possible to add buttons to the action bar or navigation bar in case there's a feature a designer wants to focus on or make readily available.

The standard navigation stack typically works best for applications that are styled and presented somewhat like a dictionary, with many pieces of related information stacked in clear and linear hierarchies. It's quite common to see this type of information presented within an application, whether the user is looking at e-mails, music playlists, or text messages. Here, it's easy to stack a large amount of information into a scrolling table and let users drill down further into a specific topic or section while also allowing for a quick swipe or touch to return a user back to the starting point.

It's worth noting that on Android conflicting opinions have long existed on how navigation stacks should work, especially regarding whether or not returning back to the previous view should be handled inside of an app using the back icon or at the system level using the standard system back button. In early versions of Android, it was commonly understood that the system back button would be used whenever the user wanted to return to the previous screen.

This has changed somewhat over the past few Android iterations, however, especially since Honeycomb (version 3.0). Currently, applications typically contain their own back buttons inside the action bar, in a style similar to that in iOS. The system-wide back button managed at the operating system level is now usually only used to jump back into an application if, for example, a video is played in the original app that requires a redirect to YouTube.

> ### tip
> Google's developer portal at http://developer.android.com has a helpful section titled "Navigation," which offers further details on how the persistent Android system-wide back button should function and behave.

If the application you're designing uses only three to four primary views or features, consider using a tab-view control on iOS or a slide view on Android. Tab bars are like the grandfather of mobile interfaces; the tool was a very common interaction method in the original days of iOS, but now it's become less prevalent, falling out of style as designers move to gesture-based interfaces or more advanced navigational stack controls. The tab control works extraordinarily well, though, because on an iPhone the tab bar resides on the bottom of the screen, where it can easily be touched by a thumb at any point. On Android, a fragment pager allows the user to quickly flick to change view content.

If you're working with an application that contains immense amounts of data—a thesaurus with thousands of words, for instance—you'll quickly find that search-based navigation is nearly essential. Although a scroll view may be used or a standard dedicated control might feel more native and expected to users, a search function will be the best way to help target desired information as quickly as possible.

Be aware, however, that search is programmatically a tough element to implement when not using criteria already included in the app's body of data. In a music library, for example, it's easy to incorporate a search function for song or artist names, because that data is already tied into the file names on the device. Song genres prove much trickier, though; that information isn't likely included in the data. And of course, search functions are inherently reliant upon a user typing terms correctly.

### note

A common way to judge an application interface—and often the best way to choose which interaction control is best for an app—is through a metric called data density. That's the amount of valuable information presented on a screen at any given time; admittedly, it's a fairly relative metric.

Take a look at the data you want to display to your user and then the potential controls. Consider which method would provide the most information on screen in the cleanest fashion. The most data-dense choice is probably a good indicator as to the best direction to take.

Some designers will contend that single-view applications are plain and boring or stand to be "improved upon" with additional features or interface chrome. Given the nature of mobile devices, this can often be the wrong attitude to have; designers should strive to remove as many screens, views, or buttons as possible to make the app experience easier and smoother. Many incorrectly believe that adding on to a simple design is the way to show the hand of an experienced designer, but minimalism is becoming an appreciated quality again; the industry has evolved over the past few years and moved back toward simple, clean styles.

Apple's design reinvention with the 2013 release of iOS 7 is perhaps the biggest reflection of that shift in approach, encouraging the elimination of excess in favor of simplicity. If your application seems as though it could be best managed with just a single screen view, that's OK (and, for many situations, encouraged). All current iterations of popular mobile operating systems use what's described as a "flat" interface structure, in which color palettes and design chrome are simplified or removed in an effort to focus on user content.

To fully understand how significant this overhaul is, consider the previously mentioned Voice Memos app, the redesign of which is shown in Figure 5.8. In iOS 6, the application contained a pair of different views, one of which was a skeuomorphic microphone. In iOS 7, however, Apple managed to simplify this app even further by ditching the faux microphone appearance

**Figure 5.8**  Apple redesigned its native Voice Memos app to focus on simplicity and clarity.

and increasing functionality through the addition of a large, clear sound-level meter. Here, the mobile giant proved once again that inside an application less is more.

# Minimizing Interface Friction

Now that you know more about the different types of apps and views available to you, let's discuss a key, overarching principle of interaction design—reducing interface friction as much as possible—and what you'll use these different views, interface elements, and app types for.

A fairly common term inside of the world of application design, friction is used to explain any scenario in which the user may be stopped or impeded when using an application. It is usually the result of some sort of correctable mistake: a poor interface component, confusing text copy, or time lost to load and perform a complex and unnecessary animation. Developers generally understand that some amount of interface friction is inevitable, but they aim to remove as much of it as possible when building an app.

> **note**
>
> When friction is discussed, it's implied that the term doesn't refer to inevitable or unsolvable problems, such as the time it takes to load an image or view a video. Instead, friction is thought of as application problems that are capable of being solved through improvements in programming or design.

The best way to tackle excessive interface friction is to focus on "touch points" inside an application: places where users will directly interact with the content and interface. Designers should sit back and question the work being done by the app after users touch each interface component. How does the app respond? Is the text on the screen or button concise, clear, and appropriate? Is there a way to minimize time spent from the point at which the user enters the application to the point at which they are satisfied and given a result? These are questions for designers to ask themselves all the way from the initial wireframe mock-up through general release.

This is also another opportunity to talk to potential users and see how they respond during beta testing. When working on a project, it's not uncommon for a designer to become overly immersed in the work and overlook interface and interaction problems that are glaringly obvious to those outside of the development team. Another set of eyes never hurts; they can find problems as simple as the wrong word or icon on a button (creating confusion) or can highlight where an interface didn't effectively point the user to a key feature (again, more confusion).

When considering how users interact with our applications, especially how they respond to different touch points, don't forget to consider that users with a variety of levels of English comprehension could be downloading your software. The app market is truly a global one, and it's increasingly shortsighted to only target users who speak a specific language or live in a certain region. Examine any icons you plan to use and the text that will be used on buttons or in tutorials. Use simple English so that a strong mastery of the language isn't a necessity to use the app, or, better yet, plan on translating the application into other languages. Either way, the simpler the words are from the start, the easier it will be to broaden the appeal of your software.

Instagram prepared effectively for users who speak and read languages other than English. As shown in Figure 5.9, using instantly recognizable iconography—rather than words—on the app's tab controller makes it easy for anyone to quickly determine how to navigate the app, no matter where they're from or how they communicate.

**Figure 5.9**   Instagram is well-known for its filters, but it also has a distinguishable interface full of helpful iconography.

# Preparing for Connectivity Failure

Designers also often overlook (or fail to put sufficient thought into) how a user will experience an app in various Internet-connectivity scenarios, including what will happen when Wi-Fi is unavailable or mobile signals through LTE networks are nowhere to be found. Does the application bounce back gracefully and maintain a fluid and responsive interface for the duration of the inactivity period, or does it screech to a halt and become unusable due to a lack of connection to the outside world? It's not uncommon for a designer to create work inside an experiential bubble, but just because you have a great LTE signal in your home or office—not to mention the latest and greatest mobile device—doesn't mean that every user will interact with an app under similar conditions at all times.

Until just recently, it was rather difficult to simulate poor connectivity conditions, but recent improvements to iOS, Android, and standard development tools thankfully have made it easy to test an application design at various potential signal levels. Thus, there's no longer an excuse not to test. Connectivity issues are a constant source of friction in many applications, so it's important to tackle the problem and ensure that it's been solved.

It sounds obvious, but it always bears repeating (both in print and in your own mind) that mobile computing is just that: mobile. As a result, making sure that apps can still be functional when disconnected from an Internet or data signal is an essential component of interaction design. Users expect to be able to launch and interact with our apps whenever and wherever they want, but designers can't always guarantee that will be possible.

When building software, designers should be looking to create something that "fails gracefully," a term often recited amongst programmers, designers, and other tech-creating individuals. For your purposes, that concept involves designing an application in such a way that when the software receives a response that is undesirable, such as a lack of cellular network availability, it clearly communicates to users what has happened but still allows them to do as much as possible while the app waits for other factors to respond as desired. Unfortunately, it's somewhat common to find applications that crash entirely when a cell signal is unavailable; obviously, it's best to avoid repeating these mistakes and to instead aim to fail in a much more graceful manner.

## tip

As a designer, it's best to heed Murphy's Law regarding mobile connectivity. What can go wrong will go wrong, so plan your design around the potential for a lost connection. In fact, a storm knocked out the power—and thus the Internet connection—as the tips for this very chapter were being written.

Because testing for potential problems has now become so simple, there's really no excuse for making an app that fails when it runs into a problem such as losing a cellular network connection. In fact, this sort of reaction could even lead to Apple or Microsoft rejecting the program during the app review process required to gain entry to the online store. Don't be satisfied with that minimum standard, though; designers should aim to go much further and provide the best user experience possible.

Because connectivity can be so hot and cold in the world of mobile devices, it's extremely common to cache all required application data locally inside an application so that it will continue to work even if a signal is dropped. An e-mail app, for instance, may download the contents of all messages locally so that the user can continue to read them even when disconnected from the Internet. In that same type of software, users often expect e-mails they write during periods of no connectivity to be saved by the application and then sent at a later time when an Internet signal returns.

It's also important to make it clear in the interface of an app when a connection is unavailable while also indicating that the application can still be used in the meantime. Often, apps use text to unobtrusively notify the user when a connection was not made properly. The best ones present on-screen information in the event that an expected result doesn't occur while also explaining that connectivity was the reason for the error. Twitter apps, for example, do this effectively by presenting a small timestamp that shows the user when data was last pulled down successfully, as shown in Figure 5.10.

No matter the interaction scenario inside an application, it's important that the software react safely in any situation in which the response from the server or user input falls outside the

**Figure 5.10**   In the Tweetbot app by Tapbots, LLC, a timestamp displaying "Last updated [day] at [time]" is used to help make it clear when the last refresh took place. (Courtesy of Dillon I. Carter)

realm of what it expected to happen. Graceful fallbacks are an important skill to learn for any designer looking to make their work better, so go out and find ways to make your application respond flawlessly for the user.

---

### IN-DEPTH

Designing for the Web carries one big benefit: Once an application is created, its front-end interface written in HTML and CSS will port over to a variety of operating systems because it can be displayed in a browser. Because such an easy method of making an app available to everyone at once exists, that has to be the preferred app design method, right?

Unfortunately, what sounds too good to be true often is, and building a Web application interface that looks and works great on every operating system is often a bit more involved than you might think.

First and foremost, Web-rendering engines tend to vary greatly, especially when being built across multiple operating systems. A font or image that renders in one way on one system may not work as planned on other systems. Thus, although you may save some time not natively preparing or coding interface assets for each platform, you'll spend much more time fine-tuning your design to each platform you attempt to support.

For example, take another look at Forecast.io, a weather application used as a Web app example earlier in this chapter. This time, however, look at it on a Google Nexus 7, a popular Android device (see Figure 5.11).

As you can see, there are many layout, image, typographic, and even feature differences when moving across devices. Although Web apps are great because they make it easy to carry work across platforms, that doesn't mean that you don't need to rethink your design based on your experience tinkering with major platforms and devices.

In short, many designers and developers often find it easier to forgo the measure-twice-cut-once approach of designing Web apps and instead program multiple native applications, especially when working on software rich in media and complex animations. Although it may be a bit more time-consuming, the hours are well spent, as it will be easier to provide the interaction experience you desire without compromising on features or quality.

**Figure 5.11**    Here's how Forecast.io looks when rendered on a Google Nexus 7 Web browser.

## Conclusion

Hybrid, modal, search, native: The words are different, but the primary goal is always the same. You want to make the best application possible while remaining true to the platform and focusing on reducing interface friction and creating a premium experience.

No matter how overwhelming the variety of application and interface types may seem, don't worry too much; you're less in over your head than you feel. Keep the primary goal—creating an exceptional way for users to interact with content and data using the interaction and interface components that make the experience as clean and consistent to the native operating system as possible—in focus and you'll be just fine.

# CHAPTER 6

# DESIGNING FOR VISUAL APPEAL

In the real world, you only get one chance to make a first impression. The same goes for the digital world; users often make quick judgments about a mobile app based on its icon and design. As a result, it's essential to develop a strong, distinctive look for your software that will catch the eyes of users and quickly indicate why downloading your app will benefit them. In this chapter, you'll find lots of tips and tricks to keep in mind while developing an application's design.

# How Appearance Changes Interactions

So far, you've read a lot about the nuts and bolts of an app's design—interaction methods and views—but haven't yet seen much about the shiny cover that envelops those elements. When building an app, it's just as important for designers to focus on the visual appeal of the software as it is to concentrate on interaction design.

An application's visual style sets the tone for the user experience, so it's worth spending a lot of time tinkering with and tweaking a piece of software's artwork in order to give it a unique look and feel. Think of the visual design of an app as its fashion sense—a carefully crafted, unique style that strives to make a certain type of first impression and speak volumes about what its intentions and purpose are.

It takes a lot of effort to develop an individual style and even more time to make sure it's consistent. The process involves constantly asking yourself questions as each design choice is made: Does this fit the style? What does this color palette communicate to the user? Does the icon blend with what's inside the app? Just as getting dressed for a night out on the town requires making lots of choices in front of a mirror, a designer must devote significant effort to planning out an app's look and style.

There are a number of different approaches to building an app's artwork. From simple, utilitarian designs to elaborate, ornate, elegant constructions, there are numerous ways to convey a mood or emotion to the user just by the way an app looks. The colors, typography, and artwork all team together to deliver a certain type of experience for a user, so it's important to ensure that a well-rounded design sets the proper tone.

Although the number of styles designers could use to construct the visual layout of an app is limitless, there are two most commonly used approaches today: skeuomorphic and flat designs.

## Skeuomorphic Design

The skeuomorphic style involves an app that retains the physical design cues of a previous or antiquated product. To see an example of this trait, take a look at the camera on your cell phone. Regardless of the brand of phone you own, it's likely that a click sound can be heard when taking a photo, an effect meant to imitate the closing and opening of a shutter. Although none of these cameras actually have a shutter that produces such a sound, the designers of each phone included that function to indicate to the user that a photo has been taken.

In interaction design, skeuomorphic constructs involve visual elements on a screen that are designed by artists to mimic a real-world object. At one point, such elements were plentiful: a note-taking application that resembled a pad of paper, a calendar app that featured animations imitating the tearing away of pages on a physical calendar, and the voicemail button resembling a reel-to-reel tape machine, for example.

The underlying goal of skeuomorphic designs isn't just to create art that mirrors a real-world object; it's also meant to instruct and inform the user about the purpose and interaction methods of an application. This isn't a new tactic either; it's been a common method in computer-interface design since the introduction of the graphical user interface in the late 1970s and early 1980s.

Apple's iBooks app for iPhone and iPad is a strong example of how effective a skeuomorphic design can be. Prior to the release of the iPad in 2010, e-books were gradually becoming more popular with consumers, but the technology had yet to be widely adopted by casual readers. To make the process of progressing through an e-book easier and more understandable, Apple implemented an intuitive page-turning animation that required only the swipe of a finger. This skeuomorphic design mimicked the behavior of physical books, making it easy for users to pick up and instantly understand how to navigate through the digital material.

The pre-iOS 7 Compass app (see Figure 6.1) employed a skeuomorphic design as well by resembling an actual physical compass in nearly every way. Although the use of skeuomorphic design was extremely common during the infancy of smartphones and tablets, especially on Apple's mobile operating system, the release of iOS 7 in late 2013 heralded Apple's shift away from the

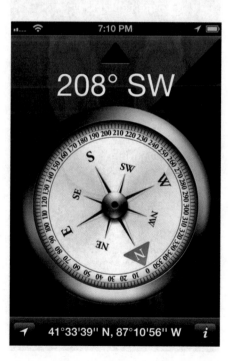

**Figure 6.1**   iOS 6's Compass app was skeuomorphic; it resembled its real-world counterpart, making the program easily understandable to users.

design philosophy. Although many apps still champion such designs today, most operating system vendors have pushed away from skeuomorphic interfaces.

## Flat Design

Flat design is the antithesis of skeuomorphic interfaces. It's the complete removal of any ornate interface and interaction design, leaving the app void of any component that does not directly provide an output for the user. Recent versions of Android and Apple's iOS 7 are the two most prevalent examples of this approach, but they both lagged behind Microsoft, which forged into this territory much earlier when it released Windows Phone 7, shown in Figure 6.2.

The proponents of flat design style contend that because computers are quite different from physical objects and abstractly depict data on a screen using pixels instead of tangible matter it makes little sense to conform an interface's look to that of pre-existing objects. Doing so, they argue, only limits the potential of a device and prevents it from achieving its optimal interaction design.

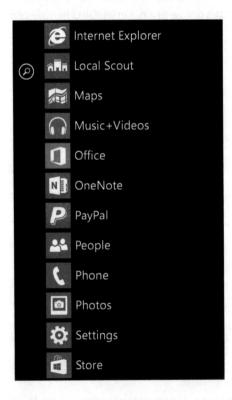

**Figure 6.2**   Windows Phone features a flat design home screen: no frills, just colored icons with large text on a dark background.

Clearly, their points are beginning to prove persuasive. Many applications and now even full mobile operating systems are jumping on the flat-design bandwagon. This progression has advanced in large part thanks to the maturity and widespread adoption of mobile computing. Generally, skeumorphic designs are easier to understand, because they replicate the interaction method of a physical object—like iBooks's page-turning function—and require little to no teaching of the user. Designers simply draw upon consumers' cognitive understanding of the real world and apply it to digital software.

But users have now reached a comfort level with mobile devices that makes such extensive hand-holding no longer necessary. Be careful, though; with a flat design there are fewer opportunities for users to pull from their own experience when navigating an app. Although designers are no longer confined to mimicking interaction methods found in real-world settings, you do have to be cautious in how you allow users to interact with data on screen. It's important that users understand the ramifications of each action and are able to quickly determine an app's purpose.

In selecting whether to go with a skeumorphic- or flat-design style, it's ultimately a matter of the designer's personal preference; there's no right or wrong choice. In the end, a designer is likely best off making a decision based on his or her own individual art style, because a better product will result from a process or technique the designer is comfortable with. It's also important, though, to meet the anticipated design aesthetic of the operating system so that the visual look is in line with the expectations of the user. This is a careful balancing act to strike throughout the design process and is one that requires an understanding of both the art design of the system and the designer's own talents.

> ### tip
> Are you still uncertain what's skeuomorphic and what's flat? Take a look at the texture and shadow in an application's art design. Flat designs tend to drop all texture and most shadow and instead use solid colors in sharp contrast to the background and buttons or text.

# Creating an App Icon

The app's icon is the first thing the user sees; before he or she ever opens the app or explores its functionality, this is the element that makes an impression, communicating a message about the style and purpose of your software amongst the thousands of other offerings in the mobile store. Although the icon is a digital product, it carries the same weight as a first handshake between potential business partners or the greeting a store employee offers a customer at the front door; it can either discourage a quality consumer experience or be the sign of positive things to come.

> ### tip
> Are you looking for inspiration in creating an app icon? There are many Web sites dedicated to exceptional icon work. A quick Web search of "great app icon designs" will turn up hundreds of pages of standout stuff curated by other designers.

As much as an often-quoted maxim warns against it, it's impossible not to judge a book by its cover (or a movie by its poster or a cereal by its box). More than we'd like to admit, consumers are attracted to an item not because of what is actually contained inside but because of what its packaging alludes to. As a result, it's essential that designers work to create an app icon that is eye-catching and appealing, helping to win the affection of users before they've ever launched it.

Before building an app icon, it's smart to first take note of the style presented by the system's icons, information generally noted in the platform's human-interface guidelines. Developers such as Apple or Google typically prefer applications with icons that look like they were cut from the same stone as its own programs so that a user's home screen or dock is composed of icons that blend well together. iOS icons, for example, are always rounded rectangles, whereas on Android there's no specific shape requirement, as can be seen in Figure 6.3.

As you begin to develop rough introductory sketches and general app icon ideas, one thing will become immediately apparent: Any icon you create, regardless of the platform it's developed for, must look good in a variety of sizes, from something 1,000 pixels square to a mere 30 pixels square. Creating a design that is visually appealing in both a very large and very small size isn't easy, so how can you go about making something that is universally attractive?

Simplicity helps; cram too much into an icon and much of it will get lost or be tough to see when shrunk down to a small size. Figure 6.4 shows a medical app icon for helping patients track the cups of water they drink in a day. The icon is scaled to the variety of sizes required for an iPhone application. Although each icon uses the same base image, its visual appearance can vary considerably when going from the largest to the smallest size. So when working to create an icon, repeatedly judge its appearance at a variety of sizes to ensure you're making something that looks great no matter how big or small it is.

To do this, it's best to draw your art in a vector format in a program such as Adobe Illustrator or in an extremely large raster format—at least 1,200 pixels square. Vector formats are ideal, as they are essentially able to scale up or down infinitely to any size; but as you've probably learned if you've ever worked with both vector and raster formats, vectors tend to be much more difficult to create, and the tools you're forced to use to make them are a bit more restricted. Thus, if you're not incredibly comfortable with vector techniques, it's better to design in a large raster format than to create bad vector art.

**Figure 6.3**  On Android, app icons appear as silhouette-style objects; unlike iOS, they don't have to use the same shape.

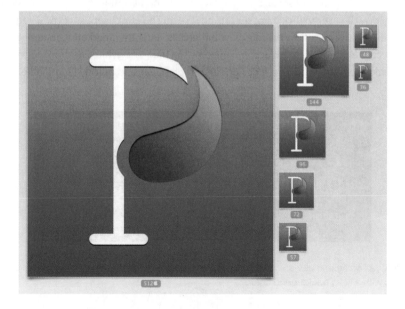

**Figure 6.4**  In this icon, the letter P formed from a water drop is clear no matter the size. (Courtesy of Ronald Yap, M.D., M.B.A.)

> **tip**
>
> Are you unfamiliar with the terms raster or vector? These two concepts are explained at length later in this chapter, in the "Building Art That Scales" section.

Once you've designed a large raster image or a vector icon, it's time to begin adapting the image to various sizes. Depending on the platform, the icon will likely need to exist in a variety of different forms (typically outlined in the human-interface guidelines). Resize the raster or vector icon to the appropriate sizes, and then save these as PNG files. At each size, though, you may notice that the artwork requires a bit of touchup work, especially at smaller sizes.

When building an icon that will look great in both large and small sizes, focus on developing an image that has a single visual focal point—an immediately recognizable shape or letter, for instance—at a size that takes up much of the icon. Some of the best icons are the simplest: clear shapes that contrast with the background color, creating a visual that is instantly recognizable, regardless of the icon's size.

You've no doubt seen them countless times already, but take another look at the application icons for popular social networks such as Facebook, Google+, Vine, and Tumblr, shown in Figure 6.5. They all consist of a powerfully colored background and a white or light-colored letter in a typography style that is consistent with the service's branding initiatives. This isn't the result of some unique trait of social networks; it's merely great design: an easily recognizable icon that allows the user to pick it out quickly on screen. The effectiveness of these logos can be seen on a daily basis; countless billboards, commercials, and other marketing materials feature a business's social-media handles accompanied by the blue-and-white Facebook logo or the red-and-white Google+ logo. These designs are simple, clear, and quickly identifiable.

**Figure 6.5**  All of these major social networks have a similar icon style, with a large, single letter contrasting with a solid background color.

If your app can't be represented by a single letter, a simple shape could also be featured promi-nently. Text-messaging applications, for example, typically use an icon that consists primarily of a speech bubble. Phone or voice-chat services often use icons depicting a telephone handset. Photo apps usually boast an icon that prominently displays a camera silhouette or a lens image.

As you prepare to scale an image down from its largest version, know that the exact sizes you need vary by operating system, what type of device you're designing for, and a handful of other factors, so therefore it's wise to visit your platform's online developer center to find out which dimensions you'll need. On most projects, expect to make between three and seven different icon sizes.

After exporting the icon to the various required sizes, you may notice that certain components or colors look less than ideal when their dimensions are reduced. Most platforms require that a general icon appear the same at all dimensions, but you can make small detail adjustments if a specific shadow or highlight suffers at a certain resolution. Be sure to verify that every-thing looks acceptable, and prepare the art asset for the programming team to include in the app binary.

# Finding a Unique Look

Once you've put the finishing touches on the app icon, you're ready to move on and tackle design for the rest of the project. When designing an app, you'll have to work hard to come up with something that sets it apart—something most easily done by developing your own unique style. In a competitive marketplace, it's essential to create something that stands out from the crowd of competitors by using a style that plays to your personal attributes and advantages.

That doesn't mean designers should stand out too much, though; the line of creativity is one that must be tip-toed along by presenting fresh, bold flavors that are uniquely your own while also providing the user with an experience that feels in line with the native platform. This is a struggle for any app designer, and it won't be something you solve after producing one or two applications. It's a constant, evolving battle to consistently improve your work while build-ing upon the huge body of style imposed by Apple, Google, and the other mobile platform creators.

As with many other art forms (or any other endeavor, for that matter), improvement really only comes through constant practice. Hard work is truly the only path for growth and success in app design.

## tip

Are you having some difficulty creating the look you desire in Photoshop? There's a multitude of great tutorials available only a Web search away. Many bloggers write tutorials for creating popular styles and visual appearances, so just do a quick search for what you're looking for, and you'll be surprised at how many resources you'll find.

There is much to be learned from the work of your competitors and app designers who came before you. Take a look at popular (or even not so popular) apps on any platform you're designing for. Assess what the icon does well and what it doesn't do well. Consider how you would work to improve it if you were given the task of overhauling the design. This will help put you in the proper design mindset and give you ideas for when it's time to start on your own project.

The best way to begin is to analyze each view of an application, and then examine how the view observes and conforms to the platform's human-interface guidelines. For example, if certain controls are required for specific content, does the app meet those criteria in every circumstance? It's likely that there will be many situations in which the interface guidelines are not followed, including on very popular applications, but by thinking critically you'll gain a lot of great interaction insight and begin to understand why a designer broke the convention in the first place.

Your goal should be to develop an ability to recognize mistakes and areas for improvement when analyzing an app's design. Strive to understand the platform and its interface guidelines so well that it's immediately apparent to you once a mistake has been made. For the seasoned designer, it's also a valuable skill to be able to analyze and determine design strategies that could quickly and simply be integrated into an application to improve interaction design.

If you can conduct a quick interface analysis of another designer's work, it's a great sign that you're improving at your craft. A master interaction designer can often look at another application for only a few minutes and easily point out places where it either follows or conflicts with the platform's human-interface guidelines, and the best can quickly offer suggestions on how to revise the app in order to meet those standards.

A trained eye can identify when a designer has complied with or disobeyed standard conventions, but it also recognizes that a good designer doesn't ignore guidelines simply for the sake of it. Instead, veteran designers know when an interaction needs to be pushed forward. In some situations, a designer may be intentionally ignoring the platform's interface rules in order to create a new type of interaction technique. Here, the goal is to implement a new interaction type only in situations in which the user's experience and cognitive flow through an app can be improved or made more efficient by way of that change.

There may be times, however, in which the designer will stray from the human interface guidelines for good reason; determining whether this decision is wise or not is a very subjective process. An experienced designer, for example, could go against the grain because he or she believes that a better solution has been found, so he or she will go ahead and implement that concept instead of following the prescribed practice.

There are many examples of designers pushing the mobile envelope and creating something valuable and influential. When someone introduces a technique or method that increases user efficiency, that concept is immediately recognizable to both users and designers, and the new process quickly becomes common.

One major occurrence of this was the pull-to-refresh design championed by Loren Brichter in the iPhone app Tweetie, which was a popular Twitter client in the early days of the iOS App Store. Tweetie created a gesture that allowed a user to slightly pull or tug the top of a data table to refresh the content contained within it. A refresh previously required a unique button, which took up space in a menu or navigation bar. But with the addition of this gesture, the menu no longer needed that button, creating space that could be used for another feature or left blank to make the overall design cleaner.

The pull-to-refresh gesture is now extremely common and instantly recognizable. At the time of its introduction, however, it was a revolutionary way to quickly update content in an app without wasting valuable screen real estate. Now, you can see the gesture inside of many apps, as shown in Figure 6.6.

Another powerful example is the technique often called "swipe from the edge," in which the user makes a swipe gesture from the border of the device or even outside its display area. Pioneered in mobile by Android and later introduced into iOS, a swipe by the user from the top of the screen now drops down a notification menu listing missed phone calls, weather fore-casts, e-mails, and other useful information. Once this idea was introduced, users and designers immediately recognized its benefit and have implemented it in countless programs since then.

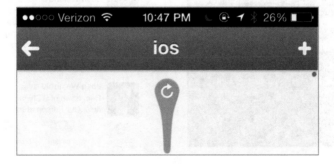

**Figure 6.6**   Pull down a table view to reveal this common visual indicator.

There are even examples of entire app companies being formed based on the principle of clashing with human interface guidelines. Take the popular iOS development team Tapbots, LLC, for example. The company was founded with a design concept focused entirely on making quasi-personified "app robots" dedicated to performing specific utility tasks. Each robot has its own unique style and structure but remains true to the Tapbots form, which both is recognizable and works to push the limits of the human-interface guidelines for iOS. The Tapbots team is well experienced in software development and mobile programming, and although their work is often bold and beyond convention it's produced in a tasteful manner that's well designed and ultimately usable by anyone with little help or instruction.

The two examples in Figure 6.7 show how Tapbots's popular app Tweetbot displays a user's timeline differently compared to the standard Twitter application, which uses the normal iOS interface conventions.

**Figure 6.7**   Although these two apps look a lot like each other, the Tapbots app (left) breaks with standard conventions (right) in many significant ways.

Just looking at this example, the differences may not be so obvious, but to the trained eye they're astonishing. Shown on the left, Tweetbot features a nonstandard tab bar that uses custom icons, with the space normally occupied by text labels instead used for small glow indicators that show when new content is available. In addition, whereas standard tabs serve only as a way to switch between different types of data, in Tweetbot they offer additional functionality. For example, holding down on a tab brings up a contextual menu that allows the user to quickly jump to other app features. Other sophisticated interface gestures (which can't be shown in the screenshot) include swiping left or right on a tweet to quickly reply to or favorite a tweet, and holding a single finger down on a tweet to bring up a menu of advanced sharing options, such as the ability to email a tweet. An application using standard interaction methods could require three or more button presses in order to achieve the same goals, but Tweetbot found quick ways to differentiate itself and create an exceptional experience.

Tweetbot takes liberties with its design that require much practice and experience to pull off, but when done correctly they're extremely valuable and do much to improve the application. Such decisions are not for a designer who hasn't read and internalized the interface guidelines, but instead for the expert who has contemplated the positives and negatives of such a design.

> ## note
> Panic Inc., The Iconfactory, Rovio, and Bolt Creative are all development studios that have created a consistent visual brand for mobile, and their apps are immediately recognizable due to their unique designs.

# Matching Art to Interaction Design

How should you go about constructing interaction designs that offer a highly polished experience that both catches a user's eye and remains true to the platform's style and structure? How does a designer create something that looks amazing yet also meets user expectations by abiding by standard human-interface guidelines?

First, focus on interaction design and interface elements in a way that makes you blind to the visual aesthetics of what you're creating. All too often, designers get ahead of themselves and focus on perfecting the polish of every pixel or color palette—a significant mistake. Focusing too intensely right away on the color and visual style of an app is akin to choosing a kitchen table and wallpaper for a house before the builders have even laid a foundation. Although it's a lot more fun to pick out furniture than it is to watch cement dry, it's unwise to choose where to put walls on a blueprint solely in order to accommodate small pieces of furniture. Your goal is to build a quality house that will last for a long time, so first focus on establishing a solid framework for the app. Details, like wall hangings and carpets, can come later.

Simple design tools—something as basic as pen and paper or more advanced like the Balsamiq wireframe tool shown in Figure 6.8—can help you isolate yourself from every visual variable in a design that's unrelated to the interaction experience. At this stage, you can determine what animation users will see as they move from one section of the app to another, where buttons will be placed, how data can be interacted with, and many other processes. Now is not the time to focus on the "pretty" aspects of the app; it's the time to focus on usability. Once you have a solid understanding of how the user will move through the app, then you can focus on making those basic assets more appealing to the eye.

Once you've fleshed out a full wireframe model, you're ready to jump forward and approach the visual design of an application. Designers tackle wireframing in various ways, but the process is typically finished after the interface of every view or screen in the app is laid out using your wireframe tool of choice along with short paragraphs connected to most if not all of the situations in which the user interacts with the app.

> ### tip
> Balsamiq is a favorite wireframing tool for designers, but others exist as well, including OmniGraffle by The Omni Group and Layout by SwordSoft.

These paragraphs should explain in fairly simple language exactly what will happen when the user activates or manipulates the content on screen. A wireframe explaining the page-curl interaction in Apple's iBooks, for example, could be written like this: "The user is presented with a full-screen view that contains the e-book text laid out in its appropriate formatting and paragraph style on screen. The user will move to the next page by placing their finger on the right

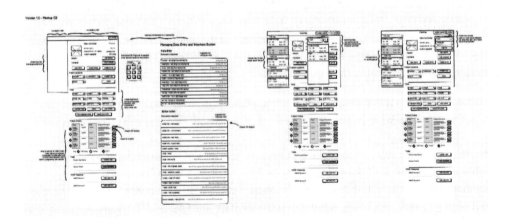

**Figure 6.8**   Simple wireframes are used so that the focus stays on what's important: great interaction design.

corner of the screen, then either swiping or dragging the page to the left side of the screen. The page-curl animation should anchor to the user's finger, allowing for dynamic 3-D movement that makes the user feel as if he is actually flipping pages in a physical book. The user can also go back to a previous page by using a similar gesture in reverse."

Once you've created a wireframe and fully explained the app's interaction methods, you're ready to move on to working on the visual graphic design inside of your application. Your wireframe is complete when you can hand it to a programmer, and that programmer has no questions or concerns on how to program or implement a design feature. Work in open communication with your programmers and continue to elaborate in your wireframe design document until you've satisfied their questions.

When creating and modifying visuals for your new application, the most valuable concept to keep in mind is design coherence, which involves making every interface attribute, animation, and piece of typography feel as if it was crafted from the same material. This is potentially the most difficult part of creating a visual look and feel, because it requires a pinpoint level of attention to detail.

In many ways, application design is like making a movie: The director and producers want to create a world for the audience that, no matter how unreal it actually is, *seems* absolutely real. Each choice must continue to facilitate the illusion of this alternative reality, making each shot feel like it takes place in the same universe, thus ensuring that the viewer remains engaged with the film. If in the midst of a Western the protagonist cowboy suddenly jumped into a sports car to ride into the sunset, the fictional world of the movie would be completely destroyed, perhaps prompting the viewer to notice other elements that are out of place.

Building an app is quite similar, as one single piece of a custom interface that feels like it doesn't belong could immediately make the user aware of other pieces that don't work well or feel awkward compared to previous app experiences.

## Crossing Platforms

If the application you're building is intended to be a cross-platform piece of software, the task of creating a coherent design universe becomes much more difficult. Now, the app not only has to blend well with the million apps on one platform but must also not seem out of place among the million apps on a competing platform with its own separate design conventions.

Even if there's a small chance that an app will eventually be ported over to another platform in the future, it's advisable to consider the design structure of all target platforms before moving past the wireframing stage of the development process, and it certainly must be done prior to working on detailed visual designs. Often, an interaction strategy that works well on one platform will hit a roadblock or hindrance on another platform.

During the early days of app markets for Apple and Android, for example, the tab bar interface method was extremely common on the iPhone yet relatively difficult to accurately recreate and implement on Android without being clunky and confusing. Because designers failed to take these differences into account, it was common to see a poor Android port of an iPhone app. These substandard programs had interfaces that contained many problems due to a development team's attempt to hastily and haphazardly fit the tab bar style into the Android ecosystem.

When fighting against this multiplatform problem, it's best to first focus on the general interaction design of each, especially on user flow, animations, and any interface pieces you plan to use.

## App Branding Guides

When you're working on your first app for two platforms, you may find yourself struggling to keep its look and feel consistent when moving to a new operating system. Quickly, you'll find yourself asking odd but important questions, things like, "Exactly what was the hexadecimal color code for the shade of blue I'm using?" and "What alpha transparency level of black did we pick for shadows again?"

If you're having these difficulties, it may be helpful to first draw up a general application-branding guide, a small handbook outlining general style decisions and themes for the app. Although branding guides are documents most commonly found in large companies—typically developed by a marketing department to ensure all corporate communications use the same logo, typography, and colors—a branding guide can be extremely valuable in the app development world as well. It's a great reference to have on hand when working to ensure that the general look and feel of the software is consistent as it moves across platforms.

In your guide, work to define as narrowly as possible exact color shades, common background textures, shadow color and blur radius, and other specific visual design characteristics. From there, you'll be able to build on these generalities and adapt them as your development progresses.

Creating these short guides, usually only a handful of pages in length, will allow you to establish a hard standard you can return to when working with design variables that should remain constant across platforms. It's important to use the exact colors and typography on Android that you used on iPhone so that users feel they get the same experience from your app regardless of which platform they access it on.

Such branding designs will also be useful if you have to hand the project off to another designer in the future or if the app sees success and you hire new designers for your operation. This reference guide will be available so that future designers on the app can also find the correct color codes or font choices without guessing, actions that often lead to inconsistency or incorrect design.

# Building Art That Scales

Once you begin the process of creating art designs for your apps, it's important to construct something that "scales" effectively at various sizes. But what does this mean for your mobile project? It's a simple concept of digital art creation, but one that will give you a leg up on the competition and help you from being caught off-guard when the mobile app landscape changes in the coming years.

Throughout the history of computer graphic design, artists and interactive designers have typically done most of their work in what's known as a raster format. The term refers to the grid of pixels that makes up an image, each filled with a specific color shade and perhaps a certain level of transparency. As computers have evolved over the past three decades, this concept has evolved somewhat, with the number of pixels available on a screen and the number of colors that can be produced on an image both increasing.

> ## note
> Common raster formats include PSD, JPEG, PNG, and GIF. If you're working with one of these, you're working in the raster format.

In mobile, the LCD panels on phones and tablets continually boast greater and greater levels of pixel density. In 2010, Apple introduced the Retina display for the iPhone 4, which at the time had one of the highest pixel display densities in the consumer market. Typically, displays are measured in units of pixels per inch, literally the number of pixels lined up next to each other on one linear inch of screen real estate. The iPhone 4 and subsequent models contained 326 pixels per inch, whereas some Android devices have since featured mobile displays with more than 400 pixels per inch.

This pixel-per-inch growth jump was significant, and with Apple's shift to a Retina display its mobile phone now contains four times the amount of pixels that had been present in the previous model, the iPhone 3GS. But with the new screen density, art assets produced for the older screen size needed to increase significantly in size; otherwise the art would look pixelated or muddy on the new iPhone screen. Android designers have long had to produce assets of multiple resolutions in order to get the best look, with each asset needing to be drawn at multiple resolutions for low-, medium-, and high-resolution displays. The general increase in screen pixel density over the past several years, however, has required even larger assets, with some Android designs needing five different redrawings in order to get the best look on each resolution display.

> tip
>
> On Android, you don't need to produce elements for every display size; create them large and the device will scale them down when needed. Be aware, though, that this action eats up the device's processing power.

In addition to needing to produce artwork at various resolutions to get the best look on each display, there may be other situations that require a designer to create various art attributes at even larger sizes. If things go well for your project, your app may need to be promoted in a marketing campaign or featured by Apple or Google in their respective stores. If you're fortunate enough to have that happen, you're going to need higher-resolution versions of your art.

> tip
>
> Google currently requires developers to send special promotional artwork when submitting an app to the Google Play Store. These images could be used as a banner on its Web site or in a prominent display spot in the store. Spend a fair amount of time on these and give them as much care as you would your app icon. Special placement in any app store is the developer's equivalent to winning the lottery.

How can you create art that will work on all of the various screen resolutions you might need down the road while also being capable of adapting to even larger sizes in the future? Many designers often think that it's best to just create raster artwork at a very large scale, perhaps at a size even larger than you'll need on the highest pixel density phone screen, but this can lead to several significant problems.

First, unless you have a very new computer with abundant RAM and processing power on which to create the artwork, your computer is likely to suffer a significant slowdown when it attempts to process and manage a very large raster file. These files simply aren't the most efficient way to create large pieces of artwork.

Second, you may find that a piece of raster art rendered at a large size will not always scale down uniformly when shrunk to a smaller size. For example, when you take a 1,000 x 1,000 pixel square and shrink it down to 100 x 100, the software you use to handle that manipulation, typically Photoshop, merely estimates how the art should look at the smaller size and then recreates the piece of work to fit the new resolution. However, because your artwork previously fit a size much larger than the new piece there will be lost pixels.

Remember that raster art actually contains exact pixels, laid out in a grid, with each holding a dot of color data. The original artwork in this example contained 1,000,000 pixels, but the new, smaller piece only contains 10,000; so what happens to the lost 990,000 pixels? The algorithms used to estimate what the figure should look like at a smaller size are fairly advanced and, in most situations, will do the job completely and accurately; but occasionally you will shrink a piece of raster artwork that looks slightly off.

It's for these scale scenarios that designers recommend creating assets in the vector format, using an application such as Adobe Illustrator. Although raster art contains a finite amount of pixels, each with a specific color, vector art is mathematically based, and each point in the visual object on screen relates to other points based on an equation. The math can be complex and is relatively unimportant, but vectors work in such a way that when you shrink or increase them in size, the lines, circles, squares, and triangles that make up the artwork all shift in size accordingly with each other, keeping their relationships more or less the same.

As a result, the art asset can essentially scale as large or as small as you want it to while still maintaining a mostly consistent look. There are some exceptions to this, especially at very small sizes, but in most situations, vector art is a much more effective way of creating art that works at multiple sizes.

> ### note
> Common vector formats include AI, SVG, and sometimes PDF. If you're working in these formats you're working with vector data.

If vector art is the key to this scalable kingdom why bother even considering something else? Why don't designers just create everything in vector? The answer, unfortunately, is a bit complex.

First and foremost, it's considerably more difficult to create art in the vector format than it is to make something in a raster format. Of course, like many questions of personal choice, this subject often leads to considerable debate, but in general creating artwork that fits an extremely rigid size structure in pixels—the kind of art needed for a mobile device with a specific resolution display—is much easier in the finite raster world. That's mostly because designers depend on specific measurements and the ability to lay out pieces in exact alignments, all of which are measured in pixels, the raster world's unit of measurement.

Similarly, adding gradients, shadows, textures, and other details as art accents—the kind of subtle keys that will create a good interface—is much more true to real-world output in raster than it is in vector. If a designer works only in the vector format, he or she may find that a creation on a computer often looks different than it does on a phone or tablet display, because the mathematical representations of the figure changed a bit based on the size or scale of a certain device.

The best plan of attack for a mobile interface designer involves a two-step approach. First, use a vector-creation program, such as Adobe Illustrator, to make the dynamic art assets that are unique to the app and will need to look great at multiple resolutions. If you're creating icons to fit in a tab or button, for example, make those first as a vector so that you can later scale them up or down in size for use on a variety of screen densities. Once the general shape and look of a piece of artwork is finalized in a vector form, you can then export the file to the various raster art resolutions required for a project, resulting in a PNG or similar file type that's optimized for any resolution. From there, you can add shadows, textures, or other detailed work that is best done at a specific resolution in Photoshop or a similar program.

Keeping this in mind, there's a third route that helps designers avoid vector or raster art entirely. Whenever possible, designers should work with their programming team to create visual interface elements in project code, because that process brings multiple benefits.

First, like vector art, interface code is typically a flexible size format and works effectively on a variety of screen resolutions. Second, creating interface components and art designs in code improves app performance significantly, because it's easier for a computing device to draw art with code than it is to draw the art when referenced from a PNG or other graphic asset.

By creating interfaces in programming code with the standard software frameworks provided by the operating system's designer, your app will be able to take advantage of any optimization added later by the platform vendor. For example, when Google moved to the new Holo design or when Apple moved to the drastically different iOS 7 it was much easier for developers to migrate their designs if they had used source code-level interface components. Designers who created all their artwork as raster or vector images needed to recreate every asset in order to adapt an app to the platform's new look.

Some designers, however, still may prefer to not have such drastic changes to an app without strong internal influence, so the design-by-coding route may actually end up being a detriment to a development team.

With the recent maturation of mobile design, many tools have been developed to help designers create more of their work in code. The practice previously was a fairly complex one, especially for interaction designers who didn't have a formal computer science background or significant programming experience. Now, though, applications such as PaintCode by PixelCut (see Figure 6.9), Hype by Tumult, and Edge Animate by Adobe have made it easier for designers to create complex visuals or animations using graphical user interface tools that are more familiar to an artist than a programmer.

**Figure 6.9**  Using PaintCode by PixelCut, any designer can work with familiar visual tools to create an app's art in code.

# Adding the Final Touches

As you continue to gain experience and become a more capable interaction designer, there are many things to keep in mind as you put the final touches on an app and grow closer to the final shipping date.

First, when creating interaction designs or app icons—anything the user will see while engaging with the app—remain focused on an often-cited principle of traditional graphic design. Aim to make something that would have looked great 10 years ago and something you anticipate will still look good 10 years from now. Good design is universal and will always look great, whereas fashions and trends come and go. Refrain from creating works that draw entirely on short-term industry fads that are likely to fade in the near future. By doing so, you'll make a solid product that will continue to stand out for reasons other than your ability to show off with the latest Photoshop tricks.

Next, don't be afraid to iterate, iterate, and then iterate further upon your design. Like great writing, design requires constant revision and persistent thought to get right. You won't create your best work on your first draft, so don't trick yourself into thinking your first pass on an interface is an unstoppable, perfect creation.

Well-regarded Apple industrial designer Jony Ive has often mentioned the vast amount of work required to get a design ready for release. It takes many poor early versions and hundreds of hours of revisions to iterate and create a functional piece of art for Apple. But Ive emphasizes that he's proud of all the failures along the way, because they ultimately helped produce the final version that the public has often been dazzled by.

This will hopefully be your experience in design as well: finding joy and value in continually improving your designs and then looking back on earlier concepts with a small sense of shame once you realize how much better your final product is. All designers make mistakes. The best designers find ways to improve on their earlier missteps. Fantastic designers are capable of recognizing where they went wrong and then adjusting and improving before their work ever goes public.

Finally, when working on a design and preparing assets or interaction outlines that you expect to integrate into your final work, always be sure to test it on a variety of devices and screens, no matter the platform you're targeting. Although Android designers are quite familiar with this idea thanks to the variety of screen sizes and device manufacturers working on the platform, it's essential even on Apple's iOS, because the LCD panels vary greatly amongst the various generations of the iPhone, iPod touch, and iPad. Although some interfaces may appear as a vibrant white on some devices, the same art could have a slightly yellowish tint on another. It's important to test on a handful of different devices under different circumstances and variables, including various lighting arrangements, to make sure that your app doesn't contain a fatal visual flaw.

## IN-DEPTH

No matter which platform your team is targeting, your app's icon will be what's front and center to the users who consider downloading it to their phones or tablets. In most app stores, only a program's name, icon, and star rating are visible to a prospective customer. It's critical to impress with just a single visual, encouraging someone perusing a long list of apps to tap yours and view screenshots and the app's description.

Take a look at the Google Play Store, shown in Figure 6.10. Here, users don't have much to go by outside of the app icon, so it's important to spend time polishing and cleaning up your design.

It's unfortunate, but most users will base a majority of their first impression of an app on the appearance of the icon. Even if it's a free app, the user will be unlikely to give it a chance if the icon is bad.

If you're uncomfortable with that pressure on your graphic design talents, fear not; there are freelance artists who are available for hire, many of whom specialize in mobile app icons. To find a talented app artist, visit popular development forums for the platform you're targeting, and ask around for people who may have references.

When looking for an artist, review his or her existing portfolio; you'll want an artist who has experience on at least three to four different client projects. Also, don't shy away from asking for references and checking with previous clients to make sure the artist is prompt and appreciative of feedback. Costs can vary greatly based on the specifics of the design and the experience of the artist, so be sure to request quotes before hiring someone.

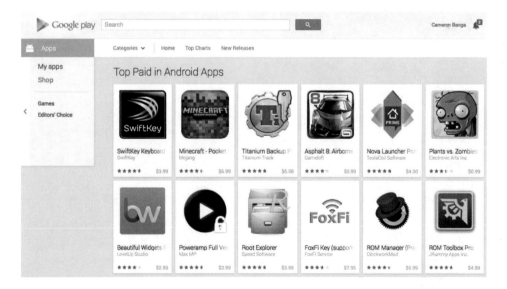

**Figure 6.10**  There's not much to judge an app on in the Google Play Market, so attractive icons help grab attention.

# Conclusion

Creating an art design that's functional yet distinctive enough to attract the user's attention can be difficult, especially when tackling cross-platform development. The best advice is to stay focused, keep the wireframe simple, and then work on visuals once you have a general interaction design established. That way, the programming team can focus on app logic and other technical implementations that require knowledge of the general app design.

By finishing the interaction design plan in the early phases of a project, you give yourself extra time to spend on the visual components. On most app projects, programmers need a final wireframe and interaction flow model in order to begin working on code. The sooner you get that information to them, the sooner you can begin perfecting the look of navigation bars, buttons, and app icons. By the end of the project, you'll be begging the rest of the team for extra time to polish up various elements, so any additional seconds you can save yourself in early phases will pay off down the line.

# CHAPTER 7

# WORKING WITH PROGRAMMERS

Unless you're both a computer science genius and someone with a penchant for quality design, you won't be able to complete an app project on your own. You'll need to play nicely with others, namely the programmers who will write the code that turns your visual dream into a digital reality. This chapter provides practical lessons on how to work with technical-minded programmers as well as tips and tricks on how to gradually get into the realm of manipulating and editing code. Although that notion may seem menacing at first, it's not that daunting once you know what you're looking for and how to make changes that produce the desired results.

# Understanding Your Programmer

As an interaction designer who's primarily focused on interface setup, chances are high that you don't have considerable programming experience. You might have a basic understanding of HTML or CSS, but it's unlikely that you're well versed in the languages of Java or Objective-C. Ideally, you're working on your project with a programmer who's more than capable of tackling the code writing necessary for a successful app.

All of this, however, doesn't mean that you shouldn't be thinking about the technical side of your application as you're designing its interface. After all, you're visualizing everything a user will see in the app, but in order for your visuals to ever get to the user some technical wizardry will have to occur. Even if you're the greatest interaction designer to ever hit the industry, it won't mean much unless you have a quality programmer working with you to turn your visuals into something users can get their thumbs and fingers on.

Once you do find a programming partner to team up with, there are a number of roadblocks you'll have to dodge in order to ensure that your working relationship remains strong. A major potential pitfall is arrogance; it's a trait many good designers (and many good programmers) in the development community are notorious for having, so do your best to avoid fitting that stereotype.

# Learning Programming Languages

Ego aside, another key issue to work through is the way you communicate and articulate your design vision to your programmer. It doesn't take long while working in development to realize that programming and design are two completely different worlds with vastly different languages; one of the only few points of unity between the two is the shared desire to produce a quality piece of software. With starkly different vocabulary in each discipline, it can be a struggle to clearly describe an interface in a way that both designers and programmers can comprehend. Bridging the language gap will be essential for your project's success.

In order to help your programmers understand and respect you, you'll need to study the language of programming in much the same way you'd learn Spanish or French in a high school or college class. Java and Objective-C, the most common languages used to program Android and iOS applications today, are called languages because they have their own syntax, vocabulary, and rules, just like any other method of speaking and writing. As you begin working with a variety of programmers, you'll quickly find that each has its own unique style that will take some time to get accustomed to—just like it takes a little while to adapt to the accent of a person from a different region of the country or world.

> **note**
>
> Although Java and Objective-C are the most popular languages used in mobile today, they're far from the only ones. Just because a programmer doesn't use one of these languages doesn't mean he or she can't build mobile apps.

Like any other language, programming isn't something you can become fluent in with just a couple of overnight cramming sessions. Instead, take small chunks of time each day to read and review the fundamentals of programming and practice expanding your vocabulary. Follow a collection of prominent platform programmers on Twitter or other social networks and consider subscribing to relevant e-mail newsletters or newsgroups, such as the iOS Dev Weekly shown in Figure 7.1. Develop a list of forums or blogs to check in on from time to time. As always, the platform you're developing your app for likely has a developer portal with ample resources—videos, documents, and code tutorials—that can help you out as well.

If you don't have a college degree in computer science or experience with formal programming courses, understanding the terminology used to address these difficult concepts only through reading e-mails or social-network posts may seem daunting or impossible at first, but don't get discouraged if programming terms aren't rolling off your tongue or flying off your fingertips in the first couple of weeks. It's extremely rare to find a mobile app development

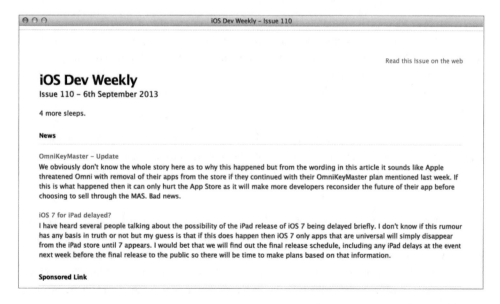

**Figure 7.1**   Keep up to date with development trends through a handful of different e-mail newsletters and listservs. (Courtesy of Dave Verwer.)

switch-hitter—someone with above-average comprehension of both programming and interface design—so you can't expect yourself to internalize everything immediately. However, by acquiring small bits of knowledge here and there you're becoming better equipped to make informed design decisions in the future.

Talking the talk is one thing, but walking the walk is another. Once you become familiar and comfortable with these not-so-foreign languages, try to act on your knowledge. Practice programming; this effort will earn you the respect and admiration of the programmers you're working with, which will pay off when you turn to them for design advice or help implementing an ambitious or atypical design plan you've cooked up. Making the effort to speak their language and understand what they do will earn you a lot of goodwill with the people who will make your vision a reality.

## From Sketch to Programmable Design

Gaining a fundamental understanding of programming's terminology and philosophy will go a long way toward helping you create design work that doesn't make code writers cringe when it's handed off to them. From the moment you begin to work on a project, one thing is certain: The end of the application development process will involve your design work being turned into computer programming code, which will then be thrown into a compiler and morphed into executable binary language, thus becoming the application users will download to their smartphones or tablets.

This chain of production is ultimately the reason why it's important to understand how programmers operate. As a designer, you'll develop documentation for a programmer, and the temptation will be to fill it with creative and flowery design verbiage. But then the programmer will need to translate that elaborate language into something more technical; like with any conversion of words from one language to another, this leads to the possibility of misinterpretation or loss of meaning.

As you learn more about programming, you gradually eliminate the potential for valuable information to be lost in translation, which will ultimately lead to software that looks and functions closer to your original design intent and will make the app a truer fit to your original interaction goals.

When striving to use more accurate technical terminology in your design documents or when discussing a problem with a programmer, don't get frustrated or discouraged when you're not sure how to explain what you're asking for; this is a common problem that affects everyone who jumps into mobile interaction design. The only real solution is to take the time to find the correct answer to what you're looking for. Learn how to accurately describe and name the interaction technique or interface asset you're looking for; don't try to make uneducated guesses or, even worse, use terminology that doesn't apply to the medium you're working with. This will only leave you with a confused programmer or will encourage the programmer to implement the incorrect interaction you accidently described.

> **note**
>
> How do you create design documentation? It's a somewhat ambiguous item that doesn't really have a formal definition, and it can vary greatly between designers. It usually involves creating a text file a few pages in length that presents wireframes, app mockups, examples of colors and logos, and notes for programmers on how the application should look and feel.
>
> Apps mentioned earlier this book, like Balsamiq, can be useful in creating design documentation. Another great piece of software for making such documents is Napkin by Aged & Distilled LLC.

One of the biggest mistakes a designer can make, for example, is to use traditional, layman's computer terms such as "double click." Although this gesture is commonly used on a desktop operating system, on a mobile device a single tap on a screen is what's used to select text or activate a button. This instruction to a programmer could either waste time with an improper implementation or lead to a poor user experience. Both are significant development mistakes that should be avoided at all costs. There's no mouse pointer or clickable button on the screen of nearly all mobile phones. When users interact with the screen, they tap, not click. Be sure to get your terminology correct, or you risk confusing your programmer. Use language similar to what's shown in Figure 7.2.

**Figure 7.2** Use words such as tap or pinch, not traditional computer interaction terms such as click.

# Describing Your Design

It's important to be accurate and clear when describing to a programmer what you want them to build. Keep reading and practicing until you're comfortable with describing your design using the most common interaction words in mobile development. When using an app, users pinch and swipe. They don't scroll or click. Practice your vocabulary and be capable of explaining your design using these words.

> ## tip
>
> As a designer, you'll need to understand the various types of gestures a user might perform as well as the proper terminology to describe those movements. Here's a short list of common motions.
>
> - **Tap**: Taking a single finger and pressing a specific area of the screen then almost immediately lifting up.
>
> - **Press**: Like a tap, but the finger is kept on the screen for a few seconds.
>
> - **Drag**: Pressing a single finger down on the screen in a specific location then moving the finger to another part of screen without lifting the finger.
>
> - **Pinch**: Placing two fingers, typically the thumb and pointer finger, on the screen then moving them closer together or farther apart while keeping both on screen at all times.
>
> - **Flick**: Pressing down on the screen then sliding a finger in a specific direction. The momentum is similar to a drag, but the finger lifts off the screen while making the motion.
>
> - **Two-finger tap**: Performing the same action as a tap but with two fingers at the same time.
>
> - **Rotate**: Placing two fingers on the screen in a similar way to the pinch but instead rotating the fingers around a center point as if they are twisting a dial.

When documenting and describing your design, use clear, simple, and concise sentences to indicate what you envision. Don't fret if English wasn't your strongest subject in school, though; this doesn't need to be award-winning writing. These sentences and paragraphs are more about implementation and less about grammar and sentence structure. A programmer isn't looking to be impressed by elaborate metaphors or ten-dollar words. He or she is simply look-ing for you to clearly articulate your design plan.

When in doubt, refer to things the programmer is likely familiar with. Lean on other applica-tions in order to clearly communicate your interaction design plan. Tell a programmer, for example, that you want new user data in your app to "automatically be pulled in and appear as if it continues on forever, the way Instagram displays photos or Facebook shows news stories," and you'll quickly communicate your point. Indicate that your app should have a pull-to-refresh function "identical to the one in the official Twitter app for iPhone," and your message will get across without a problem. These types of descriptions, similar to what's shown in Figure 7.3, provide concrete examples for a programmer to consult when implementing your design plan in code.

**Figure 7.3**  Tell a programmer in a simple way that pull-to-refresh is what you're looking for, and this is what you'll get: a gesture for refreshing content that is familiar to the user.

Although it's important to be clear and concise when describing what you want, leaving nothing up to programmer interpretation is important as well. Being as detailed as possible removes the need for programmers to fill in the blanks and hopefully leads to a truer realization of your interaction design. It's essential to state those specific details early on in the process, however, because design is a very abstract technique and programming is extremely literal.

A slight design variation that can be described in just a few words in a document could require an extraordinary amount of source code to be rewritten. Novice designers often grossly underestimate the amount of time it takes to replace source code and rework a programming problem once an implementation has already been built. The assumption that certain elements can be quickly rewritten only wreaks havoc on a project and leads to rushed design. The more a designer understands programming, the more he or she recognizes how much work it often takes to retool even the simplest elements.

This do-more-now-to-avoid-doing-a-lot-later concept is something that development teams also need to communicate to clients. It's important that they understand that spending an extra half-hour at the beginning of a project to ensure something is done right will keep project costs down. Otherwise, they'll end up paying a lot more for your team to make changes later in the game when code must be rewritten.

Therefore, be descriptive and make sure you've properly thought through all the potential design issues that may arise. Don't shy away from asking your programmers whether you've provided enough detail for them to do their job. Although you're likely to be working with them hand in hand throughout the development process, it's crucial to thoroughly discuss every aspect of your design with the programmers before a single line of code is written. Once they start, they should feel like they could write the entire application without ever needing to confer with you again.

## tip

What sort of questions should you ask a programmer to make sure they understand your design? Here are a handful of sample queries that you might want to ask to make sure you're both on the same page.

- Does the way I've integrated a segmented control bar make sense here?

- Is it OK if we integrate this custom button that I've created? Is there any special way that I should export the art assets for you?

- Do you think this custom font file will be easy enough to work into the app, or should I try to use one of the system standard fonts?

You and your team may also find it useful to build an interactive prototype through one of many specific software packages that help designers turn their ideas into something more tangible. Briefs by MartianCraft and MarvelApp by Marvel Prototyping (see Figure 7.4) are two easy-to-use pieces of software that let designers take basic Photoshop work and translate it into a mockup on an iPhone or Android, allowing for rapid prototype development. Creating a more fully interactive prototype will require more work and consume a large amount of time, thus delaying the start of programming, so be sure to fully consider the pros and cons of this tradeoff before doing so. If you don't think a prototype will get you to your desired result any faster, you may just end up wasting your limited time and resources by going through this extra phase.

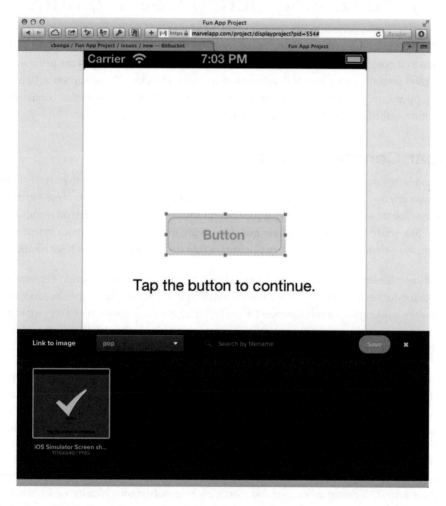

**Figure 7.4**    MarvelApp offers a simple way to create interactive prototypes of mobile apps in a Web browser.

Finally, be sure to do everything you can to grow your relationship with your programmers and ensure that strong, open lines of communication exist. If they're not comfortable creating what you're asking for, be flexible and try to understand their concerns or criticisms. It's easy to get aggressive and defensive when a programmer questions your design ideas, but when a programmer says he or she will have a tough time doing what you've planned, it's not necessarily because he or she is lazy or arrogant. Concerns are being raised because the programmer wants to be sure he or she can help build an application that everyone on the development team can be proud of.

# Communicating During Development

Just because you've gone through the preproduction process of documenting your design and handed it off to a programmer doesn't mean your work on the project is complete. In order for the app to succeed, it will be imperative for you to be in constant contact with the programming team through their phase of development up until it ships to a digital app store. Like peanut butter and jelly, design and programming are very different elements that complement each other well; they must be blended in order to effectively wrap up a project.

## Clear Communication

First and foremost, it's critical that you indicate to your programming team that you're available to answer any and all design questions during their part of the development process. No matter how well you think you've documented your design and outlined what you intend the visuals to look like, your programmers will have questions along the way. Be sure to check in with them periodically—perhaps on a weekly basis—to make sure no problems or issues have popped up.

Establishing contact on a regular schedule will help you guarantee that no design implementations or product expectations fall off track—something that can complicate the situation, especially when working with a programmer for the first time. It's much easier to make a repair or two early on when the wagon is just starting to move rather than much later when the wheels fly off the axles midway through a long journey.

Regardless of how well you do or don't know the programmers you're working with, it's important to establish a standard procedure for noting and communicating about design issues and software bugs that show up during the development process. Once multiple hands get on a project (and even when you're working alone), it's important to carefully note every issue that rears its head so that it can be adequately put to rest.

Because collaborating on design issues and alterations is such an integral part of app development, a niche industry has sprung up for apps that specifically help make communication easier. Skitch by Evernote (shown in Figure 7.5) is a popular piece of desktop software that makes it easy to quickly mark up images and graphically note what pieces of a design are broken and in need of a change.

**Figure 7.5**  Skitch makes documentation and noting change requests on images simple.

## Tracking Issues

Many programming teams use what's known as a source-code-control system to help various programmers and designers collaborate and share code. The most common technical protocols used to facilitate this process include Git, Subversion, and Mercurial. These technical tools are typically tied into full-service online businesses for which source code for the project is stored off-site on a cloud server and then distributed between team members. These control systems are also usually tied together with some type of bug-tracking software to manage issues and include a wiki site or other document-management tool for storing API and design documentation for the project.

Software development teams on the most popular mobile platforms frequently call upon the Git source-control system managed by Web sites such as GitHub or Bitbucket to manage code and project collaboration tasks. That level of trust can likely be attributed to the fact that Git was authored and managed by Linus Torvalds, the iconic programmer who was fundamental in creating the popular open-source operating system Linux.

In fact, Android is a Linux-based operating system, and iOS has a foundation in Unix, which shares many common fundamental attributes with Linux. Even without considering the Torvalds connection, though, Git is popular because it's arguably the fastest source-control system available, a highly desirable quality for teams focused on rapid iteration.

Using services such as Bitbucket or GitHub primarily offers an easy way for others to help bug-test your source code, make suggestions for features, and collaborate, typically all at a low cost. They also provide an extraordinarily easy way to manage the difficult issues that arise when attempting to share dozens of different text files and a variety of images between groups of people, especially when those files are changed quite frequently.

These tools come in handy even when working alone or when in a team of only two or three people, and despite the significant learning curve they come with they're worth the effort.

Source-management tools do much of the complex work involved in merging files and tracking changes while also providing valuable off-site backup of precious source code, although you should never use a service like GitHub as the sole safety net protecting your work. If you make a mistake in your code, Git can be a great tool for reverting back to a previous version from before the complication arose.

## tip

As with any form of important work, it's important to develop a plan for backing up your essential code and art files that you never want to lose. Most developers recommend a "rule of three" for backing up data: one drive constantly connected to your computer using routine backup software such as Time Machine by Apple or CrashPlan by Code42, a local network or directly connected drive that is backed up on a weekly basis, and a third backup protected off-site using a cloud backup service.

As you grow more fluent in a source-code-management system and more comfortable with its tools, you can discover ways to expand its uses. If you find that your team is growing larger and could use a more rigid, structured system of assigning tasks and reporting code errors or

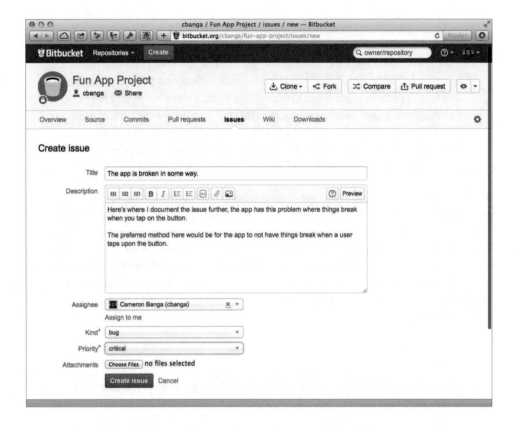

**Figure 7.6**    Issue trackers are a great way to delegate bugs and feature fixes.

bugs, you might find it beneficial to turn to more full-featured project-management solutions that also support source-code management—offerings like Assembla Inc.'s Assembla or
Atlassian's JIRA.

Figure 7.6 shows a project-issue entry created in Bitbucket, in which team members can formally document problems with code. It allows programmers to comment, stakeholders to vote
on the importance of the issue, and more.

# Learning More

You could also consider learning Markdown, a simple markup language used in a variety of
different management programs that can help you better document issues and format wiki
pages. Markdown is used heavily and almost exclusively in the creation of wiki pages on popular source control sites such as GitHub or Bitbucket. By picking up some basic knowledge, you'll
be able to include powerful formatting in issue tracking and documentation, which will make it
easier for the programmer to understand what you're discussing.

> **tip**
>
> Markdown, created by John Gruber, is similar to HTML but much simpler in style and syntax. It allows you to easily add bold, italics, bullets, and other text-formatting features that help emphasize your writing. To set a word in bold, for example, you simply surround it with asterisks, like *this*; or to note a section header, use the "#" symbol at the beginning of a line. For more information on Markdown, see this book's online links page or visit http://daringfireball.net/projects/markdown.

As you fall further down the rabbit hole of source-code management, you may also find yourself slipping into the world of command-line interfaces, using programs such as Terminal in OS X or the open-source TortoiseGit project in Windows. Although many applications are being developed to help command-line-phobic developers through the creation of a graphical user interface tool for committing and pulling source changes (GitHub and Bitbucket both have their own GUI tools), consider giving the command line a chance. It may be intimidating, but it will ultimately help you learn more about how source control works and how command-line interfaces function.

> **tip**
>
> If you're looking for help with the command line, here are some great resources to check out.
>
> - *A Practical Guide to UNIX for Mac OS X Users* by Mark G. Sobell and Peter Seebach
>
> - *A Practical Guide to Linux Commands, Editors, and Shell Programming* by Mark G. Sobell
>
> - *UNIX for the Impatient* by Paul W. Abrahams and Bruce R. Larson
>
> - *Windows 7 and Vista Guide to Scripting, Automation, and Command Line Tools* by Brian Knittel

When using a code-control system, you can easily check out a source repository during development, poke around, and make changes to the code by using an integrated-development environment such as Xcode or Android Developer Studio, test the code by using an actual device or software emulator on your computer, and then push changes back into the project that will ultimately be included in the shipping application. If you've never contributed code to a project before, especially if you've worked as a mobile designer on a handful of projects already, you're sure to find the process of contributing code to a product shipping to an app store extremely satisfying.

# Comprehending the Source Code

Now that you have a basic understanding of the tools required to contribute code to a project, you're ready to jump into the deep end of programming. The following recommendations will help you effectively manage source code and make valuable contributions to a project.

A few things to note before proceeding much further: These recommendations come from the perspective of designers who don't have a formal background in computer science and are based on knowledge gained through significant experience and many mistakes. These tips should help you tackle the problems of analyzing source code and make proper design changes even when you have little to no experience with programming or the source language used to create the software.

None of these tips are ironclad requirements; feel free to test out these suggestions then break away and experiment on your own. The idea is to find a system that makes you feel comfortable when you analyze source code for the first time—then again and again—and that will allow you to make code changes yourself and not need to rely on a programmer. Once you're capable of altering an app's code, even if only for the interface and interaction components, you'll be more capable of directly influencing how a project evolves prior to release.

> ## tip
>
> Programming is not a spectator sport. It's best learned when you get your hands dirty and dig into code. The same goes for learning command-line interfaces, UNIX commands, Git, Mercurial, or any of the other technically difficult topics that might pop up during your career as a designer. Don't be afraid; jump in and learn through experience.

## A Designer's Introduction to Programming

First and foremost, it's important to recognize that nearly all designers try to remain as far away from source-code work as possible during the design process, preferring instead to dictate directly to a programmer. Based on personal experience, this approach is inherently wrong and extremely inadvisable. By learning to work with code and knowing how to make even small changes to it, a designer gains a much deeper understanding and comprehension of how software operates. Once you can work with and understand the code that is the DNA of the application you're building, the whole software-development process becomes less abstract and significantly clearer.

Working directly in code is much like being a mechanic or using a manual car transmission; by peeking under a vehicle's hood or by physically shifting it from gear to gear, you gain a more thorough understanding of how it functions. Likewise, by digging deep into an application's code you develop a better appreciation for how your work manifests itself on the world's phones, tablets, and computers. It can even help you improve your design abilities as you find ways to create better functioning applications.

Second, take some time to learn how to use Git as a source management system. If the application you're creating is for Android or iOS, it will be nearly impossible to ignore Git. This source-code-management software is used on a significant majority of all open-source mobile software projects, and the large majority of mobile developers use it for management tasks.

Third, acquire basic knowledge of UNIX-like operating systems. In order to contribute code to a project, you'll likely need to use Git, and Git can at times be difficult to use without UNIX. After being able to successfully pull and push to source-code repositories, you can move on to attempting to edit code.

## tip

Many designers, who by no means are computer-science wizards, use the Macintosh command line frequently every day—making it important to understand UNIX. Here are a few commonly used Terminal commands and what they do when inside of a directory containing a Git repository.

- **git status**: This is used to check and see what changes you've made to a project or how far behind or ahead your project is from the branch you're working on. You'll often use this to verify what you've changed before you commit code.

- **cd**: This command is short for "change directory" and is used frequently when moving between different project folders.

- **git pull**: This Git command is used to talk to the Git server and ask if any changes have been made by the other members of your team. If so, this command pulls them and integrates them into your source code.

- **git push**: This command is the opposite of "git pull" and is used to send any changes you've made in the source code back up to the server.

- **git commit**: A commit is a group of files that you've made changes to in the source code at the same time. You'll tie these changes together with a commit message, which is a small note to let other team members know what you did with these files.

- **open**: This command is used to open a file in the UNIX command line on an operating system such as OS X or Linux. You can use "open" to edit a file quickly.

- **git help**: When in doubt, git help it out. This command will offer many insights into and details about different options and abilities available in Git.

# Writing Source Code

Source code essentially is a collection of documents that comprises everything in an application made for iOS, Android, or other platforms. Any piece of software available today typically contains dozens of source code files in various different file formats—text, images, audio, etc.—all placed together in a single package that will eventually become an application. Using an integrated-development environment (IDE) such as Eclipse, Android Developer Studio, or Xcode, these different files are tied together in a specific fashion and then "compiled" into a software binary, which is either loaded directly onto a computer using an emulator or onto the Android or iOS device you're targeting.

IDEs typically include a source-code text editor, a set of debugging tools for solving errors, and the compiler that helps create the software binary. For mobile development and in more recent and more advanced IDEs, graphical user interfaces are becoming the go-to aid that helps create interface pieces and software. Tools such as Xcode's Interface Builder allow many interface and interaction components to be added to an app with a simple drag-and-drop interface. These graphical tools are of high value to designers who don't have computer-science training, because they allow for quicker, more intricate changes to an interaction design. In most cases, though, these GUI tools only allow designers to make changes to very high-level interface and interaction pieces; to make fine, detailed changes, you'll eventually need to drop down into actual source code.

Once you begin manipulating it, you'll learn that working with code requires a fairly rigid workflow. As long as you attack programming in a structured way, you'll find success and soon feel comfortable making changes to your app projects. It's much easier than you imagine; once you get the hang of working with source code, you'll find yourself increasingly more ambitious and willing to take on new challenges.

As a designer, working with source code goes best when using the following repeatable pattern.

1.  Talk with the programmer or conduct searches yourself to find the lines of code that correspond to what you want to change in the app's design.

2.   Make small changes, usually only 1 to 10 lines of code at a time, tweaking colors, variables, and more to (hopefully) improve the application's interface and interaction design.

3.   Test the code with an emulator, a computer, or your personal phone or tablet. Launch the application and navigate to the section in which the code change should be displayed, and see if it appears correctly and responds as you intended it to. If it doesn't, jump back into the source code and make other adjustments then rebuild and see if you've gotten the fix right. Repeat until the app works as desired.

4.   Once the code works, commit it to the local source-code repository, and—depending on your team's workflow—either push to a remote repository or place a pull request at the origin repository your programming team has set up.

5.   When you're finished with a code change, move on to the next interface piece that requires an adjustment then start again at step one.

## Knowing What to Change

The most important—and difficult—part of this entire process is determining which code lines are required to make your desired change and what different properties are available to make that change. The key here is to keep constant contact with your programmer as you start exploring source-code manipulation; politely ask for help and information whenever needed regarding where to find the code you're searching for. As you start to see coding challenges firsthand, you'll begin to pick up clues as to how to spot potential problem areas.

If you're working on an iPhone app, for example, and want to change the color or font of a specific section of text you'll soon find that "UIColor" and "UIFont" are key terms to search for when you're looking to make such an adjustment. Once you know what to look for, your brain will begin to automatically search for those character combinations and help you more easily identify where they are in the code. The following is an example of some partial source code that could potentially be used in an iPhone app to create a text label:

```
cell.selectionStyle = UITableViewCellSelectionStyleNone;
[cell.textLabel setFont:[UIFont
fontWithName:@"HelveticaNeue-Medium" size:14.0f]];
[cell.textLabel setTextColor:[UIColor colorWithRed:175.0/255.0
green:41.0/255.0 blue:46.0/255.0 alpha:1]];
[cell.textLabel setTextAlignment:NSTextAlignmentLeft];
cell.backgroundColor = [UIColor colorWithWhite:1.0 alpha:0.75];
```

If you have visual design experience, there should be a great deal here that is already familiar to you. In this label, the app is using Helvetica Neue, a system font that is fairly standard throughout the design world. It establishes the numeric value for the font size in a method similar to a word processor; here it's set to 14 points. Percentage RGB color values set the color of the label, using some simple arithmetic to get a color with a red, green, and blue mix that results in a shade of dark red. Here, the text is set to a left alignment, but you could easily shift that to the center or right with a simple adjustment. Finally, the background is set as a semi-transparent white to help it stand out from a textured background.

It's as simple as that. The small set of lines above is all that's required to change the visual appearance of a text label that is seen often and communicates important information to users. Of course, this is the code for just one label, and there will be many more of these inside apps you develop; to make changes to any of them, you'll have to search through the code, locate a specific element, and then tinker with it until you get your desired appearance.

Once you master this skill, you'll no longer need to repeatedly harass your programmer to make a label a "redder red" or a "lighter light blue"; instead, you can go in and bump color levels up or down until the element reaches your heart's desire.

### warning

When it comes to committing code using a source-code-management system, you want to commit the smallest chunk of code making a change into a push. That way, if anything goes wrong and a programmer needs to search for what caused the problem he or she can roll back appropriately, and you won't lose big chunks of work due to a mistake elsewhere.

Likewise, you also want to create as meaningful and explanatory a commit message as possible so that other teammates can read through and make sense of your work in the future.

Take a look at another chunk of code and how you could manage interaction changes within it:

```
UIButton *button = [[UIButton alloc]
initWithFrame:CGRectMake(0, 0, 33, 21)];
[button setImage:[UIImage
imageNamed:@"Menu-NavBarMenuButton.png"]
forState:UIControlStateNormal];
[button addTarget:self action:@selector(editTableView)
forControlEvents:UIControlEventTouchUpInside];
[button setExclusiveTouch:YES];
UIBarButtonItem *customMenu =
[[UIBarButtonItem alloc] initWithCustomView:button];
self.navigationItem.leftBarButtonItem = customMenu;
```

This block of text creates a special, customized button in the iPhone app's navigation bar (see Figure 7.7), which then brings up a sidebar menu.

**Figure 7.7**  This navigation bar doesn't look that different from the standard iOS style, but the icon to the left is custom and implemented using the code shown earlier.

This code might look intimidating if you've never seen it before, but once you break it down it's actually quite simple. It creates a custom button that's used to slide out a side menu, similar to the navigation bar button used in many popular applications. In the example code, the button is invoked and a frame is created. The button is 33 pixels high and 21 pixels tall, set by `CGRectMake(0, 0, 33, 21)`. The two 0s at the beginning are the x and y coordinates on screen for where the button begins. Here, the button is being created at the top left of the screen. Then, the code references the image that is used to create the appearance of the button, named `Menu-NavBarMenuButton.png`.

If you wanted to change the look of the button and in turn the button image, you could do one of two things: update the button art and save over the original file, or create a new image file and add it to the project then change the string of code identifying the original file name.

The important interaction pieces here are the `forControlEvents:UIControlEvent-TouchUpInside` and `self.navigationItem.leftBarButtonItem` sections of the code. The `UIControlEventTouchUpInside` event means that the button registers the touch and tells the application to open the menu once the user releases a tap on the menu button. You could change this to respond to a specific swipe or drag gesture, but the `UIControlEventTouchUpInside` property is most likely to be used in any situation in which you want a standard button-interaction type. The `self.navigationItem.leftBarButtonItem` property means that the icon will be positioned in the standard location for navigation-bar button icons on the left side of the screen. If, for example, you wanted the button to appear on the right side of the screen, you would simply change `leftBarButtonItem` to `rightBarButtonItem`.

These are just the basics of working with source code to make contributions to a software project. If you find your experiments in this area to be valuable, though, know that you've taken a major step toward becoming a better designer capable of making a direct impact on the design development of your projects. Your programming team will appreciate that effort—not to mention the time you save them by making code changes on your own.

> **tip**
>
> For more tips and tricks on manipulating code, search the Internet for the snippets you're working with or for keywords used earlier, such as `UIColor` or `UIFont`.

Numerous blogs and forums and the invaluable http://stackoverflow.com are all dedicated to helping designers get better at programming.

---

### IN-DEPTH

Developing a standout application requires strong communication and teamwork between the programming and design teams. Here are a few shining examples of those principles in action.

- Instagram is an app that involves a variety of moving pieces yet still needs design unity across platforms. For the huge social network to be successful, it requires a strong server back end to support it, technical programming that allows for quick and attractive edits to images using unique filters, and features that remain the same across iPhone and Android. Throw in the fact that the design team must continue to outpace competition from other photo apps and that the programming team must constantly plan for new features and you have an extraordinary case study of great communication by a development team.

- What about when you add hardware engineering into the design/programming equation? Automatic by Automatic Labs, Inc. is an app that pairs with a Bluetooth dongle that fits onto the data port on your car. It's commonly used by mechanics during repairs. Using the data from the hardware accessory, the application provides an appealing interface that helps you track mileage, learn more about fuel-efficient driving, and alert family or emergency services if you're in a crash. It's another instance of a group delivering a great all-around experience, especially when you remember that the app performs exceptionally well with iOS and Android and on hundreds of different car models that have a Bluetooth hardware link.

- Ask experienced developers what type of application is the most difficult to create, and you're likely to often hear "e-mail" as an answer. It's a tough element to program around. The standards are rigid and unforgiving, there's a multitude of rare edge cases to prepare for, and users of course expect a bug-free experience at all times. Enter Mailbox by Dropbox, a delightful and novel e-mail client released in 2013 that reimagines e-mail as a to-do list. The application offers a variety of nifty programming tricks, such as the ability to time-shift e-mail so that it doesn't appear in your inbox until a future date. It paired these elements with elegant gestures and subtle design cues that were produced in an easy-to-understand way. Mailbox stands out as a wonderful convergence of quality design and programming.

# Conclusion

Programming isn't something designers have to do on a daily basis, but working with people who program will be an essential part of your work as you build an app portfolio. Over the course of your career, you'll need to get along with programmers of various backgrounds and all levels of experience.

Much like any profession that requires close work with someone of an alternating skill set, it's important to put yourself in the other person's shoes in an effort to understand the difficulties they encounter in their everyday workflow. By attempting some basic programming techniques, you can better understand how to prepare your work in a way that your programmer will appreciate, which in turn makes you a more valuable team member.

By practicing these tips, you should become more capable of sitting behind an IDE such as Xcode or Android Programming Studio and have a basic understanding of what to do. By learning how to better influence the apps you design, you're growing your potential to create a mobile masterpiece.

# CHAPTER 8

# MAKING APPS USABLE BY ALL

No programmer or designer wakes up in the morning and sets out to create an average piece of software. The goal is to make something great, and the way to do that is to constantly iterate in an effort to improve (while never harming) your application's interaction design. But how do you know what will work and what won't? Making your app easier to use requires walking a mile in the shoes of the average user—or at least spending a few hours in their eyes and fingertips. Strive to see an app the way a common consumer sees it, and you're on the path to success.

# Knowing Your Audience

Knowing what actually constitutes an improvement to an app can be tricky. As a designer, you're likely a computer and smartphone power user. You spend hours every day working with Photoshop or other pieces of complex software. You have dozens or even hundreds of apps loaded on the latest and greatest version of your smartphone or tablet of choice. You read many popular blogs and news sites for constant updates on what's going on in the world of technology.

Essentially, it's very unlikely that you represent a hypothetical average user of your app. As a result, design decisions that you think will improve users' experiences may actually end up being something the average user views as a significant regression.

The average consumer of an app you design is someone who only moderately—or perhaps even lightly—uses a computer, tablet, or smartphone. Perhaps they only fire up a laptop to manage their finances, pay bills, browse the Internet, or draft documents on a word processor. They might have only a handful of apps on their phone, and the ones they do have might have come with their device, been found on a top downloads list, or have been recommended by friends or family members.

They're far less versed in technology than you are, but you still must put yourself in their shoes if you hope to build a great product that they find appealing and useful. Although this situation is common in the development of any product—in everything from cars to power tools, the person putting the item together knows more about how to interact with it than the end user—the "appification" of software over the past several years has added a few complicating factors to this situation.

First and foremost, it's extremely rare for any app built now to come with any sort of instruction manual or lengthy tutorial. The traditional software of the 1980s, the 1990s, and the first decade of the twenty-first century was often sold in brick-and-mortar stores and came in boxes that included a booklet with a few dozen pages spelling out the program's various features and options. Today, applications are downloaded in seconds and users begin interacting with them immediately. Many even lack a Web page that offers significant details on how to best use an app. Unlike the designers of yesteryear, you now face a situation in which any user who opens your project is thrown into a dense forest—and it's your job to lead them step by step into the light.

Some developers take the time to create elaborate and detailed Web sites to help a user navigate through an application. These sites can be great tools, but they're often difficult for users to find if they don't know where to look or if they don't know they exist. In Figure 8.1, you'll see one strong example of a support Web site from the developer Tapbots, LLC.

Second, not everyone is an expert smartphone user; plenty of designers forget this, creating convoluted designs that confuse or quickly disengage a user. Too many apps include design

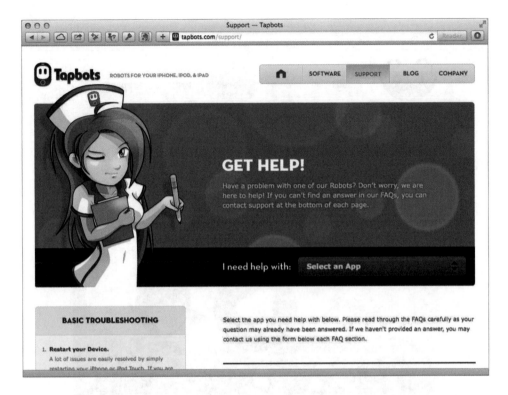

**Figure 8.1**   Here's a quality support page, offering users help with the company's apps.

patterns or interaction sequences that are seemingly made for a secret society of smartphone enthusiasts. Although there certainly is a market for apps designed solely for power users—and you may sometimes find yourself making something for that group—it's important to understand your audience and build an app that is immediately relatable and understandable for average users.

> **tip**
>
> When working on a project, consider whether or not it passes the "grandmother test." Is the application easy enough that your grandmother (who likes her smartphone but has never been a big computer user) could understand and enjoy it? If so, you've probably created an app that will work well for all users.

Finally, many designers forget that with the proliferation of the affordable, subsidized smartphone handheld devices are becoming more commonly used than computers. That means your user base will come in all shapes and sizes. From the young to the old, people are

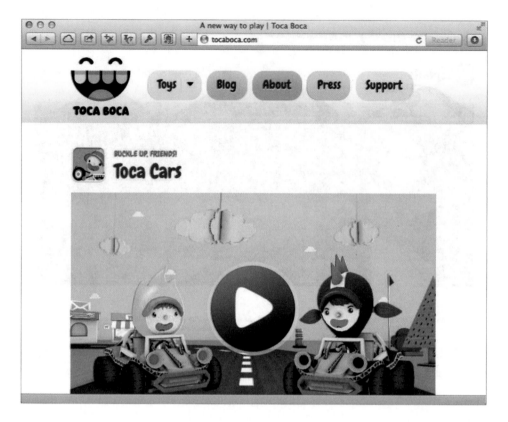

**Figure 8.2**   Toca Boca is well-known for family friendly apps and games. (Courtesy of Toca Boca.)

embracing these new mobile devices at unprecedented rates, which, although good for business, does create a number of challenges for designers.

Mobile phones and tablets are so easy to use now that they can be controlled by users that are just a few years (or even months) old. Toca Boca (see Figure 8.2) is a development studio devoted to creating kid-friendly iOS and Android apps that are fun and educational.

To understand the average users of smartphones and tablets, you must grasp the world in which they live. Like a biologist that studies desert plant life, it's difficult to understand your subjects if you've never made a trip out into the sand.

## How Sandboxing Changed Mobile

A major fundamental shift in how users experienced software occurred in 2007 and 2008 with early versions of the iPhone and Android devices and the mainstream popularity of application "sandboxing."

With a traditional computer, an operating system would give the user many files to manage and navigate via a hierarchical folder system. This technique was implemented across various editions of Windows and OS X, all featuring data stored in various folders—with common names like Documents, Desktop, and Photos—that were all created and edited by applications in the system. Over the years, users became quite familiar with this setup. They launched a program, opened or created a certain file, made changes to it, saved the file, then closed the program.

In the move to mobile, this navigation and creation method shifted significantly. Although the operating systems on smartphones and tablets still have a hierarchical structure, it's no longer one the user sees or interacts with on a regular basis. Nested directories holding files and applications have long been the norm on all mainstream computing platforms, but this practice was often considered too difficult for the average user. In order to increase simplicity and usability of mobile devices, the way users interact with content was changed drastically.

Instead of using windows and folders to navigate through information, phones and tablets use sandboxing, a somewhat complex security mechanism in which applications are self-contained and have no access to a device's file system. Essentially, each application lives as a packaged binary inside its own digitally literal and figurative box, and each remains, for the most part, unaware of other applications on the device. Each application is, with a few exceptions, unable to modify files created by other applications or can only do so when explicitly ordered by the user. Similarly, the file system is not viewable to the user, so he or she can't select a specific file to edit independently. Instead, the user must go into the application the file was created in and make the necessary change there. Figure 8.3 displays Springboard, which is Apple's tool for iOS that allows users to move in and out of different apps.

This massive change in the way people interact with technology has various pros and cons. The big benefit is that users now find devices dramatically easier to work with. Not needing to handle a file system means that users no longer need to organize files. That brings a greater sense of creative freedom because there's no need to worry about the problems that come with creating content: accidentally misplacing, altering, or deleting files. Instead, users now only need to open an app and create; all the file management happens behind the scenes.

Sandboxing also offers a multitude of security benefits for users. When apps can't directly access the files created by other apps or the operating system, it becomes much more difficult to engineer security flaws or errors that could jeopardize the user's private data or potentially harm the integrity of the device's system.

This new interaction philosophy does pose some problems for users and designers, though. The major issue is that, currently, file exchange between applications or devices is extremely difficult, especially for non-image files on iOS. Android and Windows Phone have, with better file implementations, allowed apps to communicate more effectively and hand off data through systems called "intents" and "contracts," respectively. These setups allow other apps

**Figure 8.3**  Throughout users' experiences in iOS, they never truly encounter any traditional file-management opportunity.

to take hold of specific data in order to allow users to do certain tasks. Figure 8.4 shows an example of what the user sees when an intent is brought to the forefront.

Say, for example, that a user wanted to save a single page from an academic article being viewed in a PDF reader and open it in a note-keeping application. In a traditional computer operating system, such a technique would be fairly easy, requiring only a simple "Save as" action and opening the new file in the notes app or simply copying and pasting the desired text or images.

But with sandboxing, taking that PDF page across applications will be fairly difficult and will require implementing some clear and focused design so that the user can quickly manage the process. You can use Android intents, Windows contracts, or app URL calls to send files across applications for sharing.

**Figure 8.4**  On Android, applications can register intents as a way to make it easy for applications to exchange data and files.

> **tip**
>
> Do you want to learn more about how applications on iOS can exchange data via URLs? Apple hasn't provided intents or contracts like other platforms; see the "Communicating with Other Apps" section of the Advanced App Tricks page under their iOS App Programming Guide at https://developer.apple.com/library/ios/navigation/.

The usability and security of this new application approach has another big benefit for tech-minded designers: Sales of these devices and software have soared. This rapid growth was largely catalyzed by less digitally savvy consumers who never previously bought much software as they were turned off by the prospect of steep learning curves and the risks posed by viruses or security issues.

As a result, the average level of "computer literacy" in smartphone and tablet app users has dropped, and it thus becomes even more important that applications are designed to be easily understood. Theoretically, you could develop instructional videos or immaculately detailed text tutorials to outline how to use an app. However, users will want to be able to pick up and immediately understand your work, so it's to your benefit to put yourself inside the mind of the average user and anticipate and avoid design challenges that could potentially cause confusion—all while working within the constraints of this still relatively new world of sandboxing.

### note

Sandboxing became prevalent in mobile, but it's gradually making its way back to the desktop as well. With the advent of popular desktop app stores run by Apple and Microsoft, software is now required to concede some of its traditional abilities in order to be made available for download through digital marketplaces.

Figuring out a way for users to edit files created outside your app isn't the only problem sandboxing poses. App developers are also extremely limited in what an app can do when it's running in the background and not in use. In iOS 7, for instance, applications can only maintain their activity and multitask in the background when performing one of several highly specific tasks, such as playing audio, performing a VOIP call, or using GPS to navigate for a user.

### tip

App multitasking is when an application continues to do work even when it's no longer on screen. For some apps, this is highly advantageous. It means that you don't have to keep a music player open to listen to songs, for example, or that you can continue to talk on the phone while you check sports scores. Multitasking can have some detrimental effects on things like battery life, though, so in the mobile world there are often a handful of restraints placed on how background activities function.

Additionally, apps released in Microsoft's and Apple's app stores will be subject to a relatively strict review process before being made available to the public, and applications must meet a variety of standards set forth by the platform provider in order to see a release. This typically isn't a significant issue, but it is important to read through and understand the latest rules for the platform before you begin work as some of the things that platforms don't allow can be surprising to designers and developers. Save yourself significant time by reading up on the rules before you get started.

> **tip**
>
> Were you rejected by Apple or Microsoft when you submitted your app? All may not be lost. With a rejection, you'll usually get an e-mail from the app store explaining which rules were violated and what, if anything, can be done to fix the problem. It may also be possible to appeal the decision and get approval later on.

# Interactions for the Mass Market

Despite the challenges posed by sandbox software, it has opened up the potential for small operations to design applications that can be accessed and enjoyed by millions of users. So what does it take to build an app that can find success in a mass marketplace?

To effectively design a product that will be accepted by the average user, you need a solid understanding of who this person is. The following is a generalized portrait of the qualities and traits of the average mobile user today. As it always has, this picture will develop over time, and there are many users who fall outside this norm as it is.

Nevertheless, identifying the characteristics of average users is a valuable practice for a designer as it helps you better understand the needs and expectations of your target market.

## Trait 1: Not a Computer Geek

Do you know whether your computer runs OS X Mountain Lion or Mavericks? Can you instantly name the speed of your laptop's processor? Do you know the amount of RAM in your Android smartphone? Are you currently reading an entire book on designing interfaces for mobile phones and tablets? If you answered yes to any of these questions, we hate to break it to you, but you may be a geek. Don't worry, even if you still feel like you're in the minority despite geeks' growing domination of popular culture there are many out there just like you. They just probably don't make up the bulk of the people who will download the apps you design.

Most modern users of smartphones and tablets don't know the exact specifications or technical capabilities of their devices; sometimes, they may even forget the name of the phone or tablet model they have or which company their cell contract is with. To these users, their phone or other device is a complex and valuable tech tool required to get through modern daily life, much like a car, refrigerator, or TV. They won't know the details of how their device works, because they're not required to know. They just know that it works. Thus, you should strive to create designs that allow the user to successfully move through an app without needing to know how large their hard drive is or what screen resolution they have.

## Trait 2: Only Uses a Handful of Apps

The average mobile software user typically only has a dozen or so different apps that they've downloaded on their phone. That may not seem like a lot, but it's considerably larger than the number of software programs users regularly access when using a laptop or desktop, which of course is great for anyone in the app development business. It means you're more likely to have your app purchased or talked about than software designers from a decade ago were, but it also means you're competing for users' largely limited time and attention to seek out or experiment with new apps.

Users are hesitant to go searching for new software, so your biggest hurdle will be overcoming that natural friction and getting your app worked into users' daily routines. You encourage that process by focusing on your app's name, icon, promotional screenshots, and marketing copy as those are key elements in enticing a user to click that "download" button. Take a look at the home screen of this smartphone owned by a typical user (Figure 8.5) with only a few applications. Each download of your app by such a user should be seen as a high honor.

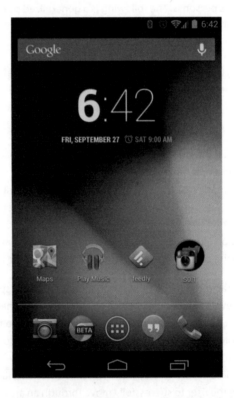

**Figure 8.5**   Many users only have ten or so applications on their device that were downloaded from an app store.

# Trait 3: Uses Apps in Short Bursts

Although mobile apps are called upon to perform in a variety of situations—in line at the grocery store, while waiting for an elevator, in the bathroom, etc.—the duration of each use of a piece of software is still relatively short. Research on the topic has found that most users spend five minutes or less per use of an app. Because that average time period is so short, designers need to focus on constructing an interface that has immediate clarity and quick usability and that won't frustrate consumers.

During production, it's best to focus carefully on the user's "first experience": the two to three minutes they spend immediately after launching the app. Consider whether the application launches quickly and if the primary direction the user takes is immediately apparent. If absolutely necessary, it could be worthwhile to consider developing a short video or interactive tutorial that can quickly guide the user through your app's processes; but be warned, these can be frustrating if they grow too lengthy.

> tip
>
> When working on a project, keep a measurement of "time until first useful response." That's how long it takes for users to engage with an app at initial launch before they're getting value from the program. This time can vary per app, obviously, but it's a great way to quantify how the interaction design is improving throughout the development process.

This trait helps explain why it's increasingly important for designs to use as many system-standard components as possible and why it's often wise to avoid diverting from the norm unless there's good reason to do so. Users quickly get impatient with mobile software, so it's paramount that they be able to pick up an app and within minutes—if not seconds—understand what needs to be done to operate it. The best way to ensure that is to use familiar interaction patterns and interface structure.

# Trait 4: Follows the 80/20 Rule

The 80/20 rule, also called the Pareto principle, has quickly become a proverb in the world of mobile development. The concept is simple: About 80 percent of your users will only use 20 percent of the features contained in a piece of software. No matter how much time goes into developing advanced, more complex tools, a vast majority of consumers who download an app will only take advantage of a small part of its potential.

Don't judge, though. Think about the word processor you last used to draft a long document or the spreadsheet you call upon to sketch out a budget. How many of those menu options and toolbar buttons have you explored? Surely there are plenty of features and settings you remain completely unaware of. Every time you open that program, you likely refer back to the same standard set of common, popular features.

Keep this principle in mind constantly as you design, and interact with your user base and test users during the development process to discover what parts of an app they turn to most often. As you learn more about which features are in demand by your user majority, you can place greater emphasis on improving the interaction experiences offered by those features. Make your most popular features the ones that are the most enjoyable to use.

## Trait 5: Likes What Everyone Else Likes

As unique and creative as your personal style may be, it won't necessarily be for everyone. Taste and design preference varies from person to person, so you're best off playing it safe and simple by opting for typefaces, colors, and iconography that are easy to read and interpret; again, avoid reinventing the design wheel with each new app.

This is why you often see strong, primary colors such as red, blue, and green in the design of popular icons, and the same goes for popular, standard typefaces such as Helvetica or Arial. Although you may enjoy your orange-and-purple complementing color theme that found a particularly creative use for Comic Sans, such aesthetic choices won't bring you worldwide acclaim. Come up with a comfortable look that many are bound to enjoy; save the radical stabs in the dark for further down the road once your design enjoys success in the marketplace.

Always remember that your average user is much like you, but not entirely like you. The mere fact that you're working on a mobile app means that you're part of a group that is significantly more computer literate than the average person. You and your colleagues are outliers and need to recognize and understand the implications of that as you design. As long as you remain mindful of this and make every effort to put yourself in the mindset of a typical user, your app is on its way toward being easily understandable and useable.

# Building Multilingual Interaction Designs

By constantly considering who your app is targeted for—and how to design it in such a way that it can find success in the mass market—you're creating the opportunity for your project to lead to financial success. But in contemplating who this average user is, it's easy to forget where this average user comes from. As mobile technology continues to permeate the globe, it becomes increasingly likely that this typical consumer is from another country and doesn't share your language or culture.

Most major platforms' app stores—especially the ones run by Apple, Google, and Microsoft—are available in dozens of different countries and on every continent not named Antarctica. The mobile marketplace is truly now a global marketplace as well, opening up the possibility that users speaking dozens or hundreds of different languages can access your work.

Foreign-language markets (see Figure 8.6 for the foreign markets available for iOS apps) remain a huge untapped resource brimming with potential revenue for developers. In the early days of computing, these markets were hard to break in to, especially for independent software-development teams. Typically, only large companies with enormous capital resources could permeate foreign countries. With app stores, it's now no more difficult to make your app available for download on the other side of the world than it is to make it available for download on the other side of the street.

When it comes to interaction and interface design, it can often be difficult to support even a few, if not a dozen or more, languages. Getting text copy into an application, fitting sentences or words onto buttons or instruction boxes, and verifying grammar and spelling is challenging in your native language, much less a foreign one. Translation services are often expensive and

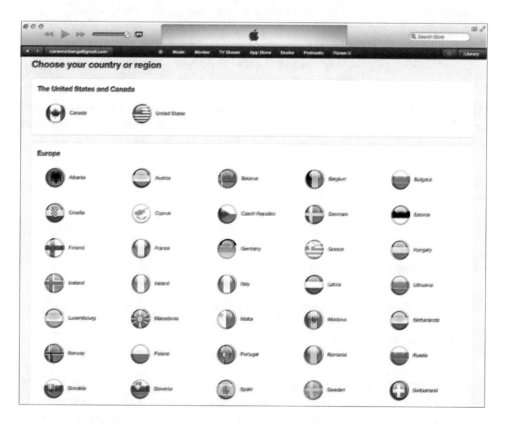

**Figure 8.6** A partial list of all the different app stores available on iOS alone is not unlike the queue for the parade of nations at the opening ceremony of the Olympics.

can lead to a wide variety of design problems; a label on a button, for example, could require just a word or two in English but need a longer phrase in German.

Luckily, the platform providers of these operating systems are learning that it's important to make strong multilanguage tools available to developers. Apple's recent IDE Xcode 5 has made it much easier for developers to juggle different languages in an app to make sure the translation of a language doesn't cause presentation issues. It allows developers to run a simulated version of an app in any target language or quickly view button previews for different text copy. Likewise, the most popular IDE to use with Android development, Eclipse, comes with its own suite of tools designed to make it simpler for developers to translate their apps with little additional work.

### note

Do you need more specific information on how to add multiple languages into your application? Methods and details can change as operating system or IDE versions get upgraded and improved, so for the latest details and procedures that pertain to your target platform, see http://developer.android.com, the Apple Development Center, or any other platform's reference pages on language localization.

Where should you look to get translations? Thankfully, there's no longer a shortage of language-conversion services available for programmers and developers looking to bring their software to other countries. Operations such as Babylon Translator and the Web service ICanLocalize make it affordable and simple to translate text in an application. Most of these services cost only a few dollars, and the end result is an accurate translation in a variety of languages performed by an expert team. The best part is that many offer extremely fast turnaround times.

### warning

**BEWARE OF ROBOTS**   It will be extremely tempting to try out an automated online translation service, but steer clear of them. Although it's easy to copy and paste large amounts of text into these services and get instant responses, the translations are often inaccurate and incomplete. Instead, seek out a reliable, human translation provider.

In the past, translation programming was often difficult, but at this point in the world of mobile technology it's a process that's much easier. As a designer, you position yourself for greater success by translating your text into as many languages as possible. Find a reputable translation service that fits your needs and budget, use the prescribed tools, and then roll out languages in your app that fit the needs of your user base.

During a recent 9magnets development project, for example, the team noticed over a weekend that traffic to its Web site from the Netherlands increased significantly after a write-up in a local blog. Although the team wasn't able to get the application translated and sent to Apple for an iPhone update as quickly as it would have liked, the developers were still able to use a language service to translate their Web site in just a few hours, allowing visitors from the Netherlands to read details about the app in their native Dutch. This significantly grew sales and, before the team knew it, the app skyrocketed to the number one spot in the Netherlands app store. Although relatively small compared to other big-developer achievements, this distinction was extremely valuable for the company and made the quick translation service well worth the cost.

If supporting multiple languages seems out of reach, or if the cost of getting your text translated is a barrier for your team, it's still valuable to reconsider your design and implement as much iconography as possible. In app development, the old saying is true: A picture is, in fact, worth a thousand words, if not more. Replacing text with pictures makes elements of your app more universal and easily understood. Even if some text will always appear in English, users who speak foreign languages will still be able to understand many parts of your app and hopefully find benefit in it.

If you're unable to offer language support in the early versions of your app, note that major digital stores offer tools that allow you to keep your software from being available in specific countries. If you know that your app will only be available in English and Spanish upon release, you can prevent it from being visible in countries that primarily speak French and German. This can be an extremely valuable tactic, especially for text-heavy apps that would essentially be useless for those unfamiliar with the language that the words appear in. This feature allows you to make an app available to lots of people without risking poor reviews or a tarnished reputation in areas that speak a language you can't yet support.

# Designing for Users with Disabilities

For all the work that's been done to improve the accessibility of apps for users in foreign countries, another group of users has been traditionally underserviced in the software industry. Just a bit of extra work by a development team can go a long way toward providing a better experience for these individuals: users with mental, physical, visual, and learning disabilities.

In mobile computing, there's a huge growth market for apps that cater to users with various impairments, and successful applications have been developed to help blind, deaf, dyslexic, and other users with disabilities to get the same enjoyment and opportunity for learning and growth from devices that other users have long taken for granted.

You might think, for example, that it'd be difficult for a blind user to fully take advantage of a device that has few physical buttons. On the contrary, there's been consistent growth among apps built to help users navigate smartphones with gestures; advanced software that reads menu options; and on-screen commands made through advanced text-to-speech libraries similar to the ones that power digital assistants such as Siri or Apple's mighty AssistiveTouch, shown in Figure 8.7.

Additionally, companies such as Apple and Google are building advanced accessibility services into each device they sell. That's led to wider industry adoption of such offerings, especially compared to traditional computers, which often required costly hardware or software additions in order to get such capability. In the past, specific programs or add-on hardware to magnify text on screen, invert colors, read text out loud, and other accessibility features would be sold separately, typically at very high costs.

This revised stance has led to a phenomenally rapid rise in accessible computing, allowing for previously unthought-of opportunities, such as displaying inverse colors for color-blind users, larger on-screen text for visually-impaired users, automatic subtitles for the hearing impaired that don't require constant screen reconfiguration, and overlay tools that allow someone with limited dexterity to use complex multifinger gestures with a single hand. These remarkable

**Figure 8.7**   The overlay in Apple's AssistiveTouch tool makes it easy for the user to perform hardware functions and complex multifinger gestures with a single finger.

developments have charted the path for a type of digital interaction that anyone can experience regardless of physical or mental obstacles.

Because Apple, Google, and others chose to hardwire these accessibility tools directly into their operating systems, little work is required to support them so long as the developer is using native frameworks and functions. Both Apple and Google have made extensive documentation available on developer sites to help designers and programmers create apps that work in tandem with accessibility settings and options; those are noted in the "In-Depth" section at the end of this chapter and in this book's online resources. Again, it's essential for designers to keep up with this information as it evolves over time.

Making sure that designs are built in a way that conforms to the platform's expected standard ensures that features are fully supported. Apple's tool that provides voiceover assistance to blind users, for example, reads a button's file name aloud for the user if no readable text appears. Thus, an image named "Button4.png" is of no use to a blind user, because the file name gives no context for its intent or function. Instead, a title like "AddNewFriendButton.png" clearly states the task it performs, indicating to the user that a social-media friend request will be sent by activating that icon.

Likewise, Google provides the ability to add content descriptions to images, which are used in coordination with Android's accessibility features, thus allowing text or voice information to be presented to users who are unable to see photos properly.

Aside from the platform-standard tools, there are also a variety of third-party applications that can help make your software more accessible to individuals with disabilities. xScope by The Iconfactory, shown in Figure 8.8, contains a variety of modes that help app designers visualize

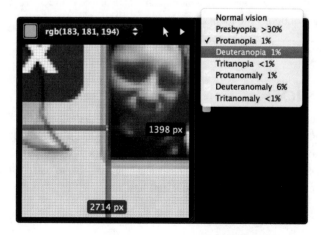

**Figure 8.8** By accessing a menu in xScope, you can see how users with a variety of color-blindness issues will see an application.

how users with various color-blindness issues might perceive an interface. OpenDyslexic, meanwhile, is an open-source font that can be included in an app to make text more legible for those with dyslexia.

By using built-in tools powered by the operating systems you're targeting, reviewing outside third-party services, and spending a few extra minutes reading, you can easily make an app more valuable to countless users that would previously be unable to use it. Once you realize that a few extra minutes verifying that a design is compliant can later bring hundreds of hours of joy to others, the added effort becomes well worth the time.

---

## IN-DEPTH

Software that helps individuals with disabilities is becoming cheaper and more readily available thanks to the rise of mobile devices. Here are a few examples of apps with interaction designs that aid accessibility.

- **Color ID Free for iOS**: This simple app allows color-blind individuals to use a device's camera to help identify the colors in photos they take. Users can access the onboard camera, hover the on-screen crosshairs over an item, and the application gives the user the name of the color shown. It's a simple way for a person to recognize the color of any item he or she is looking at.

- **Proloquo2Go**: This app serves as an augmentative and alternative communication (AAC) device for individuals with disabilities who may have difficulty speaking properly. Using the app, the user links together a handful of visual symbols in order to create sentences that the device speaks aloud.

- **BARD Mobile**: Provided by the Library of Congress, this app allows blind users to connect their devices to a Bluetooth braille device in order to access a vast library of books and magazines.

---

# Conclusion

By now, you're hopefully familiar with a variety of ways in which designers can better put themselves in the mind of the average user in order to produce applications that mass audiences find easy to use and understand. With a bit of extra work through the implementation of various language localizations and disability features, you'll be able to reach even more users and expand project revenues along with your user base.

# CHAPTER 9

# DESIGNING FOR SIMPLICITY

There's no arguing against the fact that the technology you're designing software for is a little . . . complicated. You're making programs to run on pocket-sized supercomputers and book-sized touchscreen panels. Either would have seemed like something out of the realm of science fiction just a decade or two ago. Although these devices are easier to use than ever, their limitless potential can seem a bit daunting to some users. For that reason, it's essential to strive toward creating simple interaction designs that will make your work easily usable by any potential customer.

# The Sophistication of Simplicity

So far, you've learned about the importance of usability and the need to constantly iterate upon a design to improve an application. You've also reviewed various strategies and methods that will help evolve an app's design into a complete user experience, one that will hopefully lead to a higher download rate and better user ranking.

But there's one specific design philosophy that needs to be concentrated on in detail, an overarching principle that will almost always push your design forward and bring it greater success: simplicity.

Design is an extremely difficult process, and making something appear simple and clean is much tougher than it looks. The work involved in creating a coherent, influential, workable design is vastly underappreciated by many. Design is a discipline with a variety of different ideals, paths, and preferred constructions that can lead to success. There is by no means a be-all and end-all answer to any design project, and in mobile design in particular an increased focus on simplicity has helped iPhone and Android designers create highly regarded works. Because simple designs are now setting the pace for the rest of the mobile world, it's important to have an understanding of how to follow suit on your own projects.

Ahead, you'll see why simplicity is such an important focal point in a mobile app's design and how you can integrate that into your own work. You've likely heard the phrase "keep it simple, stupid." It's a saying that rose to popularity 50 years ago as a design mantra preached to US Navy engineers regarding how they should build the systems they were working on. The notion that the best design is often the simplest design rang true for those building nuclear submarines, and it applies to smartphones and tablets as well.

## Striving for Simple Interaction Design

Why is a simple design so important? It's because a simple design is one that will always be more usable for a consumer. Simplicity creates usability. Just think about your own digital habits: When was the last time you truly enjoyed an extremely complicated piece of software? When you did encounter such a program and ran into a wall after your first use, did you eagerly return to it the next time? Or were you discouraged, choosing to let it sit on your desktop for weeks or months before revisiting it?

The same questions apply to any complex process. Automatic transmissions are more popular in cars than manual transmissions because of the simplicity they provide. The most effective TV remotes are the ones with the fewest buttons. How easy was it to reset the clock on your microwave after your last power outage? There's got to be a better way to design that button panel, right?

Simplistic designs don't always capture users' hearts because they can be rather basic. However, a good designer can clearly comprehend the task at hand, put himself or herself in the mind of the user, and develop the most effective way for future consumers to accomplish a given task. With forethought and effort, a simplistic experience can save users time, effort, and brainpower.

If you review the design in Figure 9.1 and think that it's great, it's time to look up the word "simple" in the dictionary. Experienced designers can examine this interface and find many ways to make it easier to understand.

The biggest issue with this design is that it has almost too many features and buttons; the user is given too many choices, and even getting basic use out of the app can become a daunting task. Additionally, several features seem unnecessary and could potentially be placed in different views (specifically the search bar and the hour-and-minute time selector).

In the mobile world, the two largest players today—Apple and Google—have long been regarded for their commitment to simplicity and understanding of the way complex processes impact user experiences. This philosophy didn't just start with iOS and Android devices, however; it took hold long before these companies began working on mobile operating systems.

**Figure 9.1**  This app design is a bit more complex than is usually preferred.

Apple itself was launched on the basic premise that computers were way too difficult and complicated for the average person. Cofounders Steve Jobs and Steve Wozniak believed they could use their expertise to greatly simplify the user experience so that anyone could boot up a computer and learn how to interact with it. Throughout the company's history—from the original Macintosh in 1984 and its simplification of the graphical user interface and operating system to the iPod's portability and revolutionary take on music management—Apple has long focused on distilling systems down to their simplest form.

Similarly, Google developed around the mission of cataloging the entirety of the world's data and making it available through a nearly featureless white page marked only by a few colored letters, a box to enter text in, and a couple of buttons. When some within the operation pressed to add complexity to the basic search engine, it was the guiding leadership of longtime employees such as Marissa Mayer, vice president of search and user experience, that led to the rejection of any design ideas that cluttered the simple interface.

The company realized that there is value for end users having the ability to simply visit the Web site, type the word or phrase they're curious about, hit a button, and then receive pages upon pages of information on the topic. With later products such as Gmail or Google News, the same philosophy was applied; take the most relevant and important data, strip away all extraneous pieces, and leave the user with a clean and easily manageable operation.

## tip

Google's mission statement is literally "to organize the world's information and make it universally accessible and useful." That guiding philosophy has led to some of the greatest computer science advancements in history. If your app requires a purpose or mission statement longer than Google's, it's probably worth sitting down and considering a more concise goal.

## The Difficulties of Simplicity

Developing a clean desktop interface or a simple search page seems easy, but think about the more complex products Google and Apple have introduced over the years—such as Google Maps or Apple's Siri personal assistant—and it becomes clear that making complex experiences look simple is the opposite of easy. Google's map system, in nearly the blink of an eye, provides you with the quickest route from Point A to Point B by foot, bus, train, or car. With just the push of a button, Siri can answer millions of different questions. It doesn't take much to use these systems, but it certainly took a lot to make them so easy to use.

For some, simple sounds like a bad thing. End users, stakeholders, or project managers often hear the word "simple" applied to interaction or interface and think of it as a cop-out. They see simple as being a lazy or easy way of doing things, thinking perhaps that a designer is trying to minimize the amount of work needed to accomplish a task. But once you examine a product like Google's search engine, you realize that designing and developing something simple is a gargantuan task. It's much more difficult to take something away from an interface and have it retain the same feature set than it is to add a button or slider and ultimately further complicate your interface. It's this struggle that encapsulates the difficulty of simplifying mobile design.

It's also important to recognize, though, that simple interaction design doesn't just mean removing features, functionality, interface buttons, or interaction methods for the sake of cutting things out. It means refining and stripping away things that aren't necessary until you're left only with the essential parts and features. The end goal should be an interaction design and application interface that can be understood by a user with no intervention and little instruction. The best designers keep taking out elements until all that's left is what's absolutely needed to lead a user through a process.

# Simple Design Goals

Reaching a simple end isn't an insurmountable task, even for a novice designer. Keep the following goals in mind—clarity, continuity and flow, and retention and growth—while developing a project, and you'll remain focused on achieving a simple interaction design.

## Clarity

Of all of humanity's accomplishments over the past few thousand years, mobile computing is probably one of the least natural. Is that too bold a statement? Think about it; humanity lived for centuries with a basic, uniform understanding of information and how it was developed and transferred. Knowledge was passed on orally between individuals or, eventually, written down and handed from person to person. The same held true even in the early digital age. The way computers transmitted information wasn't all that different from the oral or written traditions. But in the last decade or so, this concept was flipped entirely on its head.

Now, people have the ability to carry a device in their pockets that gives them access at any moment to all the information ever learned and recorded by humanity. These devices also allow us to connect with or talk to nearly any person currently alive, all in a matter of seconds. This is a massive paradigm shift for life on this planet; rather than any person having access to a relatively limited amount of information and contact with a relatively limited amount of people, the possibilities for learning and communication are now limitless.

Thinking about this helps one appreciate just how complicated this entire mobile process is and how much potential there is to overload a user with information at any given time. It helps you understand why it's important to create designs centered on clarity. The quantity of information now available at a user's fingertips is as overpowering as the sun. Imagine the sensation of standing outside in the bright sunlight for a few minutes then quickly walking inside a poorly lit room. Initially, your eyes are slow to react and everything appears dark and blurry, but after 15 or 20 seconds your pupils eventually respond, and everything looks clear once again.

The influx of data available on a mobile device creates a similar reaction. When a user turns on a mobile device, there's so much going on compared to what they had been looking at in the everyday world just moments before that they might not immediately comprehend what appears on the screen. It's your job as a designer to do the work for the user's pupils by building an interface and feature set that allows the eyes to adjust easily and the brain to quickly parse what is being shown.

Because this technology is relatively new—and because it's being embraced by users of all ages and technology experience levels—it's important to make your design straightforward and not confusing. Designs should be intuitive and natural. When a user opens your app and tries to figure out how to do something, the method forward should be immediately apparent. Buttons that feature imagery instead of words go a long way toward that. Interaction methods that are consistent with the rest of the device help too. When text is needed to explain something, it should be simple and direct. These devices are advanced, but the way users interact with them doesn't have to be. Clearly displaying how to use your app will greatly enhance the ease of your app's use.

## Continuity and Flow

When it comes to continuity and flow, mobile applications and their interaction designs should remain consistent for the duration of the user experience while also existing in harmony with the entire operating system.

To again use an analogy from nature, the applications on a specific platform are all part of an ecosystem, making up something like a large digital forest. Each application is like a piece of flora or fauna that exists within that area. If you're out hiking through the woods, you feel as if you're immersed in another world in which everything seems to fit together. Large trees grow side by side, flowers populate the area around them, and birds, mammals, and insects find ways to coexist in that habitat. You know what to expect in such a place, and if, for some unexplainable reason, you came across a palm tree or cactus something would seem off.

What if you had to build your own forest from the ground up? Would you know what trees to select, what flowers to line the dirt floor with, and what animals you'd need to bring in to live there? It all seems so natural when you're in the middle of it, but the proposition of creating it wholesale seems much more daunting. Each choice you make needs to seem completely natural; otherwise sightseers walking through your forest will quickly sense that all is not right.

Building within an operating system is similarly daunting. When developing an app, strive to produce a piece of software that offers continuity and flow between each different view and interaction experience while also fitting with the device's world outside your app. Android, for example, uses the font Roboto with standard Holo light or dark theme color sets. An Android app would be well served by also using this standard font and one of these set color themes unless you have a good, solid reason to do otherwise.

Achieving continuity and flow is likely the most difficult of these three simplicity goals, but it's also often the most rewarding. It can lead to many sleepless nights as you ponder what will be the right gesture or animation to trigger a user from one screen to another. You'll find it is truly difficult to present a seamless experience across every single view in your app. However, when the job is done right the user will never even notice that attention to detail, and your work will be so smooth and natural that each transition and interaction will just make sense.

These efforts to build interaction methods that flow smoothly often go unrecognized, but much like a walk along a hiking trail on a beautiful day it's the subconscious recognition of how everything fits together that is the desired result. That's what makes the experience a memorable and, hopefully, often-repeated one.

## Retention and Growth

Finally, designers want to aim to create an experience that will help the user grow and gradually learn more about how they can better take advantage of an app's tools over time. Ideally, the app will feature interaction methods in its interface that directly lead to user retention and skill growth over time.

To do this, you'll want to make the interface and the various causes and effects inside an app repeatable and clearly apparent. Essentially, this means that you should use interaction methods consistently so that they lead to the same result with every use in the app. When users click an arrow in the upper-left corner of the screen, it should take them back to the previous screen, and it should take them back each time they touch it on every screen in the app. This seems fairly straightforward, but it doesn't always happen; failure to properly consider or implement this notion leads to user confusion.

You can achieve this end by using gestures, iconography, and methods consistently throughout the entire app and in ways that are consistent with the operating system as a whole. Take a look, for example, at Figure 9.2. This sharing icon is implemented in a toolbar found inside

**Figure 9.2**  If you have experience with iOS, you've learned that tapping this icon allows you to share whatever information is currently on the screen.

many apps. Just a few years after smartphones hit the market, you now immediately recognize that tapping that icon will allow you to pass a link onto friends via e-mail or social networks.

That icon is immediately recognizable because users retain knowledge as they repeatedly use a system or observe a design. At one point in time, users must have been entirely ignorant of what that arrow represented or what would occur once they tapped it. Inevitably, they began to experiment with it, and it didn't take long to recognize it as a common part of the mobile interaction experience.

The best way to increase such knowledge retention is to stick with established patterns for icons and on-screen visualizations so that your work remains in line with what users have experienced in any other app on a certain platform.

When designing an app that requires a motion to reload or update content on a timeline, for example, why bother using anything except the now-common pull-to-refresh gesture (shown in Figure 9.3)? This systematic pull-down action to load new items in a table view is something users have come to expect. It is a motion that was easy to understand at first use, and over subsequent experiences in many different views and apps users have now come to expect this interaction principle as a means to fetch new information in a piece of mobile software.

Likewise, it would seem entirely out of place and nonsensical to use a pull-to-refresh gesture to perform the task of, say, composing a new message in an e-mail app. This runs entirely contrary to user expectations and stands in direct conflict with past experiences. Upon first use, a consumer would instantly become confused and the reflex memory they developed from other apps would be useless. Because this gesture would seem so unnatural, it's very unlikely others would follow your lead, so a user couldn't learn more about how to navigate the operating system from your standard procedure–defying decision.

To ensure that your application works within users' expectations and helps them grow in their knowledge of a platform's interface, spend time with as many apps as possible and remain up to date on human-interface guidelines. Those policies aren't created merely as suggestions; they're written as a uniform set of established principles that are the foundation for

**Figure 9.3**   When a user sees this image prompting the pull-to-refresh gesture, they've been trained to know what will result.

all designers on a platform. By using a variety of apps and keeping informed of the way they should function, you'll be well equipped to create software that piggybacks off of a user's prior knowledge and experiences.

# Interfaces That Do It Well

Let's take a look at two interfaces that greatly benefited from emphasizing simplicity: slide-to-unlock on iOS and the action bar on Android. If there were ever two examples that put to action the principles discussed in the previous section, these would be they.

When designing for simplicity, strive for the "aha" moment for the user, the moment when a setup delights and encourages continued use and enjoyment of the system. The slide-to-unlock screen and Android action bar are simple—there's nothing there that doesn't need to be—but they also offer significant functionality and information. Simplicity is about fostering an environment of clarity, continuity, and growth while also helping the user get a lot accomplished.

## iOS's Slide-to-Unlock

The slide-to-unlock interaction, shown in Figure 9.4, appeared on the very first iPhone and still exists today, albeit in a slightly different form with the introduction of iOS 7. With slide-to-unlock, before any gesture or finger touch on screen is recognized by the operating system after being awakened the user must first slide a finger from left to right across the screen.

This feature helped Apple get around a tricky situation with the first major touchscreen-based interface. Because the entire front surface of the device was operable with just a finger, developers had to take into account that not all interactions with the screen should elicit a response. There were many situations in which a user could accidentally brush the screen with a hand, so building in ways to limit the amount of times they could accidentally make a phone call or send an e-mail was essential to the success of new touch-sensitive technology.

This design was simple yet spectacular. It helped take what would be the most common task performed on the phone—unlocking the device to check messages, make a call, or open an app—and made its action extremely clear and easily understandable. A vivid animation and a clean visual design indicated to the user that the slider bar needed to be rolled across its track in order to successfully open the device. The interaction method offered a sense of flow, as the interface pieces slowly faded away and were replaced with the phone's background—but not before an affirmational "click" noise indicated the move had successfully been completed.

Finally, the gesture served as a means to train and teach the user how to interact with the interface, which was especially essential given that interacting with the iPhone was likely a user's first important experience with a touchscreen device. The interaction remained focused on the

**Figure 9.4**   Apple's slide-to-unlock mechanism, as found in iOS 6 and earlier.

three simplicity goals—clarity, continuity and flow, and retention and growth—leading to a tremendously effective design.

> **note**
>
> Do you ever sit and just play with the unlock screen on your iPhone or Android device? Take some time right now and experiment with it. Observe how the design involves animation, subtle design changes, sounds, fades, and other cues that establish a simple and coherent design.

## Android's Action Bar

Simplicity in the Android operating system design can be found in the implementation, sharing, and other interaction items on the action bar, shown in Figure 9.5. This interface item can wear many hats; typically, it's used as an anchor at the top of the screen that allows for simple

**Figure 9.5**   Android's classic action bar is where you place actionable items that depend on content on the screen.

navigation and the ability to clearly feature action items for tasks such as e-mailing the data currently on the screen.

Developing an item such as the action bar for Android is actually more difficult than one might think, mostly because of the variable width of the many Android devices. Currently, there are thousands of different Android devices that users could experience an application on with dozens of different screen resolutions to support and the potential for countless future device sizes and screen resolutions. It would simply be impossible to create an action bar that always contained a definite, finite number of items like Apple has done with the tab bar interface object on iOS.

To work with that flexibility in device configurations, Google developed its action bar to be flexible in terms of how many items could appear at any given time, and then it paired the bar with a common "more" button, presenting a simple drop-down when more items needed to be viewed (shown in Figure 9.6).

This design allows the action bar to provide sufficient functionality on both the smallest phone screen and a 10-inch tablet. It gives developers a valuable space to put buttons that execute essential actions while also offering a location for the user to repeatedly look for a one-touch

**Figure 9.6**   When the user taps the action overflow button on the action bar, further options drop down.

spot from which to send an e-mail or share a link via a social network. This bar is a continuous presence for the user, remaining anchored to the top of the screen throughout the use of many applications.

Its flexible yet predictable style and functionality presents a good pattern for user growth as well. When using apps that support the action bar, as well as apps across various-sized devices, the user is able to see that developers aren't constrained by the lowest common denominator (a device's size) but instead can build features into the bar regardless of how large or small a phone or tablet is.

# Creating Simple Interactions

Now that you know the philosophical goals you should focus your work on and have seen examples of those principles in action, how do you go about creating these experiences in your own work? The following are clear, easy strategies that, through personal experience, have guided the creation of simple interactions. They're universally applicable to any operating system and to mobile phones and tablets, so they should go a long way toward helping you create effective, simple apps.

## Learning to Say No

First and foremost, as the lead designer on any project it's critical to develop the ability to not go along with every suggestion anyone makes. As you communicate with your team or client about how to implement features into an app you're building, the temptation will be strong to simply include another button, slider, color, or other element in the project.

You should proceed with caution when adding such items, however. There will be plenty of situations in which additions will be necessary, but when those arise make sure any extra elements actually serve a useful purpose and won't just get in the way or make things more complicated than they need to be.

## Making Tasks Obvious

When you're designing, aim to make simple tasks obvious to the user. Once the app is complete, you should be able to sit with a user, ask him or her how to perform a simple objective within the application, and have the answer be so clear that the user barely has to think in order to find it. You want the routine functions of your app to be true "duh" moments.

In a weather app, for example, if you were to ask a user to tell you how to find tomorrow's forecast, the answer should be practically right under his or her nose. It's a weather app, so it clearly serves a simple purpose: to inform the user about whether it will rain or shine and what the high and low temperatures will be. If it gets much more complicated than that, you may be

**Figure 9.7**  With Yahoo Weather, you don't have to think much about how to get the weather information you need.

going about building your interface in the wrong way. The best ones keep it simple, such as the Yahoo Weather app shown in Figure 9.7.

Strive to make these duh moments intentional; use animations to clearly indicate when the on-screen visuals change, use colors or fonts to emphasize which text is the most important, or take advantage of simple shapes and figures to distinguish special pieces, such as buttons or tabs, from the background. Users should look at the screen and intuitively know where the most important information is.

## Offering Subtle Hints

Believe it or not, it is possible to make things too obvious: to be an overbearing designer, worry too much about providing an optimal experience, and end up doing too much hand-holding and ultimately annoy the user. Much like a parent that constantly calls or texts to inquire about a child's whereabouts, designers can be too present and can discourage users from enjoying and experiencing an app for themselves.

To combat this possibility, make your usability clues subtle so that users feel like they are discovering the app's features for themselves. Let them navigate through the various screens and execute functions in a manner that feels rewarding.

> ## tip
> Are you looking for the best examples of how users expect applications to perform? Check out the most downloaded calendar, calculator, and note-taking applications on the platform you're working with. These types of apps are some of the most commonly used on mobile devices, and thus these categories are some of the most competitive areas of an app store. The leaders in these fields feature some of the best modern design on any platform.

Consider an application that could be navigated in a variety of ways—say, a calendar—and how you would clue the user in on how to see various information displays. Apple's Calendar app in iOS 7 provides a great subtle movement clue. To see future or previous months on the calendar, the user must flick up or down so that the interface displays a small segment of the month's dates on the bottom of the screen. That makes it clear that the user should pull up in order to see more days. It's an obvious and simple interface clue that lets users learn for themselves.

The animations used to transition between views on any operating system are also an example of a quality subtle cue. In iOS 7's Photos app, for example, a grid of pictures is used to represent buttons for different years, months, or locations in which various images were taken. When the user taps on a group, such as the year 2014, the app executes an on-screen animation with the view zooming into the photos from that year, making them go from thumbnail size to a much larger display. Hitting the back button follows that animation in reverse, panning back out to the smaller thumbnail format. This animation helps indicate to the user how to browse their photos with the application.

## Putting Elements in the Right Location

By now, you understand the importance of proper behavior, shape, and color when it comes to the physical attributes of an app's interaction and interface methods. What about feature placement, though? Much like the real estate business, location is extremely important when it comes to app design, and you should carefully pick out a prime position for each element you include in your project.

But is the spot where an item typically appears—such as the location of the back button, so often found in the upper-left portion of a screen—always the best place for it? On both Android and iOS, the back buttons are placed properly when on the top-left side of the screen; it's easy and simple to remember.

What's wrong with Figure 9.8? The back button is in the wrong location, and if you're an experienced smartphone user this likely is a bit jarring. If you wanted to navigate back and find previous screens, you would probably have to pause and consider what to do.

Imagine if designers didn't follow any standards and the applications you used commonly had different locations for the primary back button, such as any of the four locations shown in Figure 9.9. Instead of your thumb or finger reflexively going to the same spot in order to slide back one screen, you would often need to pause and consider where to move, or even worse, you could touch the wrong spot and accidentally execute a command you didn't intend.

Like driving, walking, or typing, navigating on a mobile device is a motor skill that your brain builds muscle memory for over time, but if no pattern exists across a platform, it will be difficult to process the information and develop this intuitive ability. Don't fight against the brain; work with it, and create user interfaces that feature components in their expected location based on other apps on your operating system.

**Figure 9.8**  If you've used a smartphone or tablet before, you'd probably do a double take when you saw the placement of the "Back" button positioned in the lower-right corner.

**Figure 9.9**   Can you identify the right location for the "Back" button? Only one of these four spots is where your thumb reflexively goes when it wants to call up the screen you were on previously.

## Addition by Subtraction

It's infinitely easier to add to an interface than it is to remove from it, so going through the process of taking away or minimizing interface assets—and potentially some features as well—will often be a struggle. Each button you design, gesture you map, or piece of text you stylize will have some value to you, because it's your creation. But like great writers often must do, sometimes you have to kill your darlings.

Just like reorganizing your closet, when sometimes you have to get rid of previously loved clothes in order to make space for new ones, design often requires removing things to make way for fancy new toys. A great interface should be in a constant state of flux with small changes paving the way for better ideas and new concepts. Yes, it will be hard to throw away your previous design work, but it's often a necessary step on the path to improvement.

> **note**
>
> It's OK to constantly change your app's interface. Just look at Evernote; with their mobile and desktop apps, the note-taking giants have never been afraid to refine and tinker. This has led to a constant evolution, allowing the app to grow as its users grow along with it.

You can also realize vast improvements by removing clutter and extra interface pieces without putting anything new into the app. Fewer interface obstacles often means that it's easier for the central features and essential functions of a piece of software to shine through. A busy interface with many options makes it difficult for the user to get to the point of the program.

A finance-management calculator, for example, may have the capability of performing several rare functions that will only be called upon by a handful of power users. But if the point of the app is to allow a user to manage individual finances, these advanced features may be best left tucked away: accessible but not immediately apparent. Or, they could be removed altogether, keeping the app's focus on its most direct objective and ensuring that a majority of the potential user base will find the software accessible and easy to navigate.

These are all things to consider before the initial version of your app ships. Once the masses get their collective hands on your project, it will be much more difficult to take away features. The handful of users who take advantage of the advanced features in your app are also likely to be the most vocal, so if something disappears that they found functional be prepared to hear about it. Trim your app down as much as possible prior to release, or suffer the wrath of negative reviews and blog posts as a result.

# Simplicity through Familiarity

A recurring theme when building simplicity into your designs is familiarity: doing things in line with user expectations as a path to success. But why is this so important? Won't this familiarity lead to boring and repetitive designs? Familiarity is a great way to help users feel at home; as with a TV theme song or a chain restaurant, there's an inherent enjoyment and comfort in things that are recognizable. This applies to interfaces as well; when people become accustomed to one thing, they tend to prefer it.

Playing off of this sense of comfort is a big reason why reading and following the human-interface guidelines for any platform you're targeting is crucial. They intend to still allow for some creativity and independence, but there's a reason why every established interaction and interface principle exists. Google, Apple, and Microsoft created these standards to make the apps developed for their platforms fit well alongside one another.

# Using Well-Known Visuals

Designers can also develop familiarity for users within an app through visualizations that are immediately recognizable. In digital design, this is commonly done through the use of skeumorphism. As mentioned in Chapter 6, this term refers to a practice that involves creating an interface or visual look that mimics the appearance of a real-world object even though the app is by no means constrained by the same limitations as the physical object.

In a note-taking app, applying this concept would, for example, involve creating a yellow, lined background and a handwriting-esque font, both of which give the impression that the text is being written with a pen on a legal pad of paper. A time-keeping app that uses a standard analog watch face would also be considered skeuomorphic.

Some critics of the concept argue that it's silly to apply skeuomorphic design to digital creations, because it restricts objects that exist in an electronic realm with limitless potential to the confines of the real world. But by using real-world visualizations, an app's look can help users infer the purpose of the software or a specific function without any time-wasting instructions or troublesome, trial-and-error experimentation.

A compass app—one similar to Apple's previous compass design, shown in Figure 9.10— that mimics its physical-world counterpart makes its purpose immediately apparent to

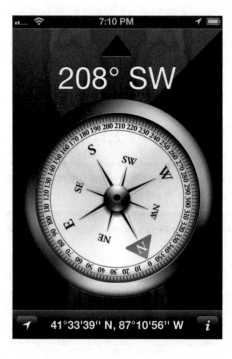

**Figure 9.10**   Apple's previous version of its native Compass application.

the user; the device can be held in the palm of a hand and used exactly like the round, metal object whose arrow always points north. It requires little or no instruction for users that already know how to work a compass, and it's the visual design cues that improve the experience.

Skeuomorphism has currently fallen out of style; many operating systems and app designs have broken away from it, sensing that users no longer need significant hand-holding to guide them through basic operations. It is, however, still a good principle to keep fresh in your design arsenal for when an appropriate situation presents itself. Like bell-bottom jeans, thick-frame glasses, or big mustaches, this design concept could quickly come back into style once you're too old to understand why anyone would ever want to return to it again.

## Following Industry Leaders

Another excellent way to retain familiarity in your design is to remain up to date on what Google, Apple, and other industry leaders do with their built-in apps. Take note of how these pieces of software change over time and how they integrate new interaction and interface components into major operating system updates. Because these companies get to work new functions and features into their apps before anyone else, their designers have already contemplated and resolved many of the common problems you'll run into, so they serve as strong examples to reference and model your projects after.

> ### warning
>
> **DON'T FALL BEHIND**   Keep up with the changes that occur on a platform every year. Currently, Google I/O and Apple's Worldwide Developers Conference (WWDC) are the leading events at which these monumental changes are announced and outlined. Always keep abreast of changes and be looking ahead, making sure that you're not backing yourself into a design corner.

It's also worth your while to download and use apps that have won design awards from popular Web sites and magazines or that have been featured by Microsoft, Apple, or Google on their respective app stores. The Web sites and teams that choose these winners, especially at bigger publications, are typically reviewers and editors that encounter an extraordinary quantity of applications, so they tend to have fairly strong opinions about what works and what doesn't.

## Going Against the Grain

Nevertheless, all this talk of simplicity and familiarity doesn't mean that you must absolutely, positively do what everyone else does 100 percent of the time without fail. In fact, many of the best applications available on any platform are the most successful because, for one feature or interaction method, a designer stepped outside what was common and made a bold decision.

When going against the grain, you must remain mindful of what you're doing and be able to back up your plan and defend your reason for breaking with convention. If you're going to go against the human-interface guidelines or common design practice for whatever you're building, there had better be a good reason other than "just because." If you find yourself at a loss for words regarding why you implemented a design the way you did, it's probably not optimal, and that's a signal to go back to the drawing board.

# Testing Simplicity

You've created a design you think is totally simple, easily understandable, and a sure-fire bet for users to love. Now prove it. It's time to measure your effectiveness and gather data that backs up your actions.

As a designer, you'll want to collect a variety of information, such as how quickly a user can move between features of the app, how long it takes valuable in-app data to load, and how easily a user can find a desired feature or function in the app. Collecting data is important so that you can objectively measure how simple and elegant a design is and then create metrics through which you can work toward improving the design in the future.

## Speed of the App

The rate at which a user can fly through your application is one of the most important factors in determining whether it's a success or failure. The time it takes to load the app or process a task inside it is often the biggest roadblock to enjoying it. Even being able to shave mere milliseconds off loading times can be very beneficial and improve user experience. You can refer to this as the "time until response" test, in which you'll look to measure the time it takes for the user to load and interact with the app.

When building assets for your app, be sure to minimize the size of any PNG or JPEG file within the software. Images and videos are heavy and can weigh down your app. Programs such as Photoshop, which you likely used to create any visual asset, include tools and saving methods that help minimize file size, so be sure to use them when exporting final versions of the files. By decreasing the size of image assets, you can shave milliseconds off loading times inside the app; although this sounds small, such speed improvements have been shown to drastically improve user experience and satisfaction.

Decreasing the final size is a tightrope to walk, though, because any compression will lead to a loss in visual quality. The goal is to make the smallest file possible without the user noticing a significant downgrade in appearance. Several great tools exist for helping compress images, including the open-source project ImageOptim and JPEGmini by ICVT Ltd.

> ## tip
> What's the difference between JPEG and PNG? They're both raster image formats, meaning that they store images in pixel-by-pixel data structures. PNG supports lossless compression and transparencies, meaning that images often look better and can have a background that is invisible, but they often take up a greater file size. JPEG is a lossy compression format, meaning it can make file sizes much smaller than normal, but there may be occasional small errors. JPEG also does not support transparent backgrounds, so every pixel must contain some color.

Likewise, aim to avoid excessive animations that need to be loaded on screen. A two-second animation in which users see text or other data move around with a cute sparkle may seem like a fun addition the first or second time, but such flares quickly become overbearing and exhausting upon subsequent uses. Be respectful and mindful of users' time when considering such additions.

Clock how long it takes for the user to get from the app's launch to the point at which they gain the value they intended to receive from the software. Ideally, you want to make the user feel as if they can get in and get out of the app as quickly as they desire.

# How the App Is Being Used

Nearly all modern applications on Android or iOS implement some sort of digital metric system in order to gain valuable data about how long a user spends inside of an application and what they do while inside the app. Tools such as Google Analytics or Flurry Analytics are key ways for developers to figure out what views or features are visited most frequently and what view or page the user was on when he or she left the application. Designers call these analytic tests "user behavior flow tests."

If you find, for example, that a specific feature page inside of an application has a high exit rate—meaning, the majority of the time, that the user was viewing a certain screen when he or she quit the app—that likely means something in the design or look of the page was difficult to understand, troublesome, or dysfunctional, and the user decided to turn his or her attention elsewhere. Use this data to re-evaluate what you've built and where to make improvements. Once you think you have an idea or two of how to improve a poor-performing page, you can try "A/B testing."

> **note**
>
> What's an A/B test? It's something that occurs heavily in Web site development. Two different interfaces are created, and users are randomly sent to one site or another. Specific interaction points are measured to see which site features options that are more preferable.
>
> As an example, a launch page might contain two different button colors for a "Sign Up" link. During this test, the development team will look to see which button gets clicked more by test users and then roll out that design for all users.

A/B testing is a strategy that is extremely popular in Web design, for which deployment and interface development is extremely fast and simple, but it's a bit less practiced in mobile, for which deployment is difficult. There are some startups that are working to create simple A/B testing inside of an application, and if you find a method that works for your team, it often can be valuable to test out two or more different interfaces in order to see which performs better with your users.

## Social Reach

Another way to measure feedback is through the good old-fashioned method of pounding the pavement to hear directly from users. Well, this method isn't *too* old-fashioned; most of the time, it now involves using the information superhighway as opposed to meeting users in person. This is called "direct feedback usability testing."

By integrating software tools such as TestFlight or HockeyApp to place feedback forms directly inside an app, even down to the specific locations where you suspect a user might have an issue, you can develop a method to speak with users directly and find ways to make your work clearer and more understandable in future versions. It's especially worth considering adding such a feature during beta testing so that you can develop solutions to common problems prior to an app's wide release.

It's also valuable to monitor what users write about their experiences with your app on social media. A variety of services are available that allow you to enter keywords—perhaps your company or app name—and be notified when someone mentions that term on Facebook, Twitter, or Tumblr. This helps you quickly learn if a user encounters a problem with your app, allowing you to reach out to the user to address the issue or to correct the problem at large.

The only problem is that most social-media grumbling won't occur until after the app has been released, so it may be too late to make significant tweaks or adjustments. This is the inherent flaw in relying upon the mass-market consumer for feedback; but, timeliness aside, much can be learned from what others are posting online.

# Dogfooding

A final and very common way to test usability and simplicity inside an application is called "dogfooding." This somewhat unappetizing-sounding term refers to a situation in which the developer or designer for a project uses the software heavily, often exclusively, to fulfill whatever purpose the application serves.

## note

Why does this process have such an odd name? Programming urban legend alleges that a manager at Microsoft in the 1980s used the phrase "eating your own dog food" to refer to company employees using their own creations. The description stemmed from a popular commercial at the time for a brand of dog chow, in which the company's CEO said that he fed their latest product to his own pets.

This sounds like common sense, but it often can be a bit more difficult in practice, especially when you're building a piece of software that has many solid competitors, such as games, calendars, or weather applications. Especially when the application is still fairly rough, you may like your competitors' apps a little bit better.

This is also why dogfooding can be so valuable. Do you like and use your app? If not, you might have a very big problem on your hands. You should be your own biggest fan, and if you find that other applications are doing a better job than you are you may need to retool your concept or approach.

## warning

**TIME IS OF THE ESSENCE**    Don't rest on your laurels after any one project or view that project as your gift to all humankind. Mobile moves at an extremely fast pace, so always remain focused on the future and on what you'll build tomorrow that will excite users, not on what you did yesterday.

## IN-DEPTH

In mobile design, simplicity shines. Here are some apps that do it especially well.

- **Yahoo Weather**: Yahoo has experienced a bit of a renaissance in recent years, largely due to the company's development of best-in-class mobile apps that focus on simplicity and usability. The Yahoo Weather app (see Figure 9.7) is the leading example of this, as it features eye-catching images from its photo service, Flickr, tied together with clear iconography and simple direction that helps the user quickly see a forecast in a visually appealing way.

- **Instagram**: Interesting social-network concepts can often be ruined through overcomplication. But Instagram (see Figure 9.11) threw complexity out the window and made its social network simple. Users post photos, follow friends and see their photos, and like or comment on photos. That's it. Through focusing on a simple, pure, photo-sharing experience, the network gained massive popularity and sold for $1 billion worth of stock to Facebook. Who ever said that you couldn't strike it rich through simplicity?

- **Super Hexagon**: It's not hard to quickly become a sucker for this game. Super Hexagon (see Figure 9.12) is extremely fun, challenging, and—surprise—simple. You play the role of a lonely pixelated triangle attempting to avoid various pattern mazes for as long as possible. If you can survive longer than 60 seconds, you beat the level. Controls are simple: Tap left to move left and tap right to move right. Game designer Terry Cavanagh has truly built a masterpiece here; he's created an experience that is so simple to pick up anyone can learn the game in 10 to 15 seconds. It's difficult enough, though, that only the persistent can master its refined gameplay.

**Figure 9.11**   Much of Instagram's success can be attributed to how simple and easy to use it is. (Courtesy of Megan E. Lee.)

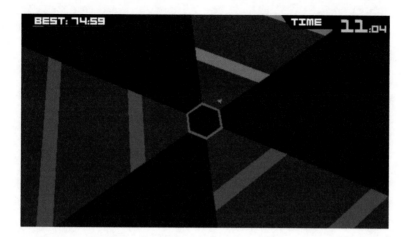

**Figure 9.12**   The extremely addicting game Super Hexagon could never be said to have ultra-advanced graphics, but that doesn't mean it won't hook you. (Courtesy of Terry Cavanagh.)

# Conclusion

When you strive for simplicity, what you're really doing is focusing on making an application as easy to use as possible for the end user through the intentional reduction of all visual and interaction components that get in the way of clarity and usability.

Over time, you'll learn the art of saying no to excess, potential confusion, and the obstacles that get in the way of an outstanding user experience. If you focus on interface clarity, experience continuity, and user growth, you'll be well on your way toward creating an application users love and are willing to share.

# CHAPTER 10

# GAINING VALUABLE FEEDBACK

Releasing an app is a public demonstration of all the design knowledge and ability you've gained and developed to date, but perform poorly and your low download count and negative app store reviews will be harsher than any grade you ever got in school. Thankfully, there's a way to anticipate problems users will have upon release. This is a test you can prepare for—by finding willing volunteers to try out every part of your app again and again and again.

# Showing Off Your Work

By now, you're familiar with the process of iterating and improving upon your design work; but so far, you've primarily only dealt with the internal struggle of how to enhance a project and improve workflow. Eventually, if you want to find success with your application you'll need to show it off to others too.

Your app can't stay on your hard drive forever. Sooner or later, you'll need to share your latest creation with clients, stakeholders, coworkers, family members, and, potentially, millions of users around the world. That thought may scare you, but a successful app will never be used just by you and you alone. Designers can't anticipate the trials and tribulations that every user might have with an app, so it's critical to get outside opinions on features and functionality.

As the designer on a project, you can often become blind to how a third party would interact with your work, and you will often develop biases about its performance because you're so closely connected to it. To build a viable mainstream product, it's absolutely necessary to gather feedback on your software from people who don't have a vested interest in its success.

> **note**
>
> Who qualifies as a stakeholder? This may sound like a simple question, but before you get too far into the development process be sure you know who will need to sign off on any beta applications before the final ship date. The last thing you want to do is work through the final few weeks or month of a project, rapidly iterating while never getting the opinion of the people who must ultimately approve the project prior to release.

How do you decide that it's finally time to push your app out into the world? Answers to that philosophical question vary throughout the mobile world, so there are a number of different strategies you could embrace. There's no universal solution, so there's plenty of opportunity to try out different approaches and figure out what works best for different types of applications.

## Protecting Your Secrets

No matter how you go about making your app available to other eyes—be it through a beta test process, a small focus group, or the public at large—it's crucial to remember that such actions mean that any mystery surrounding the message or purpose of your app will no longer be under lock and key. From the moment someone else gets their hands on your product— even if it's just a trusted group of beta testers—any secrets about your app are no longer guaranteed to be safe.

This may not be a problem for many apps. Small players in the digital marketplace aren't likely to have a large body of users anxiously seeking out details or searching for leaks about the contents of their latest project. It may not be a huge deal, then, if a beta user happens to let a piece or two of information slip about your app.

But for some—perhaps an app for a client with a well-recognized brand getting set for a big product launch or event—it's imperative to ensure that absolute secrecy is kept regarding the app's content and design. Once such an app is handed off to beta users there's the potential for other outside parties to learn critical details about the project. In these situations, it's crucial to be careful and keep beta builds under wraps until the last possible moment; only release it then to people you can trust to test it confidentially.

> ### warning
>
> **FOR YOUR EYES ONLY**   On projects for which secrecy is of utmost importance, don't be afraid to use code names and fake text inside the application to obscure its function or purpose in case the app falls into the wrong hands. Likewise, feel free to use placeholder art and dummy icons, and be sure to require all testers to lock their devices when not in use. Leaky ships don't sail very far.

Even when the features or data inside your application don't need to be kept top secret, once beta users start playing around with a product it's possible that the general public will start forming an opinion about your software. Choose beta users you can rely on and who understand that software in the preproduction stage is often volatile and will have bugs and issues that still need to be worked out. If they don't realize these key facts, the word of mouth or buzz about your app could kill its chances of success before it's available to the general public.

In this highly connected digital age, a negative or misinformed blog post or comments on Twitter can spell doom for your product upon release. You want the users who are testing your project in its infancy to help it build and grow, not to spread negative reviews that could make all your work be for naught.

## Choosing the Right Testers

Before you hand out your work to a group of testers, you want to make sure that small cluster includes only people you can rely on to give honest feedback as well as constructive criticism on how your app can be improved. Projects that go before test groups while still in preproduction often encounter a common problem: users who are too close to the developers and thus fail to give honest opinions about what needs to be done to make an app better. The testers worry too much about the developers' personal feelings in the comments they offer and don't provide valuable critiques.

Consider who you can currently count on to give you objective responses to any of life's little questions. If you ask your mother or significant other for an honest opinion about how you look in your favorite T-shirt, you'll get a very different response than if you ask a stranger in a bar. Those close to you will likely consider your feelings and give you the answer you want to hear instead of telling you when it's time to throw the shirt out and go buy some new clothes.

> **warning**
>
> **IN SEARCH OF GOOD OPINIONS**   When beta-testing software, it's extremely important to find people who offer valuable opinions and not just people who you think will love your work and agree with every design that you've created. You don't need "yes men" or "yes women" at this point; you need people who will question you and help push your product toward becoming something better.

If you choose testers who are afraid to respond honestly by informing you where your interaction and interface design is lacking, you're doing more harm to your project than if you had no testing process at all. It's essential to find a few valued peers who are willing to tell you how it is, preventing you from letting major deficiencies persist throughout development.

As you gather feedback, keep an eye on the clock. Remember that every additional person you add to your beta group means more time spent teaching a new user how to install the software, following up on problems that pop up, and checking to see how they're liking your design. When selecting a beta user, make sure this person is truly dedicated to lending a hand; you won't want people who will become bored or disinterested after a few hours.

Many users will see the opportunity of beta testing an app as something highly desirable—an honor of sorts—but it's not all fun and games. They need to understand that it will require sitting and being patient at times or replicating the same steps over and over again to isolate a bug. You want people who are testing an app solely for their own sense of accomplishment or desire to help out.

Go for quality, not quantity, when selecting beta testers. In Apple's developer program, for example, you'll be limited to only 100 users who can try out your applications, so it's important to find a reliable group, because you can't add on an unlimited number of additional users in the future if your first picks flake out on you.

## When to Share Your Work with Testers

Before you ship your work off to be judged by beta users, you need to consider whether your app is in the right condition to receive good advice or suggestions on changes that should be implemented. Often, developers rush a project into the testing process, failing to consider whether it's in a state at which the average user could look at it and determine what it will look like in its final version. If you're not to that point yet, your testers will be left confused and frustrated and will likely make erroneous or unhelpful suggestions about where the app should go in further development.

There are two things that nobody should ever see being made: sausage and software. The process through which an app is created is often messy and can be difficult for people unfamiliar with the process to understand. They simply won't recognize an app in its early stages compared to the final product. If you're not an experienced home builder, it is difficult to look at an incomplete framed structure and visualize exactly how the living room will look once complete. Likewise, it's difficult for nondevelopers to look at an app in its infancy and understand how the finished version will look and function.

Remember this ugly screenshot (see Figure 10.1)? Software can be unattractive while you're working on it, so don't be afraid of iterating and improving upon your initial design even once the first group of testers has seen it. But be careful who you let view your unappealing early

**Figure 10.1**   Don't rush to post early screenshots for the public.

work. App beauty often only runs pixel-deep, and your audience will harshly judge any rushed, less-than-perfect screenshots you post to your blog or social-media accounts.

This problem is the very reason why housing developers constructing a new subdivision will build a model house first; it's an example structure they can show prospective buyers, making it easy to visualize what other houses in the neighborhood will look like. Without this reference guide, a family looking to relocate couldn't walk around an actual building and imagine what their life would be like in that neighborhood.

Software is no different. Designers who are constantly thinking about the world of app development often forget that the average person—even someone willing to help out with beta testing—will have a fair amount of difficulty working with a project that remains in its earliest stages. These people will find it tough to offer helpful advice on what improvements need to be made before the app hits the market.

As a result, it's important to hold off on releasing an app to beta users until it hits a point at which outsiders could look at what you've built and comprehend how it will appear in its final form. Typically, this comes at the stage in which a majority, if not all, of the primary features in the app are functioning. This point is known in the industry as the "feature complete" stage, meaning that the user can walk through that function from start to finish and see the intended end result. This means that a majority of your interface design should be implemented in a way that looks more or less as it will in the final version. This doesn't mean that everything needs to be bug-free; in fact, the primary purpose of a beta-test group is to isolate and track down pesky issues that will cause problems for users.

You never want to show off your work too soon, as users will then have issues understanding the ultimate purpose of the app or will run into trouble when navigating the software. Offering up the app for beta testing too early only wastes your time and the testers' time. They will focus on issues that you already plan on fixing, leaving you to attempt to explain to them why something doesn't work the way they think it should but will eventually.

Similarly, you should not wait too long to hand off a beta build to testers. Stalling until late in the development game could mean that everything in your app will be set in its foundation, and making big changes will be extremely difficult. At this point, your design will be stuck in its current form, and all testers can do is reassure you of the decisions you've already made or alert you to problems you will be unable to fix prior to shipment.

# Devising a Beta-Test Strategy

Like everything else in app development, it's important to plan ahead. You'll want to develop a strategy before you send your first test version to your anxious evaluators. Doing so will make life significantly easier as you rush toward the final days prior to finalizing a beta version.

The last stages of a project will often be hectic. Programmers will be running tests on various issues and bugs, working to improve performance. Designers will be working on every phase of the interaction within an app, making sure the gestures perform as intended, every pixel is in the right place, the text copy has been tidied up, and every label and paragraph is clear and concise. Soon, you'll have a handful, if not a dozen or more, of beta testers using the application and recommending fixes or finding problem areas. The moving parts at this stage of the development process only increase.

Thus, if you don't have a sound plan you'll quickly find yourself overwhelmed and juggling too many balls at once. This can be a major problem at a time when you need to be the most alert and ready to adapt to anything thrown your way. Consider embracing the following strategies to help keep your head above water.

## Tracking an App's Issues

First and foremost, the most important thing you'll need to do once a group of testers start pointing out bugs is to find a solid, formal way to collect and track information on those issues. You'll need a tool that will help your development team and your testers collaborate and pass information back and forth.

Some of the best tools to help you do this are simple, Web-based issue trackers accessed through services such as GitHub or Bitbucket (shown in Figure 10.2), services you might already be using for source-code management. These sites offer issue trackers that work much like an Internet forum, allowing you to tag other users and assign issues to them directly, close out issues once they've been resolved, attach screenshots or photos to help guide a programmer through solving the issue, and much more. You can format text in these trackers using Markdown, which allows for easy and quick integration of bulleted or numbered lists, bold or italicized text, URL linking, and other text formatting that will be useful in helping to emphasize a point about a specific issue.

If you choose not to use one of these services, some test groups simply use e-mail lists to pass along information about bugs or common problems. It's a more rudimentary and basic way to handle feedback communication, but if it gets the job done for your team go ahead and do it. Be careful when you use this method, though; it can often result in a lot of inbox clutter, annoying some members of the list or leading to certain items being overlooked.

Some test-group administrators also use standard Web forums for handling the discussion of issues, creating a specific thread for each bug that users or team members can comment on. This method is commonly used with software in postrelease, either when collecting bug discoveries from a large user group or when a large public beta is available, like in larger projects that may require hundreds or even thousands of testers before the app is ready for general consumption. It works well because some technically limited common users may be intimidated by the standard software-issue tracker, and forums are much more easily understood.

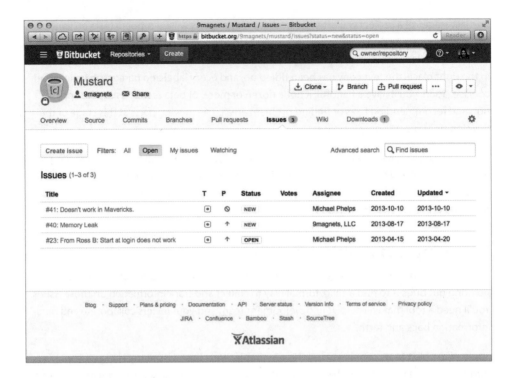

**Figure 10.2**   Bitbucket is a frequently used personal code manager and issue tracker that might fit well into your workflow.

The downside, though, is that this method doesn't make it easy to assign issues to specific programmers and designers; it's also typically unruly or difficult to manage, especially among a large number of users.

A final method, one frequently used by many indie developers, involves simple Web forms. The developer may write a basic Web site, one that includes a standard PHP Web form that when completed sends an e-mail to a programmer or designer, serving as the official way to collect feedback from test users. This often works well because there is a low barrier to entry for the test user to submit feedback; he or she just needs to click a link and enter some text. The downside comes when you must sort through a host of e-mails that could come in a variety of convoluted formats and then morph them into a formal structure that allows the programmer to determine where a problem is occurring and how to correct it. Overall, though, it's the easiest route for the beta-test user, which will likely lead to you receiving the most feedback.

## Prepping Every Build

Once you've reached the point at which you're ready to collect feedback, you'll need to figure out what the best way will be to distribute test builds of an app to users. This seemingly simple task can often become quite complex, and there are a few key points to review before sending out any build.

Again, it's important to remember that Apple currently caps the number of test users per developer account at 100. That may sound like a lot right now, but as you work on your fourth, fifth, or 100th application that number won't seem so large. This figure is also tied to the number of devices, not specifically to the number of users, so as loyal testers get new iPhones and iPads they'll be chipping away at that number.

> ## warning
>
> **KNOW YOUR LIMITS**  Depending on the platform you're working on, you may be limited by the number of test users you can bring on to a prerelease program. Be aware of these caps and how they could affect your testing cycle. Don't lose valuable potential feedback because you were caught off-guard.

The first thing you'll need to do is collect some basic information about the devices your testers are using. Regardless of the platform they're on, you'll want to know what your beta users have on hand to review your work with. Keep a list of the device type and operating system that each user tests with; this will become extremely useful once reports of the first bugs start coming in. The key to proper bug testing is replication; your programmers will want to see exactly what happens when a problem occurs in the app, and if they can't see it on the exact device and operating system the tester was using it will be a difficult issue to fix.

By knowing which operating system and device the problem occurred on, you can isolate the vast majority of variables and quickly get to the root of the problem. This knowledge will also pay dividends if your app has specific features available only on certain platforms or devices, because you'll be able to check whether users are able to use such tools.

Figure 10.3 details different platform-adoption rates for an app released simultaneously on iOS and Android. As you can see, a variety of different versions of different operating systems are used, and this graph can't even begin to display the number of different devices used (174). Monitoring these numbers, though, can help isolate potential usability or programming issues during development.

You'll also need to draw up an internal schedule outlining how often you intend to send test builds to users. Do you plan to have a new version every week? Every month? Some software teams produce nightly builds, although that's usually for larger products and might be overkill. Will you only send a new build when something substantial has been done, making it worth an update? It's a question you can really only answer with your team, and the answer will be based on your own personal workflow preferences.

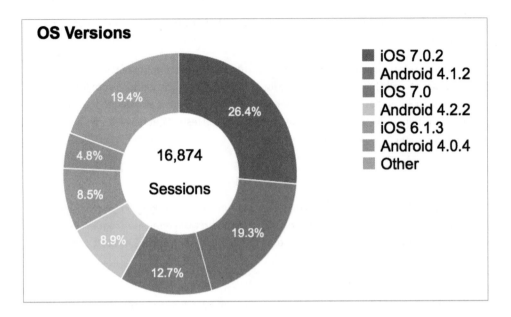

**OS Versions**

- iOS 7.0.2
- Android 4.1.2
- iOS 7.0
- Android 4.2.2
- iOS 6.1.3
- Android 4.0.4
- Other

16,874
Sessions

26.4%
19.3%
12.7%
8.9%
8.5%
4.8%
19.4%

**Figure 10.3** After you release an app, users may be downloading it on several platform OS versions at any given time.

You don't want to drown your testers with a constant barrage of new builds, but you do want them to have the latest and greatest version so they're not reporting issues to you that have already been fixed. Work with a client to develop a plan, but delivering two beta builds per week is a good target, because that total and regular schedule will give the involved parties a consistent pattern by which they can regularly expect new work.

Another important detail to include in your plans involves coming up with a consistent and internally understandable build-numbering system. Ideally, you'll want to keep that number prominent within the application somewhere so that users can reference it when reporting bugs or issues. It could be something as simple as "0.X," with X representing the sequential number of test builds that have been offered. It could also be something much more complex, maybe even including a date or timestamp to clarify to the internal team when the build was created.

tip
Are you not sure how to format your version numbers for prerelease builds? A well-tested labeling format is 0.X.(Date stamp in "YYYYMMDD" format), where X can have three potential values:

- **0.7**: Alpha build, early release. Not feature or design complete and very rough around the edges.

- **0.8**: Beta build, mature release. Feature complete but maybe not design complete. Needs much work with visual pieces, text formatting, proper text copy, and other fine details. Likely to have significant bugs or issues.

- **0.9**: Release-candidate build, near-final release. Features and designs are complete, and most bugs have been fixed. Going through final verification to make sure the app is ready for the world.

Using this system, a beta build released on April 5, 2014, would be labeled as "0.8.20140405."

You can also save yourself some time and effort by creating template e-mails that will go along with each build, as you'll often repeat many of the same instructions each time a new version is set throughout the development process. Software such as TextExpander by Smile can be a lifesaver, allowing you to store and reproduce any snippet of text with just a few keystrokes. Aside from e-mails, you could also use those programs to save instructions on how to delete an application from a variety of different versions of Android or iOS, how to reset each device, how to determine the operating system version a device is running, how to properly report bugs using your issue tracker, or a variety of other common tasks you'll be explaining frequently. Templates are extremely efficient and allow you to respond promptly to users as they ask common questions during the hectic, final testing period.

## Handing the Beta Off

Once you have a list of users on hand and an idea of how you will respond to their feedback and integrate their opinions into your software, you should consider how your beta app will be distributed to your users. Depending on the platform you're working on, this could be relatively easy or somewhat difficult. On Android, for example, you may only need to e-mail an APK file to test users so long as they have turned on the device setting that allows the use of unsigned third-party applications.

With iOS, however, you'll have a bit more work on your hands. Requirements and policies change from time to time depending upon Apple's current developer policies, so it's best to first check the developer center to find out the latest procedure.

Typically, however, you will need to collect UDID codes from each user's test device through iTunes and then use Apple's developer portal to create a special provisioning profile that

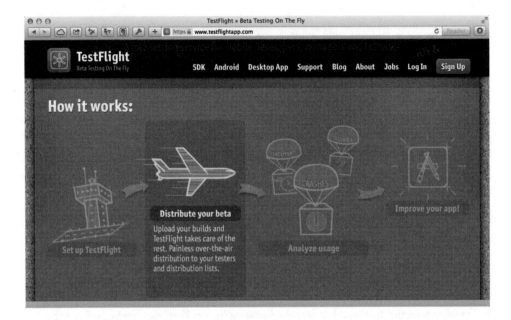

**Figure 10.4**   TestFlight's Web service was written for developers and designers by developers and designers, making it a great way to manage beta testing.

prevents the prerelease application from being installed on any iPhone or iPad devices for which you do not have the UDID. From there, you will need to get the app's compiled IPA file and provisioning profile to your test users. A couple of Web services have been built to help with this; TestFlight (shown in Figure 10.4) and Launchpad allow you to upload these files and automatically notify the user that a new test build is available for download.

Once you get your test app in users' hands, it's advisable to build a regular schedule and follow up with your test users to make sure they're using the app sufficiently and getting accurate and appropriate test data. Likewise, you may need to prompt them to fill out the issue-tracking form you selected, as most users tend to be busy and may forget to note the bugs or issues they find during their testing periods.

# Analyzing Valuable Test Data

As users report back on their experiences with your app, don't forget to take time to aggregate the hopefully useful analytic data you're collecting from your digital guinea pigs. Many programmers and development teams ship their apps with some type of crash-measurement analytics as well as with some variety of usability- or feature-popularity-measuring metric.

> **tip**
>
> As in any relationship, the connection between your team and your beta testers can be improved through solid, consistent contact. It often makes sense for the designers to be in charge of communicating directly with testers, because they will primarily have issues or concerns about the app's design and interaction. Be sure to reach out to testers if you don't hear from them for a couple of days or a week, and make sure all is going well and that they aren't running into problems. Testers will appreciate this, and building that relationship will make them feel comfortable coming to you with questions or interaction design suggestions. A strong personal connection allows for an honest and open feedback cycle, which is key to creating outstanding work.

Implementing these analytical packages can be complex and is generally beyond the technical expertise of a designer. However, most do come with simple software development kits to make it easy for anyone with a bit of basic knowledge of native programming languages to integrate advanced analytics into their app.

# Knowing Where Testers Spent Their Time

The most popular analytics services to integrate into mobile apps are Google Analytics or Flurry Analytics. Both systems are designed to track detailed user metrics on the features users love or hate.

Whereas TestFlight and Launchpad are solid ways to manage beta distribution and beta-team management, these apps are instead used to determine which features inside your application are the most popular, where users spend most of their time, how many times the average user opens the app, what countries or cities app users come from, which device models and operating systems are most popular, and much more.

Such data is valuable because it offers insight that even your most loyal testers may not tell you about. One of the first early lessons you'll learn as a software developer is that no matter how hard they try users will be unable to articulate what makes them love or hate a specific app. Analytics can give you a peek behind the usage curtain and help you better understand what is appealing and what is discouraging to consumers.

Here's one key example of the benefit of such information: A host of different development companies have done interface research regarding speed and how it relates to user satisfaction. Google is known to pride itself on how fast its search engine can return a desired result. But ask the average user, and they will rarely say that the precise speed content loaded was the determining factor between whether they liked or disliked an app. Data, though, can indicate whether long load times may be limiting use and whether any changes you make to an app improve key usage statistics.

You could, say, alter the amount of information you display on the screen at a given time, perhaps by using a compression technique to knock half a second off the initial load time. Most users would never notice this change, but analytic data could indicate increased time spent by the average user inside the app, helping support the notion that speed is important. Whenever possible, look at analytics and try to find ways to use data to guide design changes you make to an app.

## Finding Software Bugs and Crashes

Crash report analytics services—especially Crashlytics, HockeyApp (shown in Figure 10.5), or TestFlight—are also very popular and worthwhile. They provide a variety of services, including sending e-mails whenever a user experiences a crash within the app complete with a detailed report about what was happening when it occurred, what device model and operating system the user had, and whether things like language settings or localization features could have

**Figure 10.5**  HockeyApp integrates with iPhone or Android apps, allowing your team to receive e-mails when users have issues. (Courtesy of HockeyApp, Inc.)

sparked the problem. These services will be invaluable to your programming team as they offer insight that beta users may not be able to provide themselves.

Having this type of information on hand will be quite useful, because the first step in solving any bug or issue is to replicate the problem over and over. A crash occurs because of a specific event, and you'll need that same set of variables in place in order to observe what happened. It's like a basic science experiment; you need to develop a hypothesis about what happened, distill the situation down to a small set of variables, then test again and again to see what occurs. You won't be getting any blue ribbons for your efforts, but you will win over happy users.

What role do nonprogrammers play in this refinement process? Designers can contribute quite a bit in fact, because fixing bugs and resolving technical issues requires patience and a strong attention to detail, common attributes among those skilled in the visual arts. Technical bugs can often seem random and nonsensical until an obvious pattern is discovered, and your keen eye can help identify why an issue is occurring. Obviously, when it comes to pinpointing where the problematic areas of the code are and how to fix the issue you may be less of a help, but the rest of your team will surely appreciate a designer who can alleviate any difficulties that appear during the bug-testing stage of development.

## Managing Issue Resolve

As your team works to solve the various issues your testers point out, you'll want to develop an internal system of checks to ensure that problems have been resolved. Consider setting up a two-person checking system to verify that a bug in an app has been fixed before an issue can be deemed "closed."

Under such a system, the engineer that works on fixing the bug in the software code first tests the issue and verifies the code has solved the problem. Then, another team member goes in and confirms that the bug has been eliminated. If both sign off on the issue, make sure to mention it to your beta testers as something to verify once they receive your next test build.

But, you might argue, doesn't this extra step seem a little unnecessary? Your team isn't made up of children, after all, and if an engineer says an issue is resolved is there really a need to check it again? Yes. Even though this adds extra time to the process, it's essential. If there's one thing that annoys test users, it's telling them that an issue has been corrected when in fact the problem persists.

You don't go through a double-check process because you don't trust your engineers; you do it because software bugs are complex and the mobile world features a variety of operating systems and devices. Issues that a programmer thinks they've eliminated may continue to pose problems for some users. Requiring two team members to sign off before an issue is pushed aside alleviates potential pain for beta testers and, perhaps, eventual mass-market consumers.

# From Beta to Positive Changes

It's your job as a member of the creative team behind the project to judge how important each and every one of the issues raised by a tester is and how that feedback should be input and applied as you revise, add, and subtract from your app. You're the captains of the development ship and will need to determine the course toward success, locating what pieces are ripe for revision and what can be skipped. Your success will be based on your ability to read the market and anticipate user demand, so learning what users want from your product is a critical part of the development process.

Determining what to do once you've handed out a few beta builds, tackled obvious problems, and collected even more feedback on your app involves making some difficult choices. You'll likely have a variety of user bugs that still need addressing as well as recommendations for product enhancements to consider; but you'll also have a ton of user data from your analytics platforms to worry about. This creates the potential for too many problems that need attention before your planned release date. How should your team prioritize and ultimately decide what makes the cut?

It's this stage of the process that separates the good designers from the great ones. The decisions made here over what gets included in the final version of your app will ultimately lead the project to success or lock it into mediocrity.

Perhaps the most difficult thing to determine involves which proposals from beta testers require consideration and which can be ignored, at least temporarily. No matter how hard you try, it will be impossible to please every user, but issues spotted by your testers could pose problems for the general public. The key is to be selective; there are only so many hours in the day and only so many days until you release your app to the world.

When attempting to prioritize issues, aim to take user complaints and correlate them to data amassed via Google Analytics or a similar program. A request or issue that's reported often should demand your attention, because many have identified that problematic point. What's tougher, though, is winnowing down the list of concerns voiced by one or two beta testers. When such issues arise, data is extremely valuable, because it can help you learn more about these seldom-made requests and trace them back to the features they stemmed from. The elements most commonly used by beta testers should be given top priority during the refining process.

As the one creating the app, though, you know your project best. Sometimes, you'll have to trust your gut and personal preferences when it comes to putting the finishing touches on a piece of software leading up to release then go back and clear up user concerns for later versions down the road.

## Determining When Enough Is Enough

At some point, however, you have to push your app out of the development nest and hope it can spread its wings and fly. Steve Jobs was famous for reciting the phrase "real artists ship" in the months leading up to the release of the original Macintosh. If you want to have a successful mobile smartphone or tablet application, you'll first have to release it into the wild. It can't be a universal success if the universe never gets to see it.

Although the process of software development can feel as rigorous and exhausting as a marathon, development isn't usually a race with a set finish line. Your team is ultimately in control of when the project is done. With an infinite time span, you could go on forever, but it's best to set a deadline for when the project should be complete, or at the very least know when to say when and wrap a bow around your project. So what are the telltale signs that you're ready to release?

- **You've squashed all (or most) of the bugs.**

  It will be impossible for you to remove every last bug from your software, but aim to do the best job possible and make sure any particularly pesky performance issues have been resolved. Small problems can be solved quite easily as long as your team isn't lazy, and in the end doing so can prevent users from having a poor experience.

- **You're happy with what you've got.**

  You'll always be your harshest critic. If you're not satisfied with your own work, you may want to question whether it's ready to be released to a mass audience. But don't be too hard on yourself; you'll never get the app absolutely perfect, so you'll have to let it go at some point. Remember this great quote from Nintendo video game developer Shigeru Miyamoto (creator of *Mario Bros.*, *Donkey Kong*, *Zelda*, and many other titles): "A delayed game is eventually great, but a bad released game is bad forever."

  Although this philosophy isn't as pertinent in the mobile world, because it's fairly simple and fast to release minor updates, it's important to remember that you can always fix issues postrelease, but letting buggy software out into the world will turn off many users to your app, and by the time you've fixed the issue and uploaded a release to the app store the user may have written off your app completely.

- **You've addressed beta concerns as best as possible.**

  Depending on the size of your beta group, you may have a lot of features suggested to you. Within reason, you should try to accommodate these as best as possible. Place a high priority on the things you determine to be most important, and try to get as many of them done as possible before release.

- **You've prepared a launch strategy.**

  As the designer on a project, it's likely that the responsibility of creating a Web site, promotional banner art, screenshots that focus on special features, a press kit for the media, marketing e-mails, and other released material will fall to you. Make sure you have all these elements ready to go before the app is released to the world. You want the availability of this material to coincide with the release date of the app, so it has to be fact-checked, proofread, and finalized before launch day arrives.

- **You've checked your schedule.**

    This may seem like one of the silliest pieces of information offered on these pages, but don't laugh. Before you set a release date, check your personal schedule. Check your team members' schedules. Don't plan to launch an app around birthdays, weddings, holidays, vacations, or any other time at which you and your colleagues might be away from the computer. Inevitably, Murphy's Law will take hold after your app hits the digital marketplace, and you want everyone available at a moment's notice if (when) something goes wrong.

# Releasing the App

Once you've run down this checklist and completed every item—not to mention ensured that you're sufficiently satisfied with the interface and interaction design and that your programming team is content with the performance of the app's features—you're all set for release.

The next step is to prepare and submit the binary code of your software as well as any required metadata to the app stores. For Android apps, your work could be available in as little as a few hours, but for Apple software you'll likely be waiting a few days for the app to be approved. Sooner or later, though, you will be able to release your app for download to dozens, hundreds, thousands, or millions of consumers.

## IN-DEPTH

If you've never worked through an application and gone through a reiteration and testing phase, it's often difficult to understand what to expect or what the experience will be like. Here's some firsthand testimony from a fellow designer, offering his opinion on what it's like to iterate during the beta process.

James Karras is a product manager at OUYA, Inc. OUYA was released in 2012 after successfully completing a campaign on the independent crowdfunding site Kickstarter. The project allows mobile Android games to be played on large TVs using Bluetooth gaming controllers.

This is an exceptional example of iterating on interaction design. As Karras and his team looked to make hundreds of mobile Android games compatible with their upcoming OUYA, they were also looking to refine an interface that allowed users to jump seamlessly between games and menu options.

But users were having trouble with his initial menu designs, he said in an interview for this book, although that was only apparent after user testing:

For OUYA, user feedback is a fundamental part of how we run our business. An understanding of what our gamers are doing helps us to quickly adjust and iterate in order to make the best experience possible.

For example, our original design for our system menus had visual elements intentionally going off the left side of the screen. Visually, it looked fantastic, but as soon as gamers got this early version in their hands, we received complaints of overscan issues with our menu system. This occurred when, at times, it appeared as if the screen wasn't properly showing the entire viewing area, giving users the impression that they weren't seeing the full system menu. The problem was exacerbated by the fact that we had a bug with certain games that really did have overscan problems.

The solution was simple: First, divide up the gamer feedback so we understood that there were multiple problems, then pull in the design elements on the left side of the menu, so we eliminated the confusion entirely and could focus on the specific issues with games.

Internally, we didn't catch the issue because we all had inside design knowledge that parts of the menu were supposed to appear as if they were cut off. We were trained that the design "looked right." It was only by listening to gamers that we understood that confusing element of our design. Once we got that information, it made our decision clean and easy.

Since we're making a product for our gamers, we constantly turn to them for feedback to help us make the best product possible. Not only does it lead to the best outcome for gamers, it makes our jobs easier too.

Karras's team learned a hard, valuable, and necessary lesson by showing off their work to a small group of internal testers. By doing the same with your projects, you'll be better prepared to achieve success on release day.

# Conclusion

The product-development cycle for a mobile application is a lot like the human life cycle: It starts young and ambitious then grows and evolves until it's finally ready to immerse itself in the world. Being a designer during the predevelopment beta tests, meanwhile, is a lot like being in college: doomed to be awkward, uncomfortable, and brimming with a sense of overconfidence that's just asking to be humbled once weaknesses and flaws are pointed out. But over time, you and your app will refine your offerings, ultimately producing a better version when all is said and done.

# CHAPTER 11

# REFRESHING A DESIGN

Among his many other famous sayings, legendary baseball player Yogi Berra was known for his quip, "It ain't over 'til it's over." In the app design game, unfortunately, even when you think a project is over it ain't really over. Once you release a piece of software, there will be many reasons to return to it. Maybe users will find a bug you never noticed. Maybe they'll suggest a function you never thought of. Maybe a new operating system or device will come out that makes you want to update your app. In this chapter, you'll find details on how to go through the process of releasing a new version of your app.

# Improving as a Designer

Once you've shipped the first version of an app to a digital store and you're waiting for it to clear a review period and be released to customers, you're sure to experience a number of vastly different feelings. The first will likely be exhaustion.

Creating an application requires an extraordinary amount of effort, focus, and dedication—especially in the latter stages of a project when tension and stress is high as you work to perfect an app. After that sets in, you'll begin to grasp the weight of what you've done as a designer or developer. It should be a proud moment; you've taken an idea and brought it to reality through lines of code, pixels, bits, and a lot of hard work.

> ## warning
>
> **WATCH FOR BURNOUT**   Long days are no laughing matter when it comes to app development. Toward the end of a project, it's not uncommon to be pushing toward 60-or 70-hour weeks. Don't extend yourself too far, though. Give yourself a break when needed.

These sentiments and sensations will become regular occurrences, but you'll feel the effects most profoundly with your first couple of applications, when you're still becoming familiar with the full development process and all that comes with it. It's perfectly fine to feel the need to take a break and recharge after an app's release, so do whatever it takes to clear your head. But with experience comes the realization that the software-development process is never truly complete. Before long, you'll need to jump back into the routine of daily work.

If you work as a contract developer, you'll soon become accustomed to this repetitive and short project life cycle. After an app is shipped, you'll start working on another one almost immediately (assuming you're getting work regularly), and you'll start the process fresh again and again. You return to step one each time, which helps you grow as a developer and learn how to constantly improve your work. With each new project, you're able to take the knowledge acquired from previous releases and apply it to future work. If nothing else, you have the chance to make good on past mistakes.

Each time you hit the reset button and start a new project, you get the chance to clean up your shop and refine your process, working toward better organization, cleaner code, better-managed files, a smoother workflow, and other logistical improvements. You'll amaze yourself with how much you improve with each subsequent app. In a contract setting, rushing to a new project immediately after finishing one offers opportunities to constantly improve on bad habits.

Consider, for example, re-evaluating your folder layout and naming conventions between projects. Inevitably, you'll start to improperly name files and folders and get sloppy with code, Photoshop layers, and anything else that can be made messy. Your downtime is the ideal

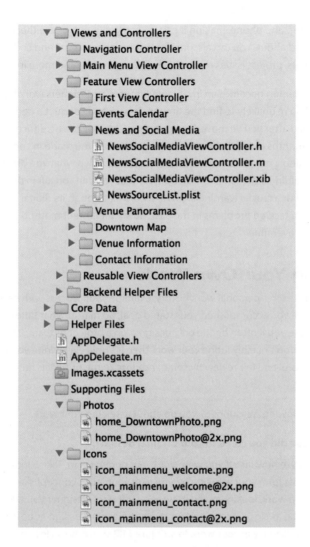

**Figure 11.1**  The file organization on this project isn't bad, but could it be improved?

opportunity to look at the way your last project ended up and commit to methods that will make your future work tidier. Figure 11.1 is an example directory layout that could be used in an iOS app project.

## Maintaining a Work Journal

A work diary is an especially helpful tool for professional app designers (and amateur coders) to get in the habit of using. Create a journal on your computer and keep track of all the work you do each day. You can use an app such as Day One Journal to jot down notes in a file that syncs between your laptop and phone, making it easy to mark your progress either in the office or when you're out and about. You can also integrate third-party scripts and code automation to make all Git commits, project issues resolved, useful bookmarks, and more indexed in the file.

Maintaining a regular log becomes an invaluable resource as designers work through multiple projects rapidly. You're unlikely to find the time to sit back and conduct a deep analysis of your work down the road after you've moved on from a project, as it can be difficult to look back at something a few months old and parse the various decisions you made in code or with an art file. But by dedicating a mere five minutes a day to writing down what you did or new things you tried you're building a personal resource library that you can consult in the future for a spark of inspiration or a crucial warning sign. As you scroll through its digital pages, you'll be able to see how you tackled problems in the past, how your current methods differ, and how much you improve over time.

## Evaluating Your Own Work

When looking back at this personal work history, examine your process with each project to determine how well you accomplished your stated goal, no matter what time constraints you were under. Because you'll often be the only designer on a project or team, it's imperative to self-critique. If you don't harshly judge your work then it's unlikely anyone you work closely with will, and a helpful and fair review by someone close to the project is required for growth as a designer.

Ask yourself the following questions as you go about assessing your work.

- **How close did you come to your original design?**

   First, analyze how far off you were from your original plan. Take a look at the final screenshots from your app side by side with your initial concept sketches and early Photoshop work. Ideally, as you grow as an interface designer you want the final application to be as close in form and function to the initial design as possible in order to increase efficiency in your workflow. Figure 11.2 shows how close the final outcome of an app may look to its initial wireframe.

- **When you diverted from the original course, why did you do so? Did it make the app better?**

   Inevitably, there will be times when your final work looks nothing like your initial sketches or concepts. When that happens, it's time to ask the most important question you'll consider as you look back on your work: Why is the final application different from your original previews? Did you misunderstand the technical requirements? Did your interaction design appear flawed once you actually saw it in code? Did the stakeholder or client disapprove of the route you were taking and force a change? Differences aren't necessarily bad, as you want to do whatever it takes to make the best app

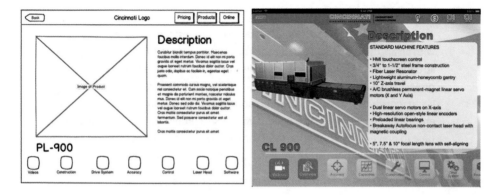

**Figure 11.2**    Just how close in concept was the initial sketch to the final piece of work?

possible; but understanding where breakdowns or diversions occurred can help you anticipate them in the future.

> ## tip
>
> Remember, it doesn't matter *if* you move away from your original design during the development process, but it does matter *why*. When looking back at your work, you should be able to recognize where you made changes for the better, why those changes were necessary, and how they helped in the long run.

- **How pleased are stakeholders, clients, and customers with the design?**

  Did your customer or client rave about the final product? Did they seem disappointed with the initial release? Obviously, the most important people to please if you want to see financial success—and ultimately fund more app projects—are your customers. If you're doing your job right, you should have a good understanding of how to meet their expectations, so these answers shouldn't be a surprise. In the end, though, it's necessary to assess your performance in this area after a project is put to bed.

> ## tip
>
> If you use Google Analytics as your analytics-tracking tool, you can track live data upon release and see how users are interacting with your app on the fly. It may seem like a bit of data overkill, but it's fun to see a surge in stats as people download and try out your app. Look at usage metrics at launch and then some time after to see if users keep with your app over time. This is a great way to judge if customers are enjoying your work.

- ■ **How pleased are you with your design?**

  At the end of the day, you should be your own biggest fan. If you're not content with an app, you won't be a happy designer or developer. The mental and emotional struggle that goes along with putting in late nights or weekend work in order to ship a project will seem less worthwhile if you're unsatisfied, and your future work will suffer if you remain frustrated by a previous app. Operate in a manner that allows you to absolutely love each app you build. If you finish a project you're unhappy with, take time to prevent this frustration from carrying over, and make every effort to ensure you're not left with the same sensation on your next assignment.

- ■ **Where are there potential improvements in your design?**

  No matter how sharp your work looks, there can always be room for improvement. Never rest on your laurels and assume your basic output is good enough. Application development is an extraordinarily competitive market, and if you're not constantly finding ways to improve your talents and become a better designer, you're destined to fall back from the pack. Always give your work a close look—and try to be objective— to find where there's room for improvement in future releases.

# Judging Who Is Worth Listening To

Do you remember that one teacher you had in high school or college who, no matter how hard you tried on a project or paper, always ended up giving you a disappointing grade below what you thought you deserved? Do you remember that you'd show that score to a friend or parent and insist that you tried your hardest, that the grade wasn't your fault, and that the teacher was biased against you? Well, prepare for frightening flashbacks. That's what it feels like to get reviews as an app developer; you'll have the same response to the user or Web site that has bad things to say about your work.

Once your app hits the market and is available to the masses, you can expect to receive feedback on the successes and failures of your work from many sources. You'll most frequently get response via user reviews in app stores as well as e-mails or social-media correspondence and through reviews by app-focused media outlets.

Seeing a poor rating for your application can feel like a punch to the gut. You're bound to make mistakes, and users are sure to pounce all over them. The best developers live, learn, and fix their mistakes. That's what makes them great. Figure 11.3 shows an unfortunately poor response one app received to its latest update. To grow as a designer, you'll have to learn to read through negative reviews and search for keys as to why customers responded poorly.

You could get a staggering, overwhelming amount of feedback soon after launch, so how do you determine what's the most important, what's worth taking to heart, and what should prompt you to consider revisions or updates? Who should you attempt to contact in order to

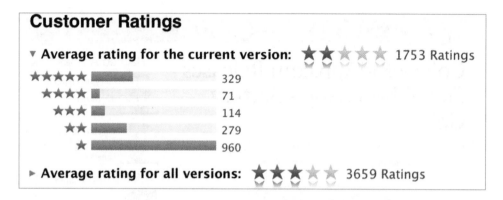

**Figure 11.3**  You will need to learn to overcome poor ratings from reviewers.

get them talking, writing, or tweeting about your product? All comments are valuable, and you should be capable of listening and willing to listen to all commentary, but you can prioritize where to focus your public relations energy. Some outlets warrant more attention, because they have the chance to influence a greater number of people.

## Review Web Sites

Most of your focus should be given to popular app review Web sites (such as AppAdvice.com, shown in Figure 11.4), online influencers in tech (users with tons of Twitter followers, those who write for tech Web sites, etc.), bloggers, and traditional news outlets. These reviewers have the opportunity to reach a wide audience, so it's not uncommon to see developers aggressively reach out to such users over e-mail or social media.

When contacting these valuable users, provide a press kit to help them with the writing or reviewing process. For a mobile app, this should typically include high-resolution screenshots of the app, a large image of the app icon, the text description that appears alongside the app in digital stores, personal contact information in case the writer has follow-up questions, a bullet-point list of key features, a test user account or login credentials (if applicable), links to the application's download location, a free download promo code (if available and provided by the app's current store), and any other information you think might be valuable to someone reviewing or otherwise writing about your work.

Compress the kit as a ZIP file, then make it available to any reviewers or press members who might give the app a test drive. Post these materials online too; there's nothing more frustrating for a journalist or reviewer than going to a digital-media operation's Web site and not finding the necessary images, descriptions, or other information needed when researching a product. This small effort goes a long way toward making life easier for people who can spread the word about your app.

**Figure 11.4**  If you want to generate buzz about your app, you'll have to work hard postrelease to gain some media traction. (Courtesy of Tyler Tschida.)

---

**warning**

**DO A DOUBLE CHECK**  When creating a press kit, don't forget to include all of your contact information and a link to the application along with a free download promo code (if applicable and available from the app store you're selling through). Potentially great launches can be ruined by simple yet devastating mistakes. Cross all your t's, dot all your i's, and make sure the media has every last bit of information it needs.

---

Don't be afraid to e-mail journalists or contact them through social networks. Even though unsolicited messages are likely to have a low impact and reviewers are often inundated with random e-mails, it's always worth a shot. Make every effort to stand out from the crowd when writing these messages; keep them short and to the point, mentioning only the key differentiating features that make your app appealing to the journalist's readers or viewers.

Because cold-calling (or, more appropriately, cold-messaging) can bring minimal results, consider reaching out to these key sources prior to the moment at which you need something from them. Introduce yourself to people who can help with the promotion of your work when attending development conferences, trade shows, or local, digital-related events. When seeking a review or published article about your app, it's better to be working with people you know and who trust your work. When the opportunity arises, take a deep breath, swallow your nerves, and cheerfully introduce yourself to journalists and publishers from your favorite Web sites.

## App Store Reviews

When users are considering downloading or purchasing an app, they look to the simplest place possible for details about prior users' experiences: the review section of digital app stores.

On the Apple, Google, Amazon, and Microsoft online stores, users can submit brief reviews along with a personal rating for any app. These reviews can be especially tough to stomach for application developers, because it's difficult to scroll through feedback you have no control over, no role in screening, or any ability to respond to by directly helping users having problems with your product. You can't even respond to criticism in most app stores—with the exception of Google's, as shown in Figure 11.5—so you're powerless to correct reviews riddled with inaccuracies.

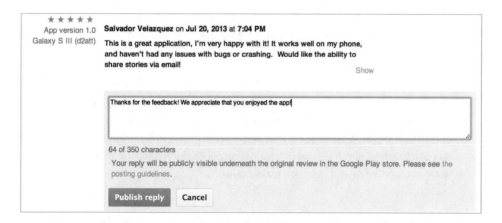

**Figure 11.5**   Google gives developers the opportunity to respond to reviewers' criticisms, something you and other designers would surely like to see adopted by other app stores as well. (Courtesy of Salvador Velazquez.)

These reviews often amount to nothing more than rants or support questions submitted in the wrong forum, making the entire experience frustrating and difficult for the developer. But unfortunately, these comments can have an astonishingly large impact on sales, because they're the last bits of information any end user sees before they decide to tap that all-important "buy" or "download" button.

> **note**
>
> Take comfort in the fact that some portion of an app's success is based on nothing more than plain, dumb luck. Try as you might to ensure that users love your app and rate it highly, you'll also have to rely on luck in order to find success in the digital software marketplace. Sometimes, an app enjoys enormous success because the right person stumbled across it at the right time and spread the word. Other times, maybe you end up near the top of the results for a common search term. Do the best work you can, push your app into the marketplace, and see what happens.

There's not much you can do with these reviews besides live and learn from them, and use them as indicators of what parts of your application needs updating in the future. Most users will never go out of their way to make a formal feature request, but they will leave notes and comments in these reviews; take a look to find out what's suggested frequently, and use that to identify spots for improvement.

## Personal Messages

Users may also try to contact you through personal e-mail or other forms of direct communication, including Twitter, Facebook, or instant-messaging services. These are flattering feedback methods, because it means the user took time to reach out personally and privately to let you know what he or she thinks about your work.

> **warning**
>
> **USERS WANT TO CONTACT YOU**    Users will take advantage of any method possible to contact you—even calling your personal cell phone to complain about a bug or missing feature. If you make information public, people will use that method to get in touch. Be careful what you make available.

Your application may only cost a dollar or nothing at all, but these users took their own valuable time to write a personal e-mail looking for clarity on an issue they had or to let you know about a feature they desire. You should place a lot of significance on any feature request or identified bug that stems from a personal e-mail or similar type of communication. The author clearly cares about your product, so even if the issue they raised wasn't a concern of yours during development, it's worth examining further because a user felt it was important enough to contact you about it.

Research, as well as anecdotal evidence, seems to indicate that personal referrals can account for a large percentage of the downloads and purchases of an application. The users that personally e-mail you show they've already made a huge investment in your product and are likely willing to carry that passion into their daily online or real-world lives and suggest your app to people they come in contact with. By going out of your way to accommodate any features or bugs they let you know about, they'll come to appreciate and respect you as a developer even more, making them passionate, loyal customers who are willing to check out your future work.

## Avoiding Negativity

Criticism is not the same as negativity—and it's important to be able to distinguish between the two. When working in the online world, you'll encounter one trait of online users that is increasingly frustrating and difficult to accept: an insistence on including harsh negativity when assessing anything. As you scan e-mails or Web reviews of your product, you can easily become overwhelmed by the sheer amount of harsh putdowns.

Although the anonymity provided by the Internet can be a great quality, it can also be a major drawback, especially in the way it changes behavior. If you go to a restaurant and get service that's slightly below average, you don't spend a long time belittling the waiter or shaming the manager. That'd be rude and unnecessary, making you and everyone around you embarrassed or uncomfortable. But on the Internet, where nearly every user has a pseudonym and there's no fear of public confrontation, humans adopt a shockingly unrestrained attitude and become more harsh and offensive than they ever would be when talking to another person face to face.

While reading through and considering feedback, separate the constructive criticism from the unproductive negativity. A user who offers helpful comments is letting you know about a potential downfall or issue with your app but doing so in a way that allows you to understand the problem and develop a path toward resolving it. Critical users are tactful and polite, contributing a thoughtful assessment that helps you improve your work. Destructive tactics such as personal attacks or harsh language only seek to tear you and your app down, offering no opportunity for learning, growth, or improvement.

In the end, there's not enough time in the day to worry about people who only want to discourage you or dampen your spirits, so do your best to only focus on giving time and consideration to individuals willing to help you get better at what you do and, as a result, make better experiences for the very users who are reviewing your products.

# Turning Requests into Changes

Along with all the criticism—helpful and discouraging—will also come many requests for additional features or user-generated ideas of features users would like to see added. As you scour through feedback, you're sure to come across many suggestions of how outsiders think your work can be improved that almost always require significantly more work.

Dealing with these feature requests should be managed in a way similar to how you dealt with bugs in the development process, meaning that you'll need a formal method of processing this information. As you receive suggestions, you'll want to turn them into reviewable data and create a standard procedure for how to decide what should be worked on immediately and what can be saved for a later version.

The issue tracker you used when dealing with bugs—a service such as GitHub or Bitbucket (see Figure 11.6)—may still be the best tool available to accomplish this task. Whenever a user

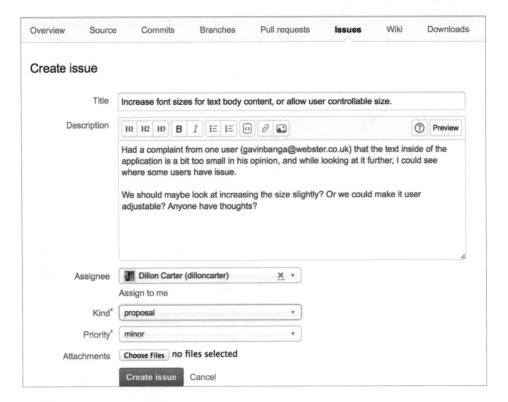

**Figure 11.6**   Most trackers contain specific tags for proposed features and allow users to vote on the ideas or suggestions they think are best.

makes a request, you should file an issue ticket just as you did for a bug, and then you can tag that issue as a feature request and manage it just as you did with any other issue throughout the project's development. You can then keep track of and eliminate duplicate requests, set milestones for when you plan on implementing requests, and leave comments or attach photos that can help teammates in the programming and design phases down the road.

Whenever you receive user feedback, be certain to report and track that information immediately. The longer you wait to process feedback through formal channels, the more likely it is that information will be lost or forgotten. Direct user feedback is arguably the most important and influential information you'll receive throughout the development process, so it's essential to take it seriously and ensure you get as much utility out of it as you possibly can.

Although your issue tracker can help you sift through multiple reports of the same issue, pay attention to elements that generate repeated inquiries. A number of requests on the same subject or feature should indicate to you and your team that there's demand for a certain function within your app (see Figure 11.7). In the software industry, it's often said that one bug ID or feature request is isolated and not important, but if the same thing is spotted or asked for twice it likely means that dozens of users are thinking the same thing but have not come forward. If you get multiple messages covering the same territory, note this increased demand and consider working it into an update soon.

Postrelease feedback is also an important way to double-check the key decisions you made throughout the development process. As you get responses from users, see if they relate to any changes you made while planning out your app. If users request a feature you cut or are complaining about things you added, it's a red flag that a move you made along the way was a mistake. Learn from what your users bring to your attention, reflect on where you went wrong, and incorporate this revised approach into your next project.

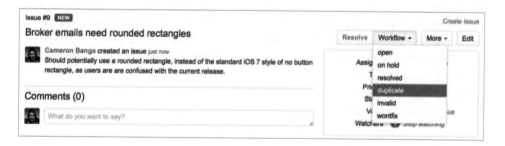

**Figure 11.7** Consider creating individual suggestion tickets for each user request and marking duplicates in your tracker. This takes a bit more time, but it offers much more detail on what precisely is being requested by each user.

# Preparing Users for Design Changes

The update and revision process isn't all sunshine and rainbows, unfortunately. At some point in your career, you're going to have to release a new version of an app that removes a feature or makes a drastic change that users might not take kindly to. Making such decisions will be extremely tough, as doing so involves determining when to cut an element loose because it's holding the rest of the app back or it's simply not functioning as intended anymore. In order to make an improvement that benefits 99 percent of users, you'll have to do something that angers the other 1 percent.

> ## note
>
> If you haven't worked on many software projects before, the idea of removing features may seem absurd. Why eliminate anything? It's nothing more than lines of code! As your project totals grow, however, you'll learn that keeping up with code over various operating system upgrades and new device releases involves considerable work. Eventually, all good things must end, and you'll find yourself in a situation in which you have to cut out a feature that someone enjoys.

When faced with these situations, feedback coupled with solid analytics will help you make an informed decision about how to improve your app while angering as few users as possible. If services such as Google Analytics support your notions of which features are rarely used or underutilized, you can make statistically supported calls about where to focus your improvement efforts or where you can afford to cut code or resources.

The development team at 9magnets, for example, worked on an app for a pro sports franchise awhile back in which addition by subtraction proved possible and effective. In the section of the app that showed the team's upcoming games, there was a single view deep in the schedule page that was rarely used and grew difficult for the developers to make look right on the ballooning variety of Android screen sizes. By taking a look at user statistics on an analytics platform and talking with users directly, the team determined that the page was rarely visited and was used only when a person needed more information about where a game could be seen on TV. With this information in hand, the developers were able to include that small detail in a more prevalent place on the schedule page, which both increased user satisfaction of the application and helped navigate around a design challenge.

Although to outsiders it may seem illogical to ever remove functionality from an app, there are many reasons why a development team might want to cut features from an app after it has hit the market.

First, you may want to remove a feature to replace it with something similar or make room for a revised user interface. Second, the feature could have become an unexpected nightmare to support and simply might not be worth the time required to keep it from breaking down. You may run into such circumstances when a new operating system comes out and drastically changes the interaction methods you've designed and built around. As you find a way to conform your app to a platform's new specifications, you may be forced to drop certain elements in the name of conversion simplicity. Finally, there may simply be situations in which you're reworking your code base for a new version of an app, and you need to start from scratch in order to make the product cleaner and more functional. At that point, certain features won't be worth the effort if only a small number of users are taking advantage of them.

No matter how underused you think a feature is or how much you believe it won't be missed, there's sure to be a section—however small—of your user base that will sorely miss it once it's gone, and they'll let you know it. There are ways, though, to prepare yourself and your users so that there's minimal backlash or pushback from consumers when you take away a feature some of them grew accustomed to using.

The most important thing you can do is create a plan or strategy for users who will be affected so that when they approach you with the issue you already have a game plan that will help them see the minimal impact the change has on their lives. If you remove a feature they've depended on, but replace it with a similar one that accomplishes the same outcome, let them know about it. If all it takes to reach the same end is a small change to their personal workflow, point this out to them. If absolutely nothing else works, direct them to another app—even from a competitor—that they can turn to achieve what your feature previously did.

It's also worthwhile to make it easy for users to export data from an app in a standard format— a TXT or CSV file—so they can take the work they've produced in your program and move it to a different piece of software that might better suit their needs after you remove support for a certain feature. Offer as much warning as possible regarding any changes on the horizon, including blog posts and e-mails that can educate users about the reasons for, significance of, and extent of any changes in functionality. You don't want to surprise users when suddenly, after a small update, everything looks or works differently than what they've become familiar with.

## note

Data portability is a concept that involves making the user-created information in an application available in files readable by either humans or computers. This allows the user to leave an app with data in hand if they find a more effective alternative. It's not required, but it can often be an easy way to build goodwill with your users, as they will trust you with their data because they can always export it and go elsewhere if need be.

It may seem counterproductive or unnecessary to spend so much time caring about a small subsection of users, especially if it means you're encouraging them to download a piece of software from someone else. But remember, recommendations are often the most important spark that fuels downloads and revenue. By caring about the users affected by even a small change, you show you care about their well-being more than you care about any revenue you gain from them; ultimately, that will make them more likely to support your future projects or encourage others to try your products.

As in any business, the customer is always right, and their feelings are always important. Be appreciative that your users are showing concern when they contact you with frustrations or questions over the removal of a feature they depended on. Be sympathetic and understanding. Never blame users for the anger or confusion they express over your decision. Don't ignore them either, or their discontent will only grow. Be honest and empathetic, and you'll prove capable of keeping any backlash to a minimum.

# The Resubmission Process

As you prepare your team for the update process and ready your app for resubmission to the appropriate app stores, recognize that this process is not the same as the one you went through upon original release. There are a handful of significant differences you must be aware of as you get set to release a new version of an existing app.

First, you've got to prepare for the high expectations of your established user base who, after some time getting to know your app, will have higher performance standards than your original beta testers. They could be reliant upon your app to perform any number of functions throughout their day, so they won't have the patience for radical new interaction models or daring redesigns. They want familiarity and consistency with modest improvements; they don't want to relearn an app each time you feel like putting out an update.

This could prove to be a challenge for development teams as you work on applications with a long lifespan, because users will develop an expectation of continued support across new operating system versions and device styles. The mobile landscape will continue to change, as evidenced by recent releases of a larger iPhone, a dramatically different visual design in iOS 7, and the proliferation of Android phones and tablets. Users will demand that you stay on top of all these changes and adapt your product to each new platform or device.

As you do so, be conscious of the simultaneous responsibility of appeasing old users but hooking new users. You want to keep existing consumers happy and comfortable with an app they've come to enjoy, but you must also make an app that is continually drawing in fresh customers. With every update, your application must remain coherent and appealing to these two distinct sets of users. It's a struggle to keep an app looking brand new and full of improved features while not pushing reliable users outside their comfort zone, but that's why you're the one making the app and they're the ones using it.

Similarly, you must be cognizant of the fact that your application must maintain a brand over time, even for users who haven't downloaded or used your app before. Be careful not to make significant color, icon, or name changes as you prepare future releases. Every development team will get the itch to change their primary icon style or dream of testing out a new color if an initial launch isn't immediately successful. Users, though, have come to associate your app with a certain look, even those users you may not think are aware of you. If someone goes looking for your app but can't quickly recognize it by the logo, color, or style they connect it with, they may move on, never giving your app a longer look. Visual changes, although exciting to your team, may have negative consequences for user-base growth.

## IN-DEPTH

When it comes to Hollywood blockbusters, sequels are rarely better than the originals. That's not always the case in the world of digital apps, though. With the opportunity to improve on design, interaction methods, and functionality, the second iteration of an app can often be better than the first. Here are a few that have done that particularly well.

- **Grades 2**: This sequel—which allows students to track their grades across several classes—from iOS development studio Tapity saw extraordinary success, building upon the original version through better artwork, more features, and tighter interaction design. The work was highly regarded, even winning a coveted Apple Design Award.

- **Plants vs. Zombies 2**: This cult hit mobile game by PopCap Games took a bit of a different route than its predecessor, which was originally released for desktop computers and video game consoles then later ported over to mobile phones. Because the phone apps—with simple gameplay and clear interface setups—were such a success, the developer actually went ahead and launched the sequel for mobile first, targeting iOS and Android platforms. The plan was a success, leading to one of the biggest app launches of all time.

- **Fantastical 2**: This iOS calendar application has long been considered the gold standard for scheduling, with its powerful ability to parse natural language into calendar events. Just type in "Stop for coffee with Mallory at 2 p.m." and the app will add an event to your calendar for 2 p.m. titled "Coffee with Mallory." The sequel added greater performance, a reminder function, cleaner visual design, and the ability to view maps of event locations. These additions made it a huge success after its release.

## Conclusion

By following this long set of suggested steps, you'll be able to design, develop, test, release, and revise an application. Don't be too humble when a piece of software you design finally hits the app store; it's a remarkable achievement. Building a complete mobile application from start to finish is an impressive feat. You should be extremely proud.

After completing your app, it's time to go back to the beginning and start this difficult yet rewarding process all over again. If you stay committed and focus on continually improving, you're sure to have a long and successful career as a mobile interaction designer.

# STANDOUT APPS

There's no better way to learn than by checking out concrete examples, especially when working to improve your mobile app design. But where should you begin? This appendix aims to highlight some of the best-designed multiplatform mobile apps. These products are extraordinary programs that function on both iOS and Android, remaining true to their respective platforms while still producing an exceptional mobile interaction experience. Check out these apps as you look to grow as a mobile designer; they're excellent standards to learn (and perhaps borrow) from.

**Figure A.1**   No matter your platform, 1Password offers a quality native app.

# 1Password

If you've never heard of 1Password, consider downloading a copy of it as soon as possible. It provides an extremely valuable service that helps to secure your different Web service accounts, your banking information, and other digital valuables. If you store valuable information on the Internet—and who doesn't these days?—you'll sleep easier at night using a service like 1Password (Figure A.1).

Because 1Password looks to push and revise the way users handle their passwords, it's necessary to provide quality and useful mobile applications for both Android and iOS. Not only must the applications be available, but they should also be designed to be a frictionless experience that's easy to use and extremely responsive. The team behind this app has done a great job of providing apps focused on the user, regardless of platform.

# Amazon Mobile

There's no better online shopping location than Amazon.com, and what's true for the Web rings true for mobile as well. Amazon is just as spectacular on phones and tablets as it is online, thanks to a speedy and powerful mobile browsing experience augmented with additions only possible on mobile, such as the ability to scan physical barcodes and check a product's price (or even buy that product) on Amazon.

Amazon's applications are great cross-platform references because their design shows successful tactics for handling interaction and features at scale. These apps are used by millions of consumers on a variety of different phones and tablets, and the company's business is dependent on the app to satisfy consumer needs and sell more products.

Because these apps are a significant sales tool for the Internet's largest merchant, you know that the interaction methods and interface principles inside its apps are the result of hundreds of hours of work and discussion, and no decision was taken lightly.

# CNN News

Modern news programming is a 24/7 beast, requiring stations to race to put out content first over a multitude of different media types. Written articles, videos, audio, and photography must all be shared on a variety of mediums: TV, the Web, social media, and more. Mobile apps are just another complicated variable to add to that equation, as seen in Figure A.2.

**Figure A.2**  Formatting on-screen views to look great when handling photos, videos, text, and other content can be tough, yet CNN makes it look easy. (Courtesy of Francisco Velazquez.)

CNN has done a fantastic job with its mobile applications, providing as much news as it possibly can in a design that's comprehendible and simple and in a way that suits the needs of and differences between Android and iOS. It's a fantastic release no matter the operating system or form factor you're using.

# Coach's Eye

Coach's Eye is a bit of an outlier on this list. Whereas most apps listed in this appendix are produced by large, established corporations or teams, Coach's Eye is made by a team known mostly for niche video that doesn't have the big budget of a large multinational company.

The app is built to solve a difficult technical problem as well: How do you accurately and easily allow a user to dissect video of golf or baseball bat swings in a way that offers a clear indication to the coach of how the player is performing? Plenty of technical design restrictions arise when discussing an app that lays graphics on top of videos. Throw in multiple platforms and you really have a task to tackle.

The team behind this app solved the issue by focusing on simplicity and creating an interface that directs and guides the user how to complete his task. Once video has been taken, well-designed and simple tools allow for the overlay of various editing and markup aids to help coaches teach athletes the proper way to perform their tasks on the field. In porting its iOS app to Android, the team maintained the look and notable features of the Coach's Eye brand while also focusing on simplicity and ensuring a great experience on both operating systems. If you plan on integrating video into your app, this is a strong example to use as reference and inspiration.

# Evernote

Mobile devices have given a big push to the note-taking market, as users saw their new, constantly-in-hand, always-online devices as a great way to jot down notes during the days. Evernote has been the best performer in this market so far, with apps for all leading mobile and desktop computing platforms. They've brought successful apps to market on iOS, Android, and Windows Phone 8 as well as traditional Windows and Macintosh computers; they even have a Web browser version.

The product has been built from two steadfast principles. First, it's been extremely reliable regardless of platform, even when performing complex tasks such as syncing large notebooks across multiple devices or operating systems. Second, its world-class design team has excelled at providing unique, intuitive, tailored interaction experiences on all platforms. On a mobile phone, you get a great experience for working on the go, and on a tablet, you get an experience catered toward situations in which you're likely to use a larger screen.

Evernote is perhaps the best example of cross-platform design excellence fit and finished for individual platforms. Obviously, it's created by a large company with many resources, which allows for a lot of time to detail each app to a specific platform. You, on the other hand, are likely to have a variety of constraints pressed upon you that will make it impossible to reach its level of support, but it's a great piece of software to aspire to.

# Facebook

Facebook has gone from a college dorm startup to the largest social network in the history of the Internet—now with more than one billion users—and the company's stock has become a darling of Wall Street, sparked by growth and monetization of its mobile applications.

Facebook was an early leader of the HTML5 app format, in which Web standards components were integrated into the mobile application and development practices, leading to a mobile app that relied little on platform-specific interface and interaction models. Instead, Web tools were used so that much of the interface and interaction design could quickly and easily be ported between iOS and Android. However, this created a somewhat lackluster experience for the user, as the Web components were not as fast as those of a native interface, meaning that the lagging user interface would often be unresponsive in loading images or user comments.

The Facebook team overhauled its applications, going native for iOS and Android in 2012. This led to a much better user experience, with faster load times and an interface that was more responsive to touch. As a result, in-store reviews rose significantly, and users were much happier with the sleeker, speedier app compared to its slower, less native predecessor. Going native also gave Facebook the opportunity to innovate with new features, such as the creation of Facebook Home for Android (shown in Figure A.3), allowing for constant communication with users even when outside of the Facebook app.

Facebook represents great interaction design because of the wide variety of content types available for consumption, expertly formatted for smooth mobile viewing and interaction.

**Figure A.3** Facebook Home introduced "Chat Heads," a persistent icon bubble using nifty physics that allows users constant chat capability with their friends.

Facebook has photos, videos, text statuses, calendar events, and much more. The high number of information types available here means that no matter what type of data you're looking to display in your app, Facebook probably has taken something similar and made it look great.

# Flipboard

Flipboard was a hot name in Silicon Valley after its release for the original iPad because it offered a fun and interesting way to quickly flip through a variety of news stories. "Flip" here was meant literally; the app had a unique and novel animation in which a user would use a finger to flick around stories set up like cards in a poker deck. The app made reading the news on the iPad a unique experience that felt new to the platform.

Over time, Flipboard has brought its magic to Android and the iPhone, porting its fun animations to smaller screens. It's a great example of targeting multiple platforms with a unique style and interaction method.

Flipboard offers a ton of value as you learn to tinker with animation, complex art layering, shadowing, variable-length typography, and photography. Take a look at how its team has managed small, animated transitions and visual presentations; there's much to learn here.

# Google Chrome

Google's Chrome Web browser is a strong example of an application that has adapted well to multiple operating systems. Web browsers are among the most highly used applications on any operating system or device, and mobile is no different; various programs allow users to view any Web site from their phones or tablets.

Google has built Chrome to be a minimalistic browser focused on speed and simplicity. On both iOS and Android, the browser is designed to place rendered Web content front and center. Whereas many designers and developers focus on adding features and increasing complexity, Chrome is a testament to interface design that serves a strong purpose while also allowing the app's content to be front and center.

Open the browser and visit your favorite site, and you'll see how the application is focused on bringing Web content to the forefront. Paired with a strong feature set, such as bookmark syncing with the desktop app, the browser delivers a top mobile experience.

# Google Maps

Having maps and navigation information constantly available has become one of the most important features on smartphone devices, as users can now look up critical location information anywhere they can get a cellular connection. Google quickly became the Internet's leader in online mapping, and its Google Maps applications for Android and iOS cemented its claim to the top spot, bringing easy-to-use mapping data to both platforms.

The Web search giant has seen success with both Google Chrome and Google Maps because it's worked hard to meet the interaction conventions of each specific platform. If you ever work on an application that requires cross-platform integration of location-focused data, Google Maps is an excellent example you can build and learn from.

# Instagram

Instagram is a remarkable photo service that began on the iPhone a few years ago as a simple photo-taking/filtering/sharing service, but it quickly evolved into one of the most popular and powerful social networks in the world. The network was purchased by Facebook reportedly with a $1 billion dollar combination of cash and stock options, a huge amount for such a site.

The network grew so quickly and commanded such a price because it was the best and easiest way on a mobile phone to share stylized photos with friends on the Web, Android or iPhone devices, and social networks such as Twitter or Facebook. In short, Instagram became valuable because it was the best tool for photography on a mobile phone. Why? Because on both iOS and Android the application had a simple and intuitive interaction method that empowered users to take wonderful photos quickly and easily. If simplicity is your target, you'd do well to have your arrow land on Instagram (shown in Figure A.4).

The team at Instagram focused the bulk of its efforts on presenting beautiful photos and letting others view those photos simply and easily. Speed is key in any interface, and Instagram made it easy to keep scrolling and scrolling through compelling images.

**Figure A.4** Instagram only does photo sharing, and it does it really well. (Courtesy of Kenneth B. Sothman.)

# Instapaper

Instapaper (shown in Figure A.5) offers one of the best mobile reading experiences, allowing users to quickly save Web pages for reading later offline via an iPhone, iPad, or Android device. The service is invaluable for users who travel often or commute to work and desire ample reading material.

The app is renowned for its simplicity and its focus on fantastic design, with industry-leading typography and legibility. Regardless of platform, the app has strived to provide the most well-presented reading experience possible on mobile, and has succeeded with flying colors. If you're building an app in which users will be reading large bodies of text, this app is a great example of how to best format and present clear, legible text.

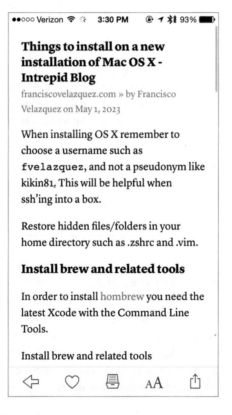

**Figure A.5** If you're working with typography, study and learn from Instapaper.

# MLB.com At Bat

So far, this list has included a variety of great utilities and social networks, but where are the entertainment apps? If you're a sports fan looking for examples of phenomenal cross-platform software, take a look at what Major League Baseball has developed over the past few years with their MLB.com At Bat application for iOS and Android.

MLB has done an amazing job of bringing an assortment of entertainment content to mobile: live game video, short highlights, condensed games, radio broadcasts, news stories, player interviews, standings, scores, and much more. No matter what device you're on, you'll always get great, platform-perfect interaction from this app.

When looking at ways to best format and manage rich media content, check out MLB's mobile work for inspiration. They've done an extraordinary job, and you'll learn much from their example.

# Twitter

The popular social network Twitter went public in 2013, powered largely by successful growth on its Android and iPhone mobile apps. Like most free social networks, the service survives on ad revenue, and the designers on the Twitter team have worked extensively to integrate ads into their app's mobile experience.

The iOS app was long the gold standard for the service. The official app was a re-release of the independent app Tweetie by Loren Brichter—which Twitter itself acquired in 2010—long considered the far-and-away best way to blast 140-character updates from an iPhone. The mobile team did some minor redesign work to better match the color and feel for Twitter's brand, but the initial release of the official app for iPhone looked much like its forefather.

Twitter followed up with constant iterations to the interface and an eventual port to Android that featured a similar interaction style. As for interaction methods, Twitter excelled with the tab bar–style interface made popular in iOS, but that is unavailable as a standard interface component on Android. To counter this, the team designed a slightly modified take on the action bar, allowing for a similar experience that feels more at home on the platform. This lets designers port over much of their interaction work and visual styles from the iPhone to the Android. Because changes or updates can then be applied to both versions of the app, the similarities allow for rapid release cycles and other timeframe benefits.

Twitter stands out because its designers have accepted vastly different interaction expectations on Android and iPhone. They've focused on optimizing versions for each platform, with a coherent and distinct focus on the content people want: tweets on their timeline. The interface does a great job at keeping its primary goal as the focal point, then adding secondary features as need be.

# TuneIn Radio

Another great example of entertainment gone multiplatform, TuneIn Radio (Figure A.6) provides access to hundreds of radio stations on the go. The design may seem simple and easy to
jump across multiple platforms, but it can truly be difficult in practice, especially when juggling
such large groups of data. With hundreds of stations nested into a variety of categories, geo-
locational tie-ins, and more, it's not an easy app to port over to new platforms.

The developers of TuneIn Radio, though, have done a fantastic job of adapting their work in a
way that stays true to the brand and feel of the application while keeping complexity low and
functionality high. If you're looking to design cross-reference apps that handle a large quantity
of options or data, this is a great reference for interaction guidance.

**Figure A.6**   TuneIn Radio offers a great example of how to organize and structure large quantities of
data and menus.

# Wolfram|Alpha

Wolfram|Alpha is one of the most interesting search engines available on the Internet—primarily because it's less of a search engine and more of a knowledge engine. Enter in a math problem, and it will solve it. Ask for a US president's birthday, and it will give you the date along with the day of the week it occurred. For a variety of complex questions, Wolfram|Alpha will send back extremely detailed responses.

It's these fact-filled replies that make the production of this multiplatform application difficult. Through a couple of operating systems and many different device sizes and form factors, responses need to be presented in a legible and coherent way whether the output contains short bursts of text, long strings, photos, digital graphics, etc. If the sheer variety of potential different design formats required doesn't make you sympathetic toward the app's design team, just imagine the potential outliers and edge cases they have to prepare and design for given the quantity of data they're working with. If you're bringing a reference app to iOS and Android, this is a great study guide.

# APPS FOR DESIGNERS

You can't be the best carpenter if you don't have the best tools. Luckily, it doesn't take much effort to assemble a strong toolbox. Throughout this book, a handful of apps have been mentioned in passing, but this appendix is a quick reference of the ones that are more than worthwhile to look at when building your own designs.

Note that some of these tools are only available on OS X; but if you're on Windows, fear not. Many of these apps are available for that platform, or other apps exist that can perform similar tasks.

# Adobe Photoshop

If you've ever done any visual design, either for print or digital mediums, you've inevitably heard of (or hopefully used) Adobe's Photoshop. Even if you haven't, the application is so popular that it's become a colloquial verb, with even your mother knowing that images are manipulated by "Photoshopping" them.

There have been many other applications that attempt to perform similar work as Photoshop, and many of these tools are phenomenal at providing similar functionality for a quarter of the price (or even less). Pixelmator by the Pixelmator Team has become a leading competitor for pixel editing, if you're looking for an able alternative.

If you're new to the world of design, however, Photoshop takes the cake. There are thousands of art technique tutorials available on the Web, and nearly all of them assume that you have Photoshop as your graphic design tool.

If you plan on working in mobile for the long haul, invest in Photoshop or, even better, Adobe's Creative Cloud suite of applications. They're simply the best software available for creative types, and they will be your primary tools for pushing pixels.

# Balsamiq

After completing some technical documentation, you'll often jump into a wireframing application to lay out the interface in detail for your programmers, detailing each interface component that will be implemented on every screen throughout the app. This way, once the programmer goes to create the app, they'll understand exactly how the different views and buttons should interact with each other and flow.

Balsamiq (Figure B.1) is a great tool to do just that, as it's available on a variety of platforms, offers a variety of prepackaged mobile stencils and wireframe assets, and provides a simple visual style that shuns ornamentation in favor of clarity. It helps designers quickly build wireframes that can be shared with stakeholders and programmers while empowering your team to iterate extremely quickly based on what you hear back. It's an invaluable tool to help document how you expect a user to interact with your app.

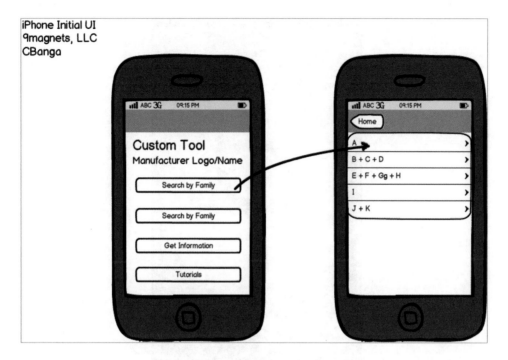

**Figure B.1**   Wireframes allow you to quickly put together an idea of how you want an application to flow between views and functionalities.

# Bugshot

Bugshot is a simple, handy, iOS-only application—by Marco Arment of Tumblr and Instapaper fame—that serves a single purpose. It allows you to take any screenshot from your iPhone and iPad and quickly annotate it with arrows or boxes or even blur out confidential information you don't want shared, such as the contents of a private message.

In Figure B.2, an arrow has been pointed at a shadow that needs to be fixed, and some location text has been blurred out because a client has made the team sign a non-disclosure agreement; thus nothing critical will be made public if this image leaks out.

**Figure B.2**  Bugshot makes it easy to quickly mark up screenshots for teammates.

Designers use the tool on an almost daily basis when working on design iterations and creating bug reports for programmers. If some formatting is wonky or something goes awry visually, take a screenshot and load it into the app so you can quickly point out what you want to bring to your programmer's attention, making both of your lives easier.

## Dribbble

Dribbble, owned and operated by the aptly named Dribbble LLC, is less of a tool and more of a social network located on the Web at Dribbble.com. It's a community of designers taking time to showcase and preview their latest work to fellow designers in hopes of gaining feedback and critiques.

The Web site can be a great place to pitch your work to others who make a living pushing pixels and to obtain evaluations from designers who have worked on app and Web site designs for large, successful projects. It can often be invaluable to hear feedback on your interface or inter-action design from peers, many of whom have worked at large startups, and Dribbble offers this service for free.

Dribbble is also a great source of inspiration for when you're fighting designer's block. Thumb through work done by your peers and see what they're dreaming up. Often, it can be a great way to see what's new and popular; don't copy, but do be inspired.

# Icon Slate

When designing mobile apps, you'll inevitably need to create a variety of icon sizes to go along with the app code you ship off to the Google Play Store, Apple App Store, or other mobile market. Most platforms require three to five different icons of various sizes. Often, the required sizes change as new operating system versions or devices are released, making it hard to keep track of the requirements.

Icon Slate by Jeremy Marchand helps make that process easy for you by indicating the latest size specifications for each mobile platform. It asks you to pick an image to be fitted into the various size requirements, lets you preview your icon at each respective size, and then neatly exports art files into a folder for insertion into your app project.

Although it's a great tool when building iOS or Android app icons, it can also be used to build a variety of desktop operating system and Web icons as well. If you're picking up design projects for other digital mediums, this app can often lend a hand in other ways.

Icons are often one of the most important things you'll create in any design, so it's important to have a tool that helps you design them extremely well. Icon Slate is the tool you'll need to do your job correctly.

# MindNode Pro

Many designers are big fans of the art of mind mapping. They tend to be visual people, and when working with a variety of technical programming concepts, feature sets, design com-promises, and stakeholder requirements mind maps are a great way to combine feedback and requirements into a simple, well-organized visualization. All parties can then follow along thanks to a structured, clear format.

> **note**
>
> Unfamiliar with mind mapping? This process was discussed in Chapter 4, and designers can find a lot of value in its practice. Fun fact: This entire book was outlined in MindNode Pro.

MindNode Pro by IdeasOnCanvas GmbH allows for easy creation of mind maps using fast keyboard shortcuts. Just hit the tab key to break off into a child branch or press the return key to spin off a sibling branch. Do you have a structure that helps you visualize the task at hand? Feel free to add color or text styles to get your point across.

Consider starting projects with mind maps as it's a great way to reach a middle ground with involved parties. For creating a basic early design document that's easily understood and discussed by designers, programmers, and managers, MindNode Pro should be your tool of choice.

Mind maps are a quick way to get ideas into a tangible format so they can be shared and discussed with other team members. They aren't the only way to do it, though; some designers use slideshow tools such as PowerPoint, word processors, or even pen and paper to get their ideas into a form that can be exchanged with others and built upon.

# Pngyu

Inside any application, you're likely to have dozens, if not hundreds, of various art file assets. Most commonly, you'll be using PNG files, the format preferred by Apple and Google for use on iOS and Android, respectively.

PNG is a lossy format, although many applications tend to produce PNG images with inefficient compression, which can account for a significant amount of fluff in file size. On mobile platforms, where megabytes can make or break an experience, it's imperative that you optimize for file size and create the lightest-weight app possible.

Pngyu is an open-source utility that compresses PNG assets and makes them lean-and-mean digital fighting machines, cutting away anything that's unnecessary. You should always throw PNGs through some sort of compression tool before shipping a file app because it can cut away as much as 20 to 25 percent of the application's binary size with no loss in quality.

# Skitch

Skitch by Evernote is quickly becoming a favorite of iOS and Android designers who are looking to transition as much work as possible to the vector format. In the early days of mobile, raster formats were more than adequate, but as the industry moves toward higher resolution displays and various aspect ratios, many designers are trying to create as much as possible in the vector format in order to future-proof their work.

Skitch has become the go-to tool for icons and visuals that can benefit from vector construction thanks to its intuitive interface and powerful filters and shading tools. If you're looking to create a high-resolution app icon that could be later blown up to fit even on a billboard if necessary, Skitch is a great tool to use.

# Spark Inspector

Spark Inspector by Foundry376 is a tool that is only usable for iOS development, but it's extremely valuable in helping to design interaction and interfaces for the iPhone and iPad. Spark Inspector is a runtime inspection tool that allows you to view interface files in a pseudo-3-D state in order to better visualize layers and then make changes directly to interface files and see the results live in the iOS simulator running on your Mac.

The workflow it offers is a game-changing method of editing iOS interfaces. Traditionally, a designer would make a change to an interface file, recompile the application for testing, see how the change looks, and adjust if necessary. Spark Inspector, however, allows you to make changes live and see them implemented immediately. There's no need to recompile, which is a time-consuming process, especially when applications become larger and more complex. For any designer tackling an iOS project, Spark Inspector is a worthwhile tool that soon pays for itself many times over.

# xScope

As a designer, you'll spend a lot of time measuring pixels, zooming in on specific parts of the screen to get a close-up view of animations, and verifying or editing colors. Luckily for you, xScope by The Iconfactory is built by designers who also spend a lot of time counting pixels and overanalyzing animations.

The tool measures pixel dimensions, provides multiple on-screen rulers or guides, zooms in to show pixel-level detail, shows how your app will look for users who have color blindness, and even mirrors art assets to your phone or tablet to test color accuracy and visuals, as shown in Figure B.3.

xScope is an invaluable tool that designers use daily. Using it to measure distances is amazing; when working on interaction design, you'll often find yourself trying to space pieces specific pixel distances apart, which can be difficult or impossible to manage with the naked eye.

**Figure B.3**    xScope lets you see a microscopic view of apps you're building, getting a better perspective on details such as shadows, spacing, and alignment.

# ARTWORK REQUIREMENTS FOR ANDROID AND IOS

Of the platforms on the market today, two standout in the mobile industry. Android and iOS account for a vast majority of the mobile devices currently in use, and nearly every popular app targets these platforms first. Thus, it's likely these operating systems will be where you focus your initial development efforts. This appendix is a quick-look guide for important technical requirements of each platform: layout icon sizes, suggested image formats, art file naming conventions, and other technicalities you'll need to know about as you begin designing.

# Android

Much of the previous discussion on art decisions and design tactics has used general terms, attempting to provide resources and tips that would be valuable no matter what platform you target. But there are some specific art and detail requirements that exclusively apply to Android. Let's take a look at some of these.

## Icon Sizes

For Android, you'll be working with what are called launcher images for your application icon. The launcher image is the first thing users see on the device after they download an app, and this icon sits on the user's home screen, waiting to be tapped to launch your software.

Android works on a scaled ratio system, with assets created for different display densities based on some mathematical logic. All Android phones can be categorized by screen density: medium (MDPI), high (HDPI), extra high (XHDPI), extra extra high (XXHDPI), and extra extra extra high (XXXHDPI). That can be a bit confusing, but it essentially allows for assets to be scaled up depending upon density. In the past, it was common to support low-density displays, but today Google recommends that you ignore this antiquated size.

With these different sizes, you'll basically be creating icons at different multiples of the MDPI size, which is 48×48 pixels. For more information on the scaling (called 2:3:4:6:8 scaling), see this book's online resource links or the iconography section at http://developer.android.com. For Android icons, you'll need to produce the following sizes:

- MDPI: 48×48 pixels
- HDPI: 72×72 pixels
- XHDPI: 96×96 pixels
- XXHDPI: 144×144 pixels
- XXXHDPI: 192×192 pixels
- Google Play Store size: 512×512 pixels

Icon images must be placed inside a square art file at these specific resolutions, but there is no requirement that your icon be square shaped. This means you can create any sort of shape that suits the taste of your app. Google recommends the images be front-facing, as if the user is slightly above the icon—essentially, how it would look if you were seeing the icon on a shelf.

## General Art File Format

iOS and Android both use PNG art assets whenever possible for a variety of reasons. First, PNG is a lossless format, which means that when the image is saved from its original source the file size will be compressed as much as possible, but the image will not be degraded to a lower quality.

This is in stark contrast to the common image format JPEG, which you're undoubtedly familiar with from photos on the internet. JPEG is a lossy format, which means that the image will be more significantly compressed, but only by sacrificing quality. Sophisticated algorithms are used to compress the image further, and the decrease in quality is unnoticeable to most users; but if you kept saving a JPEG over and over again, you'd begin to see color blurring and pixelation in the image.

PNG also has the benefit of supporting an alpha channel, which means that a pixel will hold no visual data and will technically be invisible. This is great for assets like shadows, as you'll want them to be partially transparent, making it look like a shadow hangs in the background behind your image. JPEG does not support an alpha channel, which means you're unable to make parts of images transparent or partially transparent. This is also especially true for many icons or buttons, which you will want to be ovals or circles.

# General Art File Management

Android also uses what's known as a ratio scaling system in order to resize art properly for different screen sizes and pixel densities.

The medium DPI (MDPI) size setting is considered the baseline size for working with Android, so all of your artwork will be modified based on how large you want the asset to appear in the medium density. You'll then use a different multiplier for each density:

- Small Density Ratio Multiplier: $0.5\times$
- Medium Density Ratio Multiplier: $1\times$
- Large Density Ratio Multiplier: $1.5\times$
- Extra Large (XL) Density Ratio Multiplier: $2\times$
- Extra Extra Large (XXL) Density Ratio Multiplier: $3\times$
- Extra Extra Extra Large (XXXL) Density Ratio Multiplier: $4\times$

This means that if you create a button you want to be 30 pixels wide by 50 pixels long on a medium density screen, that same button should be redrawn at $45\times75$ for large density displays, at $60\times100$ for large density displays, and so forth.

Because the multiples system can be a bit confusing due to starting at a small baseline and multiplying up for larger displays, it's important to note that it's never a good idea to just create the medium screen size assets and then use Photoshop or a similar tool to enlarge the icon for a bigger screen. The multiplier system makes this tactic seem intuitive, but it will lead to pixelated and poorly rendered images. Instead, determine the sizes you need to create, then begin by making the largest image first and scaling down as necessary.

## Naming Conventions

In Android, it's recommended that the platform's standard file structure be followed, with a specific folder structure used to contain and hold different code or asset files. You'll have a "res" directory for art resources, and you'll place images inside various "drawable" folders.

These various folders (an example is shown in Figure C.1) for drawable images will have different appendixes, such as "-mdpi" or "-xhdpi," and images for corresponding screen densities should be placed in the appropriate folders with the same file name.

## Other Tips

A somewhat valuable tip for Android is that the operating system will scale your assets up or down as necessary if you don't want to create assets for all the various screen densities.

If you're serious about your app design, create and export drawable resources at the appropriate size for each respective density. The Android Asset Studio, provided by Google at http://developer.android.com, will also help determine the proper file sizes for various art assets in a project.

**Figure C.1** In a standard folder structure for an Android app, you'll be placing artwork in the specific folder for the screen density you're targeting with the image.

You can save time, however, by not creating assets for screen sizes such as the rarely used small density (SDPI) or extra extra extra large density (XXXHDPI), and instead let the operating system scale for these sizes. This will produce less optimal designs for these screens, but it will save work you would on assets that few users will see, allowing you to focus on more pressing interface problems.

# iOS

Like Android, iOS requires that art resources be handled in a specific way. In this section, you'll find the details of those requirements.

## Icon Sizes

Unlike Google, Apple doesn't use any sort of mathematical scale for icon sizes required per app. Instead, they use arbitrary sizes that are best fit to their purpose. This allows for sizes that better fit their specific context, but it can more difficult to keep track of.

Although Android icons can be any shape, Apple requires you to create images that can fit into a rounded rectangle shape. As with any other art asset on iOS, you must provide an additional, high-resolution icon for Retina display devices, which you will denote by appending @2× onto the end of the file name.

For each icon, Apple requires square shapes of the following resolutions:

### Required Icons

- Icon size for App Store and Web: 1024×1024 pixels
- iOS 7 icon size for iPhone and iPod touch: 60×60 pixels
- Retina iOS 7 icon size for iPhone and iPod touch: 120×120 pixels
- iOS 7 icon size for iPad or iPad mini: 76×76 pixels
- Retina iOS 7 icon size for iPad or iPad mini: 152×152 pixels
- iOS 6 icon size for iPhone and iPod touch: 57×57 pixels
- Retina iOS 6 icon size for iPhone and iPod touch: 114×114 pixels
- iOS 6 icon size for iPad or iPad mini: 72×72 pixels
- Retina iOS 6 icon size for iPad or iPad mini: 144×144 pixels

### Recommended Icons

- Spotlight Search icon, all devices: 40×40 pixels
- Retina Spotlight Search icon, all devices: 80×80 pixels

- Settings icon: 29×29 pixels
- Retina Settings icon: 58×58 pixels

### Newsstand Icons

Newsstand icons can vary in aspect ratio, giving a look that mimics the aspect ratio of a standard newspaper or magazine, depending on the publication. But all must fit these requirements:

- iPhone or iPod touch scaled long-edge length: 60 pixels
- Retina iPhone or iPod touch scaled long-edge length: 120 pixels
- iPad or iPad mini scaled long-edge length: 76 pixels
- Retina iPad or iPad mini scaled long-edge length: 152 pixels

These icon sizes are all accurate as of this book's publication, although Apple does have a history of changing these requirements as time goes on and adding additional icons such as the Spotlight search icon. Keep up to date on documentation to ensure you're meeting the present standards.

Both iOS 6 and iOS 7 requirements are listed here, but note that iOS 4 and 5 have the same requirements as iOS 6, although it's currently rare to support OS versions that far back. If you intend to only support iOS 7, you do not need to include icons sized for iOS 6.

Finally, note that the corners of your rounded rectangle app icons will be cut off by iOS when viewed by the user, but you should provide them as complete squares that include art even in the corners of the icon. You should have no pixels using the PNG alpha channel.

## General Art File Format

Exactly like Android, on iOS you'll ideally use PNG for any asset you can, as it's beneficial for the same reasons. The ability to provide greater image quality and an alpha channel will be valuable in designing pixel-perfect apps.

Apple has also provided additional optimizations in iOS that help the operating system render and display PNG images faster and more efficiently than images in other file formats. This extra bonus gives you even more reason to create iOS design assets as PNGs instead of in other formats such as JPEG.

Finally, when working with PNG it's also important to understand compression's influence on output. When working with Xcode to create iOS binaries, the IDE will help you perform a PNG compression to minimize file sizes. That being said, Xcode does not do an extraordinary job with file compression, and although this tactic is better than nothing you can do better with file compression.

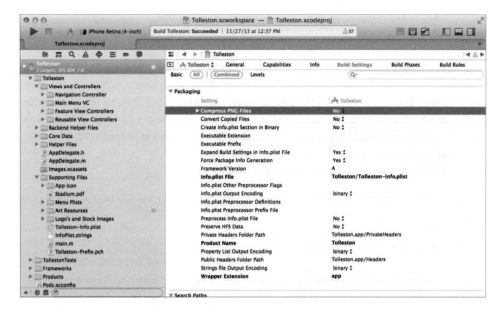

**Figure C.2**    When building projects, consider turning off PNG compression and using a third-party solution for additional optimization.

In order to achieve that end, first turn off automatic compression in Xcode. To do this, turn off "Compress PNG Files" under Packaging in the project's Build Settings panel (see Figure C.2).

After turning off compression, consider using a third-party compression solution, such as the independent Pngyu utility. ImageOptim and TinyPNG are similar services that also do a great job with compression. Most compression tools are derivatives of the UNIX compression library pngquant and work better with specific file types or sizes, but overall they will do a much better job at compression than Xcode's built-in tool.

## General Art File Management

In general, iOS allows you to be rather laissez-faire regarding how you manage art assets. Xcode handles images and allows you to use its grouping property to create a psuedodirectory nested structure to organize image assets. Images will reside inside the project directory, as created by Xcode, but will have little structure outside of that and will be placed without organization inside the folder after being imported by your IDE.

Most developers place image assets inside the group titled "Supporting Files," made by Xcode at the creation of any new project, but there's no requirement that you do this. You could follow this standard and then create a few simple nested groups to organize the images as best fits the specific project. Consider making one group for icons used in menus, another for photos, another for background images, etc.

Note that with iOS, you don't deal with the variety of screen densities that you do on Android. There are currently only two densities available for an app to be rendered at: regular resolution and Retina resolution. In every iOS circumstance, the Retina resolution is equal to exactly twice the resolution of the regular screen, making the math incredibly easy. A button that is 30 pixels tall by 50 pixels wide should be created at 60 pixels tall by 100 pixels wide for the Retina screen. When adding Retina files to an application in Xcode, append the "@2✕" suffix to the file name, and the operating system will do the rest of the work for you.

Here's an example of pixel size and file names for a hypothetical button inside of an app:

- Button.png: 30✕50 pixels
- Button@2✕.png: 60✕100 pixels

On screen, this button would appear to be physically the same size on a non-Retina device as on a Retina device. iOS will pick the correct version for the user depending on the device; you only need to create both images.

## Naming Conventions

There is no required standard as to how your image files should be named when adding them to an iOS project. You can apply whatever convention or style you prefer. Something like "OpenDocument.png" for opening a user's text document is more than acceptable and in many cases is recommended.

That being said, inside iOS Apple has built a wonderful accessibility suite of tools to help users with disabilities enjoy and use their devices to their full capacity. One tool in particular, called VoiceOver, will read text aloud to users who have difficulty reading or who are blind.

When using VoiceOver, any button in the interface will be read to the user as the image's filename, unless you've done a bit of additional work to optimize for accessibility. This means that if you use simple button names that clearly describe their purposes—something like "EmailSharingButton.png" or "PrintDocument.png"—they will be clear to a user of VoiceOver and require no additional work from you. This is a win–win scenario, allowing your application to be usable to a larger market base while giving users with disabilities the ability to experience your work.

## Other Tips

When laying out art assets in an XIB interface file or in code, you use an X-Y coordinate system to specify to the operating system where the image should be placed. Imagine that; all of those high school classes on geometry are finally going to be of use.

If you want an image 100 pixels down the screen and flush with the left side of the screen, place it at the (0,100) point, either in Xcode's Interface Builder by dragging the image into position or in code by using something like the following:

```
UIImageView * imageName = [[UIImageView alloc]initWithFrame:
CGRectMake(0, 100, 30, 50)];
```

Here, you're placing an image that is 30 pixels tall and 50 pixels wide at a point that is equal to the start of the left side of the screen and 100 pixels down from the top of the view.

When working with Retina assets, use the same coordinates and sizes of the pre-Retina standard coordinates, and the operating system will scale up. If, for example, you want a 60×100 button to look great in the same space on Retina, keep the same coordinates and do no additional work or make any changes.

This holds true when working on an iOS 7 app for iPhone or iPod touch, for which there is no supported non-Retina screen and, in essence, no need for non-Retina assets. Instead, continue using the original resolution grid in the sizing and mapping of your art assets.

# INDEX

## PERFECTING INTERFACE DESIGN IN MOBILE APPS

## ESSENTIAL MOBILE INTERACTION DESIGN

Cameron **BANGA**
Josh **WEINHOLD**

# FREE
# Online Edition

Your purchase of **Essential Mobile Interaction Design** includes access to a free online edition for 45 days through the Safari Books Online subscription service. Nearly every Addison-Wesley book is available online through Safari Books Online, along with over thousands of books and videos from publishers such as Cisco Press, Exam Cram, IBM Press, O'Reilly Media, Prentice Hall, Que, Sams, and VMware Press.

Safari Books Online is a digital library providing searchable, on-demand access to thousands of technology, digital media, and professional development books and videos from leading publishers. With one monthly or yearly subscription price, you get unlimited access to learning tools and information on topics including mobile app and software development, tips and tricks on using your favorite gadgets, networking, project management, graphic design, and much more.

## Activate your FREE Online Edition at
## informit.com/safarifree

**STEP 1:** Enter the coupon code: IOGTOXA.

**STEP 2:** New Safari users, complete the brief registration form.
Safari subscribers, just log in.

If you have difficulty registering on Safari or accessing the online edition,
please e-mail customer-service@safaribooksonline.com

 Addison Wesley  AdobePress  ALPHA  Cisco Press  FT Press  IBM Press  Microsoft Press  New Riders  O'REILLY

 Peachpit Press  PRENTICE HALL  Que  Redbooks  SAMS  SAS Publishing  vmware PRESS WILEY wrox